EARLY YEARS ESSENTIALS

Early Years Essentials offers a wealth of evidence-based strategies and ideas to enhance the learning and development of young children. Linked to the EYFS framework and drawing on a wide range of case studies from across the sector, it shows what excellent provision looks like in practice alongside summaries of key research.

Each chapter includes a 'pondering question' which offers the reader the opportunity to reflect on their own knowledge, as well as providing a framework to consider how to enhance their own teaching skills. Covering all aspects of early years practice, the chapters include:

- The indoor and outdoor learning environment
- Observation, planning, and assessment
- Working with parents and carers
- The prime and specific areas of learning
- Adult-child interactions
- The characteristics of effective learning
- Inclusion and diversity
- Child and practitioner wellbeing

Including reflective questions and key takeaways in every chapter, this essential text will support student and practitioner knowledge and understanding of how the EYFS principles can be effectively embedded into best practice.

Jayne Carter is Director of Ignite Education Ltd, providing consultancy for practitioners within the early years and primary sector. She uses coaching as a model for change, facilitating professional conversations which are focused on empowering others and generating growth in knowledge and skills. She is also the Programme Development Lead at Partnership for Children.

Poppy Gibson is a lecturer in education at the Open University. After nearly two decades working in education, Poppy's research now focuses on wellbeing and mental health in childhood.

EARLY YEARS ESSENTIALS

Linking Theory to Provision in the Early Years

Jayne Carter and Poppy Gibson

LONDON AND NEW YORK

Designed cover image: © Getty Images

First published 2026
by Routledge
4 Park Square, Milton Park, Abingdon, Oxon OX14 4RN

and by Routledge
605 Third Avenue, New York, NY 10158

Routledge is an imprint of the Taylor & Francis Group, an informa business

© 2026 Jayne Carter and Poppy Gibson

The right of Jayne Carter and Poppy Gibson to be identified as authors of this work has been asserted in accordance with sections 77 and 78 of the Copyright, Designs and Patents Act 1988.

All rights reserved. No part of this book may be reprinted or reproduced or utilised in any form or by any electronic, mechanical, or other means, now known or hereafter invented, including photocopying and recording, or in any information storage or retrieval system, without permission in writing from the publishers.

For Product Safety Concerns and Information please contact our EU representative GPSR@taylorandfrancis.com. Taylor & Francis Verlag GmbH, Kaufingerstraβe 24, 80331 München, Germany.

Trademark notice: Product or corporate names may be trademarks or registered trademarks, and are used only for identification and explanation without intent to infringe.

British Library Cataloguing-in-Publication Data
A catalogue record for this book is available from the British Library

ISBN: 978-1-032-82583-0 (hbk)
ISBN: 978-1-032-82581-6 (pbk)
ISBN: 978-1-003-50526-6 (ebk)

DOI: 10.4324/9781003505266

Typeset in Interstate
by SPi Technologies India Pvt Ltd (Straive)

"Pedagogy in the early years is not theory in isolation—it's a tapestry woven from curiosity, evidence, and wholehearted connection."

Jayne Carter

"In every small moment with a child lies a seed of lifelong impact. Early years is where possibility meets purpose."

Poppy Gibson

CONTENTS

List of contributors ix

1. **Introduction** 1
   JAYNE CARTER AND POPPY GIBSON

2. **Learning environment: Indoors** 4
   JAYNE CARTER

3. **Learning environment: Outdoors** 19
   JAYNE CARTER

4. **Effective partnership with parents** 33
   POPPY GIBSON

5. **Prime area: Physical development** 46
   POPPY GIBSON

6. **Prime area: Personal, social, emotional development** 64
   POPPY GIBSON

7. **Prime area: Communication and language development** 79
   JAYNE CARTER

8. **Specific area: Literacy** 94
   JAYNE CARTER

9. **Specific area: Mathematics** 108
   JAYNE CARTER

10. **Understanding the world** 123
    POPPY GIBSON

11. **Expressive arts and design** 135
    POPPY GIBSON

12	**Observation-assessment and planning cycle**	147
	JAYNE CARTER	
13	**Quality adult-child interaction**	160
	JAYNE CARTER	
14	**The characteristics of effective learning**	173
	POPPY GIBSON	
15	**The importance of implementing EYFS principles as a whole school**	183
	JAYNE CARTER	
16	**Protected characteristics in the Early Years**	196
	POPPY GIBSON	
17	**Wellbeing**	213
	POPPY GIBSON	
	Index	229

CONTRIBUTORS

Agnes Kosek, Lecturer in Educational Psychology, on Early Years Programme and on Accelerated Degree in Primary Education at the University of Greenwich
Alexander Walsh, Speech and Language Therapist
Alison Fleetwood, Service Manager–Family Hubs, Early Years and Talking Together, City of Doncaster Council
Amber Browne, Crisis Care Practitioner, Northumbria University
Amy Marrison, Reception Class Teacher, Catton Grove Primary School Norwich
Amy Stancer, Headteacher St Giles Nursery School, Lincoln
Andrew Moffat, PD Lead, Excelsior MAT, CEO No Outsiders charity
Angela Hodgkins, Senior Lecturer, Department for Children and Families, University of Worcester
Angie Barkworth, EYFS Leader, Bricknell Primary School, Hull
Anne Rogers, Early Years Consultant
Carys Jennings, Curriculum Tutor, The Open University
Catherine Hitchcock, Headteacher at Donhead Prep School, Wimbledon
Catherine Mather, Early Years Personal Tutor
Cazzie Jude, Executive Leadership Coach & Early Years Consultant
Chloe Higgins, Teacher at Lark Hill Nursery School
Chris Williams, Founder of 'Chatta'
Claire McKie, Founder of DfE England and DoE W Australia Power Phonics Reading and Spelling Program
Claire Plews, HE Counselling Curriculum Coordinator–University Centre Weston, EdD Researcher University of Bristol
Courtney McAllister, Postgraduate Researcher
Crystal Cunningham, Literacy Specialist and Curriculum Designer
Danielle Kelly, Early Years Lecturer, The Trafford Stockport College Group
Danyah Miller, Storyteller, writer, trainer
Deborah Haddon, Early Years Specialist and Lecturer, Nottingham College
Declan Dowkes, Lecturer in Early Years and Education Studies, University of Brighton
Diana Wilson, Headteacher at a Primary School, formerly Head of EYFS
Dr Diane Boyd, Honorary Research Fellow School of Education University of Hull

Eleanor Milligan, Lecturer in Education, University of East Anglia
Emalee Caton, Early Years PANCo Lead Tutor, National Day Nurseries Association, Reception Class teacher
Erica McGinley, Maths Consultant
Erin Skelton, Senior Teacher at Worksop College | Chief Strategy Officer, Bright Field Consulting
Fey Cole, FE Curriculum Manager for the Department of Health, Life and Personal Sciences
Fryn-Myers Baird, Independent Schools Queensland, Early Childhood Project Advisor
Glenn Denny, Nursery Manager, York
Graeme McAvoy, Doctorate of Education (EdD) Student at the University of Strathclyde
Hannah Baker, Co-CEO Partnership for Children
Hannah Foster, Reception Teacher
Hannah Robinson & **Kelly Thompson**, EYFS Lead & EYFS Class Teacher, Park Academy
Helen Bartle, Assistant Headteacher at Ackton Pastures Primary Academy
Helen Battelley, National Early Years Active Start Partnership (NEYASP)
Holly May Andras, University of Cambridge
Dr Jackie Musgrave, Associate Head of School, The Open University
Jake Balding, Early Childhood Educator in Training-Anglia Ruskin University
Jane Dorrian, Early Years Lecturer, The Open University
Janine Ryan, Freelance Early Years Consultant
Jayne Carter, Director of Ignite Education Ltd
Jess Gosling, Phase Leader Early Years with Year 1, British Nursery School of Wilanow, Poland
Jessica Wythe, Lecturer in Early Childhood Studies at Birmingham City University
Julie Taylor, Nursery Class Teacher within a Primary School Setting
Karl Eaveson, Nursery Manager
Kate Gingles, Independent Early Years Consultant
Katie White, EYFS Teacher, North Cockerington CE Primary School
Kelsie Lee, Primary Education graduate
Kierna Corr, Head of Nursery, Windmill Integrated Primary Schools and Nursery Unit, Dungannon, N. Ireland.
Laura Douglas, ITT Leader, L.E.A.D. Teaching School Hub, Lincolnshire
Lauren Wilcock, School-Based Nursery Teacher, Latchford St James CE Primary School.
Lesley Boyle, Senior Lecturer, Initial Teacher Training University of Hertfordshire
Lily Sheikh, Early Years Practitioner
Lisa Kelly, Foundation Lecturer, Chester University
Louise Monange, Director of Nursery Operations The DEN Nursery Group
Louise Smith, EYFS Lead, Coldfair Green Primary School
Louise Turnbull, Programme Leader for Early Years provision, Burnley College
Lucy Fox, Early Years Leader
Lucy Hennell, Experienced Primary Teacher
Dr Lucy Parker, Deputy Headteacher Ludwick Nursery School
Lyndsey Farmer, Vogrie Outdoor ELC

Marianne Hixon, Early Years Teacher
Melanie Yates-Boothbyx, EYFS Lead, SENCO and Nursery Teacher. St Peter's.
Michael Charles Fransen Cresswell, Tutor in Education at Coventry University
Michelle Yeung, Year 1 Teacher at Sha Tin Junior School
Millie Overton, EYFS Class Teacher - Old Leake Primary Academy.
Mx Maxwell Davies, Lecturer Arden University
Natalie Quinn-Walker, Public Health Lecturer and Deputy Course Lead MPH
Natalie Weir, PhD researcher, University of Derby
Natasha Nechat-Murphy, Teaching Assistant, London, United Kingdom
Nick Robinson, Nick Robinson Sports Coaching
Nicola Carvell, Assistant Headteacher / EYFS Specialist Leader of Education, Cornwall
Nicola Wallis, Practitioner Research Associate: Collections & Early Childhood, Fitzwilliam Museum, University of Cambridge
Paul Silver-Wolfe, Educator at Little Wild Tribe
Paulette Luff, Senior Lecturer, Anglia Ruskin University
Peter Foulds, School Improvement Advisor - Maths, Lingfield Education Trust, NCETM SD Lead & LLME
Rachael Summerscales, Founder of Honest Childhood
Dr Rachel Briggs, Reflective supervision in education practitioner: Reflected and Balanced
Rachel Lehart, Childcare assessor / Lecturer
Rachel Summerscales, Founder of Honest Childhood
Rebecca Walsh, Early Years Practitioner
Rohit Sagoo, PhD Researcher, University of Bedfordshire
Roisin Casey, Assistant Head of Early Years, Clarion School Dubai
Sam Robinson, Programme Lead and Lecturer in Early Childhood Studies
Samantha Dholakia, Coach, Consultant, Trainer: SPD Tuition & Coaching
Sandra Beale, Science Communicator to 0-6, Founder of Toddler and Early Years STEM
Sarah Clough, Head of Engagement, Cast Theatre
Sarah Eastaff, Director (Arts and Education) darts, Doncaster's Creative Health charity
Sarah Guscott, Higher Education Practice Tutor and Lecturer at Inspire Education Group
Sarah Roebuck, Programme Leader in Higher Education University Campus Doncaster (Former PVI Nursery Manager)
Dr Scott Michael Steele, Lecturer in Law, Anglia Ruskin University Peterborough
Simon Airey, Visiting Teacher
Sophie Dent, Humanitarian Support Manager - Local Government Authority
Sophie Smith-Tong, Teacher, Mental Health and Wellbeing Lead and Founder of Mindfulness for learning.
Stephen J Morgan, Nursery Teacher at Summer Lane Primary and also Early Years Coach and Mentor
Steve Mackay, Deputy Headteacher Thundersley Primary School
Susanne Rice, Childminder and owner of Little Puddings
Tamsin Grimmer, Principal Lecturer at Norland College, Early Years Consultant and Author
Tara Paxton and **Lisa Greenerm**, Childsplay Nursery, Newcastle

Thalia Krassam, Trainee Primary Teacher
Tobias Hammond, Early Years Expert
Tracy Hopkins, EYFS Associate Headteacher-Transform Trust
Tricia Mohamed, Early Years Consultant: Play Practitioners
Troy Jenkinson, Freelance Lecturer, Children's Author and Equality, Diversity, Inclusion & Belonging Specialist
Vicky Cook, EYFS Lead, St Peter at Gowts' C of E Primary School
Dr Viki Veale, Senior lecturer; Early Years and Primary Education (St Mary's University, Twickenham)
Yria Polydoropoulou, Deputy Head

1 Introduction

Jayne Carter and Poppy Gibson

Welcome to *Early Years Essentials: Linking Theory to Provision in the Early Years*.

Early years education is a remarkable and dynamic field, full of opportunities to shape young minds, nurture curiosity and lay the groundwork for lifelong learning. It is a phase of development, characterised by rapid growth, exploration and discovery. Yet, despite its profound significance, pressures placed on Early Years practitioners often face the challenge of translating theoretical insights into practical, meaningful provision. The interplay between pedagogy, child development theory and the lived experiences of children in Early Years settings is at the heart of quality education—and ensuring that research informs practice is key to delivering the very best for our youngest learners.

The inspiration for this book emerged from countless conversations, reflections and observations gathered over time. As Early Years practitioners, we continuously share ideas, strategies and insights that contribute to the richness of our field. My notebooks are brimming with practical suggestions and thought-provoking discussions... these ideas deserve a wider audience! It became clear that there was a need for a dedicated resource that not only captures the wisdom of experienced educators but also presents actionable approaches that can be adapted for diverse settings. *Early Years Essentials* is the result: a compendium of practitioner-led provision ideas that seamlessly bridge theory with pedagogy, ensuring that learning environments are informed by both research and real-world expertise.

At the core of this book is the belief that effective early years provision is driven by knowledge, intentionality and professional reflection. Each of the seventeen chapters revolve around a central ***'pondering question'***—a guiding theme designed to provoke meaningful reflection on key aspects of early years education. These questions encourage practitioners to critically evaluate their own approaches, inspiring thoughtful discussions and deeper engagement with pedagogical principles. As co-authors, we use these pondering questions as a foundation for exploration, weaving together research, case studies and professional experiences to provide a holistic perspective on each topic.

The case studies included throughout this book reflect the invaluable contributions of Early Years professionals, whose dedication and expertise bring learning to life in unique and inspiring ways. It has been a privilege to gather insights from educators across private, voluntary and independent settings, as well as practitioners and teachers within schools, childminders, consultants and advisors. The diversity of voices represented ensures that this book speaks to the wide range of experiences and perspectives within early years education. The shared wisdom of contributors highlights not only best practices but also the creative and adaptable nature of early years provision.

Early years education is not a one-size-fits-all approach. Every child is unique, and so are the settings in which they learn. Whether you are an experienced early years leader, just beginning your journey in the field, or responsible for training the educators of tomorrow, *Early Years Essentials* is designed to provide inspiration, structure and practical guidance that can be tailored to individual contexts. The suggestions and strategies outlined in this book aim to support professionals in creating enriched learning environments that foster curiosity, independence and emotional resilience in young children.

The structure of this book ensures accessibility and usability. Each chapter is designed to provide both theoretical grounding and practical applications, encouraging readers to engage with research while considering how it translates into daily practice. By blending evidence-based insights with real-world examples, the book seeks to empower educators to plan a curriculum that is informed by secure knowledge of child development, effective pedagogy and the realities of early years provision.

In early years education, the role of the practitioner is multifaceted—it requires a balance between guidance, facilitation, observation and responsiveness. Learning unfolds through rich interactions, carefully curated environments and thoughtfully designed experiences that encourage exploration and meaningful engagement. Children thrive when they are given opportunities to follow their interests, build relationships and develop the skills that will serve as the foundation for their future learning. The chapters in this book explore these vital aspects of provision, ensuring that educators are equipped with the tools to create high-quality, research-informed learning experiences.

Central to our philosophy is the recognition that young children learn best when they feel secure, valued and engaged. Relationships lie at the heart of effective early years practice, and this book emphasises the importance of creating environments that support not only academic development but also emotional and social growth. The research and strategies explored throughout the chapters reflect a commitment to holistic education—where children's well-being, confidence and sense of belonging are nurtured alongside their cognitive development.

In the pages that follow, you will find inspiration drawn from the vast and varied expertise of early years professionals who bring learning to life every day. Whether exploring the intricacies of indoor and outdoor learning environments, the role of meaningful interactions, or the importance of partnerships with families and communities, this book provides insights that can strengthen and refine your own practice. The hope is that readers will not only take away practical strategies but also feel encouraged to reflect on their own approaches, question assumptions and deepen their engagement with the principles that shape effective early years education.

We hope *Early Years Essentials* will serve as a valuable resource, equipping practitioners with the tools, knowledge and inspiration to create learning environments where children feel empowered, supported and excited to explore the world around them. Whether you are reading this book to refine your existing practice, develop new strategies, or seek fresh perspectives, we invite you to engage fully with the ideas presented, reflect on their implications and adapt them in ways that best serve your children.

Thank you to the many contributors who have shared their expertise, experiences and insights. Your dedication to early years education is evident in every idea, strategy and perspective included in this book. We appreciate and value the collective wisdom of practitioners who make a difference every day, ensuring that children's early learning experiences are rich, meaningful and full of possibility.

Here's to fostering new discoveries, supporting children's development and celebrating the incredible work of early years educators.

Jayne & Poppy

2 Learning environment
Indoors

Jayne Carter

Introduction

Whilst it is, without doubt, important that the learning environment is an aesthetically pleasing place for our children to be welcomed into, having a pleasant-looking indoor environment only provides some part of the whole early years jigsaw. Its importance is paramount in providing a pathway for children to participate in learning. This chapter provides valuable opinion pieces from our contributors; these provide a unique window to how they have purposefully planned for an indoor environment which drives provision, promotes engagement and provides a space for learning.

Pondering question: how can the learning environment move from decoration to a place of adventure and discovery?

It is interesting that the current EYFS statutory framework makes no direct reference to the learning environment and its importance in the provision shared with the children. In the non-statutory guidance 'Development Matters' there are only two citations of the learning environment: one included in Chapter 2: seven key features of effective practice point 4 Pedagogy: helping children to learn: 'A well-planned learning environment, indoors and outside, is an important aspect of pedagogy', and two, ideas to incorporate mathematical activities for children between 3 and 4 years old: 'Use small numbers to manage the learning environment.' The additional non-statutory guidance 'Birth to Five Matters' in the chapter on 'enabling environments' provides more guidance on the role of the indoor learning environment. Significantly, this guidance highlights the importance of planning a well-designed environment which nurtures the holistic development of the children. The guidelines provide a number of key recommendations:

1. Children thrive within environments that support their individual and diverse development needs.
2. Enabling environments offer children security, comfort, choice, engagement and opportunity.
3. Children's learning is best supported when they have opportunities which allow for movement and action, creativity and imagination, independence and collaboration.

4. Open-ended resources enable children to access and combine processes of development and learning.
5. Inclusive spaces are nurturing and supportive of all children.
6. Within an enabling environment, knowledgeable practitioners optimise the development and learning potential of every child.

The significance of 'purpose' when planning an effective indoor learning environment

Underpinning all of these recommendations is the understanding of the **purpose** of the learning environment for teaching and learning. Practitioner subject knowledge is a vital component here to move from a place of decoration to one of adventure and discovery. How both the adults and the children are able to use and operate within the environment should be at the forefront even at the initial planning stage and as we prepare for the arrival of our new children. Key questions at this stage could include 'what do I want the room to say/mean/represent for the children? How can I ensure that the room supports learning and entices children to even want to explore and discover within it?' This is a very different approach to collecting lots of resources and hoping that the learning fits into them. Flipping the narrative so it leads and directs professional thinking ensures that the learning environment is assigned a role which is just as significant as that of the curriculum or the role of the adult. The Reggio approach supports this view, assigning the learning environment with the title 'the third teacher', stating that its importance is fundamental for children to demonstrate their own feelings, ideas and learning. Children are supported to investigate, discover and explore following their own desires and motivations within an environment which provokes these dispositions and inclinations. "The Reggio approach reminds us that the environment is not just a backdrop for learning; it is an active and essential component of education," (David Hawkins, 2023).

Who owns the learning environment?

When exploring the recommendations suggested by 'Birth to Five Matters', despite being presented as individual statements, the words child/children are prominent in each of them. As it should be! The learning environment is **their** learning environment, a space which belongs to them rather than the adult imposing their expectations, preferences and direction of travel. Let's look at each of these recommendations, delving into the reasons why and how children can be the leaders within their learning space.

1. Children thrive within environments that support their individual and diverse development needs.
   The addition of the word '**all**' may further enhance this recommendation. For all children to feel that they are able to thrive within their environment, it follows that every time they venture into it, they are able to explore resources which they like and are interested in. Like any group of children, there will be some at specific and different parts of the learning journey than others. This diversity needs to be acknowledged not only by all

the adults in the room but clearly shown within the choices made within the learning environment. The learning environment should be a space where everyone can access, be immersed in and be both supported and challenged. Without this dedication, only some children will be able to fully engage with the activities/experiences with the indoor provision, isolating some of their peers.
2. Enabling environments offer children security, comfort, choice, engagement and opportunity.
Deciding on these aspects as significant in the role of the learning environment truly nurtures a holistic view and increases the potential and importance of the environment in children's learning. Consider our spaces at home. We may have a variety of areas which provide different experiences, offering us choices to fill immediate or planned needs or desires. For example, there may be a space for conversation and collaboration. There may also be a space which offers periods of solitude, quiet and rest. We understand the importance of this variety for our own lifestyle dynamic and as educators supporting children at the very start of their life's adventure, why wouldn't this also be a consideration for our youngest learners? The concept of opportunity included in this recommendation is such a positive aspiration for the learning environment and one which I believe evokes a sense of true possibility—anything and everything is achievable for your children! So, what does an opportunity-rich learning environment look like? As well as the careful planning of continuous provision based on both the learning aspects included in the curriculum and the skills/dispositions included in the characteristics framework, applying similar thinking and plans to the enhanced provision offers a high range of opportunity.
3. Children's learning is best supported when they have opportunities which allow for movement and action, creativity and imagination, independence and collaboration.

Learning from the children in the development of the indoor learning environment

How can the learning environment ensure that all aspects of this recommendation are catered for? By committing to them as an unconditional part of your aspirations for your children and dedicating to this commitment in deciding what you plan, how you support them and how you encourage them to meet their individual goals. Let's explore each of these pairings in turn. How often do we consider how children are able to move and be active within their indoor environment? Many of these considerations may be impacted by the physical space we inherit and short of knocking down walls, we must work within the space we have. I am reminded here of the research carried out by Maria Montessori and her subsequent Early Years Centres. Fundamental to her approach is the idea of the body and mind being intrinsically connected. Current scientific explorations have named this as 'embodied cognition'. Montessori went on to advocate for an early years ethos which moved away from the maybe more simplistic form of movement consisting solely for the purpose of exercise or recreation, to that of being an integral learning method for children. 'A virtuous circle begins where the mind and the body develop together: the more I can explore with my body the more I know and the more I know, the more I can explore' (Maria Montessori Institute, 2024). Embedding this belief into the development of the learning environment directs not only the choices made of the type of resources to be included but also has influence in the way that these resources are organised and arranged. When considering how creativity and imagination can be included in provision, it's useful to explore these learning aspects in a little more detail. This detail should then influence and direct the type of resources to be included in the learning environment by giving some structure to how both the adults and the children interact with them. I firmly believe that nurturing a child who sees the possibility in experiences around them provides them not only with the pleasure of taking joy in the creative world but also embedding crucial skills and dispositions to embrace problems and situations with enthusiasm and positivity.

Learning versus resources

When including opportunities for independence and collaboration, I would suggest that our thinking is directed by these two aspects of learning rather than being led by the resources or the organisation of the learning space. Simply making space for children to play together or just providing single-spaced resources is not sufficient for many children to understand what they are able or expected to do. Again, they may look inviting (and probably have taken a considerable time to put together), which provides a pleasing decoration to the room. These aspirations of collaboration and independence need explicit and clear explanations and time taken to show the children what playing together entails. All children bring their own experiences, their own personal stories, with them into your setting which may or may not include knowing what it means to socially play with one or more other children. Cooperative play often won't magically happen simply by placing children together!

4. Open-ended resources enable children to access and combine processes of development and learning.
   What is so unique about the 'open-endedness' of resources which are so powerful in promoting learning for our youngest children? Consider these two scenarios; (1) children engage with a resource which looks inviting, the children like it although it has limited flexible learning opportunities. The same children engage with this resource time and time again and appear busy in their play. (2) a resource which hasn't a defined or planned use is included in both direct teaching opportunities and within the children's learning environment. Children are able to return to the resource over and over again with different children accessing it over time. What makes this difference between how children use the resources? The thought from the adults of the purpose of this kind of resource is a key consideration. **Just** providing open-ended resources is important but without the investment in helping children to know what to do with them—how to explore the potential of a resource through being a play partner alongside the children and offering guidance—stifles this experience for children. Single function resources can produce single function learners—they have no reason to think outside the box or to move away from the narrowness of the resources they are playing with. There is limited challenge or in fact motivation to explore and discover new things.

5. Inclusive spaces are nurturing and supportive of all children.

    Inclusivity, a cornerstone of a quality EYFS ethos, curriculum and practice, absolutely must be a crucial consideration when starting to plan the learning environment and is included in any ongoing evaluation of the effectiveness of this environment on children's learning. As well as physical adaptations to guarantee that all children can access their learning space successfully, the model of inclusivity should also respond to the wider view of the child as both an individual in their own right as well as their place within their own family culture. Thinking of your children and families as a rich tapestry, where there are boundless opportunities to learn from and about each other could support the choices made for provision. Again, learning first **then** provision ensures that play is not only purposeful but also that children can see themselves as special as they play.

The role of the practitioner in the indoor learning environment

6. Within an enabling environment, knowledgeable practitioners optimise the development and learning potential of every child.

    The role of the adult within early years cannot be underestimated. The adult, their care, guidance and skills are, in my opinion, the main reason for the success of the child's experience within the setting. The learning environment should be a mirror to show what is important for that adult, including how they engage with the children when playing together. Child development, we know, propels the practitioner into the role of a pedagogical guide. I propose that this secure understanding of child development as a vehicle in ensuring the youngest children achieve their very best personal goals also includes the purpose of the learning environment as an equal partner within research and expertise and not as a second consideration.

In this first contribution, Fram Myers-Baird, Early Childhood Project Advisor, explores the significance of honing a personal authentic view on the role of the learning environment.

Fran Myers-Baird: creating purposeful environments through beauty, aesthetics and authenticity

Designing environments for children can be subjective depending on educators' knowledge, understanding and interpretation of what quality environments look, feel and sound like within an early childhood service. When educators incorporate peer-reviewed literature and contemporary research to plan purposeful environments, this will foster and enhance children's learning, development and wellbeing.

Australia's robust system for regulating early learning emphasises the importance of providing children with a welcoming, safe and inclusive environment. These elements create a foundation to transform educators' meta-cognition around purposeful environments, shifting thinking towards an intentional and sustainable place that promotes learning. When children's strengths, culture and interests reflect the environment, this will promote competence, exploration, and play-based learning (Australian Children's Education and Care Quality Authority, 2018).

Finding inspiration to create a sense of wonder may require educators to listen and view the environment from the children's perspective. When an environment has been designed with intentionality, consideration and care, it stimulates play, creativity and imagination. Authenticity helps children to make connections, understand the purpose and broaden their perspectives of the world to instil lifelong values. It is our responsibility to bring the rich beauty of the world through aesthetically designed environments that further affirm children's rights.

When planning an environment, educators should incorporate place-based pedagogy to respect and draw on the views of children, families and community to ensure the environment reflects the context of the service. During the curating or reigniting process of an environment, educators are encouraged to observe, analyse and reflect on what they hear, feel, see and smell within the current setting. This is to ensure the environment design is authentic and purposeful to build on children's developmental strengths and mitigate vulnerability.

When designing an environment, consideration needs to be given to how educators can enhance flexible use, flow and interaction within or between indoor and outdoor spaces. This may include rethinking how the service utilises the environment and resources holistically across indoor and outdoor settings; for example, provoking children's interests through introducing natural elements within the indoor environment such as the use of sand, soil, grass, wood, minerals and metals.

When examining and reflecting on the current environment, consider how educators' values, their interpretation of theories, biases and philosophy may influence the environment design or resources offered. As educators, we use a variety of worldviews or theoretical perspectives to inform curriculum decision-making. How do educators within your service connect theory to practice?

Building on the key aspects included in Fran's submission, Tobias Hammond, Early Years expert, offers more reflection on how to successfully plan for an engaging indoor learning environment.

Tobias Hammond: tools for supporting the learning environment

Learning environments can often be a hard place to negotiate as a practitioner.

Ofsted's three Is come from the Early Years Inspection Handbook, 2019. The three Is stand for Intent, Implementation and Impact. We as practitioners can use this tool to support our own practice. We need to see this as a tool of support in our skills toolboxes as early years practitioners. I interpret them as the following: Intent standing for—what is the intent of the said learning opportunity; Implementation—what is available, what is needed for the environment/learning and how long will that take; and Impact—what has been the impact on our young people in our care.

However, when I think about the three I's, I personally would like to add another one-inclusion. We all know in the early years that inclusion is the golden thread. Therefore, it should be the thought behind everything we do.

An example of using the four Is can be used when we see trends in the early years. A trend we are seeing more of is table talking in areas. They are normal plastic little screens with a printed sign in the middle. You can often see them in early years environments with things such as 'who can build the biggest tower' and so on. We can use the four Is to support this and to see if it is really needed in our own environment. So first, what is the intent? Do we want someone to gain a new idea or skill? Implementation: can our children read a sign/is it age appropriate? How much time is it taking the staff member to do? Then we can ask what the impact is going to be. If it was simply words/decoration and put in a 3-year-old setting, perhaps it is not going to have a greater impact on learning and development. Inclusion: can all our young people learn from it?

The third contribution in this chapter comes from Helen Bartle, Assistant Headteacher at Ackton Pastures Primary Academy. Her passionate and personal view on developing her own learning space provides useful and practical ideas for development.

Helen Bartle: creating an intentional learning space for early years

Presented with an early years space to develop I wanted to create a really intentional space that would enable all children to thrive and develop. I was keen that it be inclusive, support the development and needs of all in an oasis of calm where all could learn.

To provide some context the space is large, with a very high ceiling, and because of this the display boards are very high, above adult height. The setting caters for children with a variety of needs, and I wanted the space to be right for everyone—this was crucial for me.

I started with the walls, floors and ceilings, before moving onto the furniture and soft furnishings. The colours chosen in the classroom were done so to promote a sense of calm and cleanliness. I chose plain, neutral colours for the walls, displays, furniture and baskets (that matched), to reduce pattern and the sensory overload. The floor was changed to a dark wood-effect colour so that it is cosy, inviting and comfortable for the children to play on at low levels.

The furniture was then added with the layout of the room being carefully considered to create spaces for children to work together and that also had sufficient space to play in. Areas are clearly defined by the placement of furniture, using open low-level shelves and pieces with higher backs that create nooks to aid self-regulation. The home 'corner' is in the centre of the room in an L-shape so that children can move and play in and around the space whilst also it also feels cosy and inviting. Home corner units are purposely at a low level so that play can happen over and around the space.

I then added some colour through soft furnishings. Pale green rugs, blankets, cushions and beanbags were added creating a cosy aesthetic, and also creating textures to touch, stroke, envelop and soothe. Fairy lights and angle poise lamps were to highlight areas and resources and create warm lighting without the use of the harsh ceiling strip lights.

Finally complimentary pale coloured voile drapes were hung across the length of the ceiling, halfway down the wall to lower the ceiling on a budget, whilst still allowing the natural light from the roof windows in the room. The drapes lowered the acoustic footprint and created a calmer space for all. Displays have been kept deliberately sparse to reduce the sensory overload whilst still reflecting our curriculum learning and values.

The room itself is large, but we have created a room off the main space to create a quiet, calm space that all children can access should they wish to. These spaces contain sensory toys, dark tents, soothing lights, beanbags, rugs and cushions. It felt important that within such a large room we had a smaller breakout space.

Whilst the space is ever evolving with new children, new resources and new contexts, what I hope to have created with the physical aspects of the space is one that is calm and inviting and that works for all our children, so that everyone can play and learn without fear or anxiety.

Continuing the thread of understanding the purpose of the indoor learning environment for our youngest children, Louise Monange, Director of Nursery Operations: The DEN Nursery Group shares a fascinating focus on incorporating STEAM into the learning environment.

Louise Monange: introducing STEAM into the indoor learning environment

Creating an exciting and adventurous indoor environment for children is vital in fostering a culture of exploration, creativity and active engagement in learning. Such an atmosphere should stimulate curiosity and support open-ended play, facilitating children's experiences through discovery and inquiry. A unique and effective way to achieve this is by integrating STEAM education (Science, Technology, Engineering, Arts and Mathematics) into the learning environment.

Reimagining traditional play areas can transform them into dynamic, interactive learning experiences. Instead of mere sand and water play, these spaces can evolve into science and experimentation zones filled with magnifying glasses, plants and opportunities for colour mixing. Engineering principles can be seamlessly introduced as children construct structures with sand and water, encouraging comparisons with creations made from building blocks or varying materials. This incorporation allows for hands-on navigation and interaction, enabling children to engage with their surroundings in a more profound, meaningful way.

Integrating natural elements into learning environments enhances opportunities for adventure and experiential learning. We can create scenarios where every play adventure tells a story. For instance, children can recreate the tale of the *Three Little Pigs*, using materials like straw, bricks and sticks to build their interpretations of the pigs' houses. This hands-on experimentation invites discussions about stability and strength, prompting children to collaborate and problem-solve, thereby nurturing communication skills and supporting social interactions.

In a STEAM-rich environment, the philosophy of provocations beginning with prompts that spark curiosity opens paths for children to steer their learning journeys in various directions. For instance, introducing robots as a provocation might inspire children to design and build their own using recyclable materials. They can further enhance their learning by utilising apps that teach simple programming concepts or engage in coding exercises. This flexibility and responsiveness to children's interests transform the learning experience, making it more engaging and adventurous as children realise that their passions drive their exploration.

Ultimately, crafting an environment that transitions from mere decoration to adventure through STEAM requires thoughtful design and intention. Practitioners should create spaces that invite exploration, nurture curiosity, facilitate collaboration and remain responsive to children's diverse interests. By embedding STEAM principles into physical spaces and integrating them into daily practices, educators can transform early learning environments into thriving hubs of discovery and excitement. In this setting, children are not just passive recipients of knowledge; instead, they become active participants in their learning experiences, cultivating a lifelong love for inquiry and exploration. Through this approach, we provide a solid foundation for children's continued growth in creativity, critical thinking and collaboration.

The next contribution in this chapter, written by Kate Gingles, an Independent Early Years Consultant, encourages us to reflect on our own ethos of high-quality EYFS practice.

Kate Gingles: good practice never goes out of style!

I have worked in the EYFS for over twenty years and, having moved between schools and year groups frequently, this September saw me setting up a new classroom for at least the eleventh time! I found some photographs of my first-ever classroom as an NQT in 2003. What's interesting is how much has remained the same and the aspects which have changed.

The book I turned to for support time and again as an NQT was *Planning Children's Play and Learning: Meeting children's needs in the later stages of the EYFS* by Jane Drake (2013). I remember how the chapter on planning the learning environment and quality areas of provision supported me to set up that first room, dividing the space into defined areas and organising a rich range of resources within them that could be independently accessed. Looking at it now, I can see it still influences my practice subconsciously many years and several versions of EYFS later!

Of course, some things have changed in my environment. Gone are the bright coloured backing papers and perfect displays that I carefully spent my summer creating, ready for the start of term, to be replaced with neutral colours and working walls. Alongside the new additions (natural resources, real-life objects, hessian, glass jars for paint, beautiful wooden shelving, ten frames and Numicon to name just a few!) many things endure, because they are, and always will be, what works best for children and what makes the EYFS work.

- A clear purpose to each area so everybody (children, staff, SLT, governors, parents) can see what it is for
- A large quantity and range of resources so that children can make choices about what and how they learn according to their own interests
- Enough space in each area for children to work together and for adults to get in and support their play
- Carefully labelled resources so that children (and adults) know what goes where
- Open shelving and shallow storage containers so children can see what is available to them
- Resources sorted in a way that provides further opportunities of learning; for instance animals in the small world area sorted by type, paper stored according to properties in the creative area, counting resources sorted by colour or size
- Opportunities to promote independence, for example pouring or mixing own paints, selecting own snacks, aprons, wellies and waterproofs to access when needed
- Writing/mark-making opportunities in all areas
- Opportunities to celebrate and showcase children's learning, their voice and their interests
- A direct access to the outdoors

The EYFS learning environment is a special place. It is more than the third teacher, it's the space where learning happens and memories are made. As teachers, it is our second home, as it often is for our children, so time spent developing it is always time well spent and an investment in quality.

Cazzie Jude, an Executive Leadership Coach and Early Years Consultant, effectively builds on the ideas shared by Kate and shares her own thoughts on what works well when developing a learning environment indoors and the proposed impact on both practitioners and children.

Cazzie Jude: 'wake the giant: Designing Early Years classrooms that support teachers and engage learners'

Creating the right learning environment in the early years can significantly reduce the stress on teachers and teaching assistants while enhancing children's engagement. However, what constitutes the 'right' learning environment? As an Early Years specialist and inspector, I have visited schools where little attention is given to the classroom learning environment. There is a distinct lack of resources and the resources available are not arranged in an appealing way to stimulate curiosity in young learners. During free-flow play, children are often left to 'go and play' without clear expectations or accountability. This misses a crucial opportunity for purposeful engagement.

Kathryn Delany, in her article "Waking the 'Third Teacher': the Whys and Hows Te Whāriki: Principle to Practice", discusses how the environment can be an active part of learning, stating, "Waking the giant is challenging. But like most sleeping beings it can be tussled, uncovered, shaken, and awoken. When awake, this giant is powerful and informs the kind of learning that happens in our early childhood education settings" (Delany, 2018). So, how can we 'wake the giant'?

Creating a natural environment

A natural classroom environment with wooden tables, chairs and furniture is essential. It provides a calming, inviting space that connects children to nature. Using wicker baskets for resources, incorporating bamboo or hanging fake leaves can make indoor spaces warm and comforting, especially on days when children cannot go outside. These natural resources and calming colours help create a visually appealing space that can have a calming effect on both children and adults.

Organising resources

To foster independence, resources need to be easily accessible to children at their level. If resources are stored in baskets, they should have labels or photographs to help children identify and return items independently. A common mistake is labelling the basket but neglecting to label the shelf where the basket belongs. This small step can make a significant difference, helping children to self-resource efficiently and reset the learning environment at the end of the session.

Learning centres

Learning centres should be thoughtfully designed to meet children's developmental needs, ignite their curiosity, and stimulate their imagination. Each centre should have a clear purpose, reflecting both children's interests and academic themes. It's important to arrange the centres strategically, ensuring noisy areas are separated from quiet ones. Centres should remain available to children as long as they are purposefully and meaningfully engaged. Teachers should focus on keeping them appealing and refreshing them with new invitations and provocations.

To further enhance children's learning, ensure that centres include open-ended resources that allow children to use their imagination and explore. Writing materials such as clipboards and paper should be readily available throughout the classroom to encourage children to write or draw their ideas and plans. Children also need opportunities to revisit their projects. Labels saying 'Under Construction' can be used so that children can return to their work, and others know not to pack it away. Plan your centres in advance and actively engage with them. Teachers should demonstrate how to use each centre effectively. The centre can be mirrored on the interactive board, with a child or adult modelling its use, either in real time or through a prerecorded video. Train children to reset the room by knowing where resources go and understanding the expectations for taking care of both the resources and the environment.

A well-designed learning environment not only engages children but also supports teachers and assistants by fostering independence and responsibility. By taking the time to plan and create stimulating, organised spaces, educators can 'wake the giant' of the learning environment, transforming it into an active participant in children's education.

The next contribution incorporates the notion of 'common play behaviours'. Tracy Hopkins, EYFS Associate Headteacher: Transform Trust, tells us about how a shared understanding and commitment to planning the environment has led to improved progress and outcomes for the children in EYFS.

Tracy Hopkins: using common play behaviours to develop skills through continuous provision

In our Trust we have developed an early years vision statement titled 'What does excellence look like in the EYFS?', recognising that each of our schools are 'united but uniquely different' and that every child is unique in their experiences, languages and cultural backgrounds. Using the common play behaviours as a common ground, while being able to individualise based on our contexts, we ensure that our continuous provision is enabling and challenging for the children.

In early years education, the role of play is paramount. It is through play that children explore, learn and develop essential skills. Integrating common play behaviours into continuous provision—providing a consistent, stimulating environment throughout the day—ensures a robust framework for children's development and the opportunity to develop, and extend skills.

Common play behaviours encompass a range of activities that children naturally engage in. These include role-playing, constructive play, sensory play and exploratory play. Each type of play contributes uniquely to a child's development:

- Role-playing allows children to explore different social roles and scenarios, enhancing their understanding of the world and developing social skills and empathy.
- Constructive play, such as building with blocks or drawing, fosters creativity, problem-solving skills and spatial awareness.
- Sensory play, involving activities like playing with sand or water, aids in sensory development and fine motor skills.
- Exploratory play encourages curiosity and cognitive development as children investigate and learn about their environment.

Continuous provision involves creating a well-organised and resource-rich environment where children can access various play and learning activities throughout the day. By embedding common play behaviours into this provision, we create a dynamic and engaging learning environment.

For instance, a classroom might include designated areas for different types of play—such as a role-play corner, a construction zone with building materials, a sensory table and an exploratory science area. This setup allows children to choose activities based on their interests and developmental needs, promoting autonomous learning and sustained engagement.

In our Trust we have devised a simple document (not a checklist) of the skills that children may display in each area of provision and the resources that may facilitate this to extend their skills even further. For example, an emerging skill in the construction area may be that children are building simple towers. For this, we would need to ensure that children are provided with stackable building blocks. As their skills develop, children may build horizontally and join their buildings together. For this, we would need to provide resources such as planks and larger blocks to make bridges and other constructions. An extended skill may be more elaborate building. For this, we would need small blocks.

Incorporating common play behaviours into continuous provision enriches early years education, supporting comprehensive development and fostering a love for learning. By creating environments where play is central, we are ensuring children thrive. This approach not only aligns with the natural ways children learn but also prepares them for future educational success and lifelong learning.

The penultimate contribution in this chapter comes from Carys Jennings, a Curriculum Tutor in the Open University in Wales (PGCE). Here Carys reminds us of the importance of including children in the planning of their learning environment and offers a valuable insight to how this promotes high levels of engagement and learning.

Carys Jennings: involving children in their learning environment

Creating an environment that encourages curiosity and interest and one that reflects children and adults' intentions to learn and flourish is a joy for a practitioner. When thinking about the impact an environment has on us as adults, if we do not feel comfortable or safe in an unfamiliar or undesirable space, the same is tenfold for a young child.

Co-construction of learning spaces is not a new idea. However, listening to and observing children within different spaces can potentially reveal a myriad of new understandings about the learners in our care. An example of this was with a 5-year-old boy who had joined the reception class having moved from Luton. 'He doesn't speak Welsh', his mother shared, 'we speak English at home.' He was joining a Welsh medium school. Mum was originally from the area and her parents, who were also a support to the family were native Welsh speakers. After a few weeks he settled in and showed curiosity much like the other learners, he engaged well with the environment. He was particularly taken with the 'Ready steady cook' kitchen that was the role play area for the second half term of his schooling.

After a few observations it became clear that the young boy did indeed speak and understand some Welsh, especially the vocabulary relating to cooking. He would describe his actions or ask others to pass equipment in a knowledgeable fashion. Clearly, he felt safe and understood the context of this special space. Having discussed these observations with his parents, it became clear that often his grandmother would collect him from school, and they would undertake some baking or cooking activity during that time; this was clearly something he enjoyed, and he learnt new vocabulary with ease as it was within a context that 'made sense' to him.

Having noticed this the adults enhanced the kitchen area with additional resources to support and further engage the children, adding new packets of ingredients, utensils, cookery cards and books and note pads to create lists for shopping.

The culmination of the kitchen activities was participating in an actual cooking session with the cooks in the dining hall. We'd asked them would they be willing and able to host the event; they were delighted and helped during the session, creating pizzas and rocky road pudding slices. This brought about a whole new set of relationships with the wider staff community within the school.

From a role play environment to a real kitchen gave the children opportunities to co-operate, handle resources, learn about safety and food hygiene, interact and develop new skills in a purposeful –it was something they talked about for weeks, months and even very recently (16 years on), whilst walking down the street in our local town a familiar face approached: 'Hi Miss'. After a brief chat before parting his words were–'Remember pizza and rocky road day Miss?–awesome!' Job done, I thought.

In the final contribution for this chapter, Dr Viki Veale, Senior Lecturer: Early Years and Primary Education, from St Mary's University, Twickenham, reminds us of the transformational impact the learning environment has for children's overall development.

Dr. Viki Veale: theory into practice: re-shaping the indoor environment to transform behaviour

Some time ago, I was invited to visit a four-form entry setting that was concerned about behaviour in their Reception. The setting had invested a great deal of money into renovating its outdoor environment, which was beautiful, but the real problems were in the classroom. During the renovations, the school had installed a beautiful rainbow coloured canopy to provide shade in the outdoor area and as I was led from room to room, the light filtering through the windows shifted from cool, calming purple, blue and green to a warm invigorating yellow to an angry red. Perhaps unsurprisingly, it was in the red room that concern was highest! In addition to the angry red light flooding this room, the class mat was brightly coloured and busy, the walls were covered in printed resources designed to promote literacy, high frequency words hung from the ceiling and the storage spaces were overflowing with an abundance of mismatched plastic resources and puzzles with missing pieces. It was completely overwhelming.

The use of neutral colours and natural resources creates a peaceful, tranquil space where children and practitioners feel relaxed and comfortable promoting harmonious relationships (Jarman, 2024). *The Curiosity Approach* highlights that decluttering enables children to see available resources and use them purposefully (Bennett and Hellyn, 2021). Removing the plethora of plastic toys not only aligns with today's sustainability goals but also draws on the Montessori approach which emphasises the use of real objects (Isaacs, 2014). The careful curation of resources and use of natural materials is also emphasised by Steiner, who believed this practice better enabled children to make agentic choices about how to pursue their interests (Nichol, 2016).

Returning to the setting some years later, I found it transformed. The rainbow canopy was gone, replaced with a neutral sunshade in a natural fabric. The classrooms had been stripped out, all the broken toys and puzzles with missing pieces removed and the resources were now carefully curated and displayed to spark curiosity. Natural elements had been brought in with class plants, branches and loose parts. The garish display boards were now backed in hessian, the brightly coloured matt replaced with a soft grey one, and gone were the ceilings dripping with high frequency words: in short the whole setting had been transformed. The practitioners had worked hard to put theory into practice, and the result was an indoor environment that was calm and pleasant, where positive relationships were flourishing and where children were able to learn effectively.

In conclusion

This chapter has explored the significance of the indoor learning environment in early years education, emphasising its role beyond aesthetics to actively support children's learning and development. It highlights how purposeful planning transforms spaces into environments that drive provision, foster engagement and encourage discovery. Drawing from a range of guidance and perspectives from various experts, the chapter underscores the importance of inclusivity, open-ended resources and the practitioner's role in shaping a meaningful space. The overarching message is that the learning environment should be owned by the children—designed to empower their exploration, nurture their creativity and support their individual needs while reflecting the values and expertise of knowledgeable practitioners.

Summary of key points

- When designing and evaluating the indoor learning environment consider the purpose of it in promoting holistic learning, including the aspects included in the characteristics framework.
- Ensure that resources support the consolidation of known knowledge and skills as well as offering the experiences of new discoveries.
- Model how the provision areas can be used, using these frequent opportunities to introduce the play patterns, use of language and application of knowledge and skills.

- Consider how to include the children in the further development of the learning environment. How can their views and ideas be authentically listened to?
- Incorporate opportunities to perfect the impact of the learning environment: is it continuing to engage children, provide support and challenge? Does it still enable children to show you their achievements?

References

Australian Children's Education and Care Quality Authority (2018). Guide to the national quality framework. https://www.acecqa.gov.au/sites/default/files/2024-03/Guide-to-the-NQF-web.pdf

Bennett, S. and Hellyn, L. (2021). *The Curiosity Approach*. Available at: https://www.thecuriosityapproach.com (Accessed: 13 September 2025).

Delany, K. (2018). *Waking the 'Third Teacher': The Whys and Hows Te Whāriki: Principle to Practice*. Educational Leadership Project. https://www.elp.co.nz/files/delany_k_waking_the_third_teacher.pdf

Drake, J. (2013). *Planning for Children's Play and Learning: Meeting Children's Needs in the Later Stages of the EYFS* (4th ed.). London: Routledge. https://doi.org/10.4324/9780203762080

Hawkins, D. (2023). Reggio Emilia quotes. Number Dyslexia, Available at: https://numberdyslexia.com/reggio-emilia-quotes/#:~:text=David%20Hawkins (Accessed December 2024).

Isaacs, B. (2014). *Bringing the Montessori Approach to Your Early Years Practice*. London: Routledge.

Jarman, E. (2024). Targeted use of colour in learning environments. Available at: https://elizabethjarman.com/wp-content/uploads/2018/04/the-cfs-approach-and-targeted-use-of-colour.pdf (Accessed 4 July 2024).

Maria Montessori Institute. (2024). Why Movement Is So Important for Children's Development. [Online] Available at https://www.mariamontessori.org/news/why-movement-is-so-important-for-childrens-development/?utm_source=chatgpt.com (accessed 13th September 2025).

Nichol, J. (2016). *Bringing the Steiner Approach to Your Early Years Practice*. London: Routledge.

3 Learning environment
Outdoors

Jayne Carter

Introduction

Do you enjoy being outdoors? The wealth of research exploring the many benefits of a well-planned outdoor environment for young children is vast, extensive and significant. Findings, such as those shared in this chapter, highlight the unique contribution being outdoors makes to core aspects such as physical skills and appreciation of nature/the wider ecosystem as well as the positive effect on mental health and wellbeing. Contributions included in this chapter show how this research moves into implementation in a variety and type of settings.

Pondering question: what can the outdoor environment offer to children to deepen their learning?

All research and thought pieces currently available explore how the outdoors not only contributes to the child's experience of being an early years learner but effectively presents the multitude of decisions taken by the adults in settings or schools. What is absolutely crucial is the commitment of all practitioners in not only understanding the purpose of 'being outdoors' but embracing the distinct characteristics it offers to both the children and themselves as the adults also participating in the outdoors. In their insightful research study, Scollan and Farini (2021) advocate for a shift in the view of the outdoor learning space, moving from the notion of an 'enabling environment' to 'an environment which enables'. This subtle yet significant change of emphasis moves the onus from the environment simply being present as the child interacts with it to a much more direct, responsive and vital function in the learning process. The 'adult-centric vision' of an enabling environment, where the decisions are fundamentally made by the adults on behalf of the child, can, according to Scollan and Farini, stifle the very intention of the environment – it ceases to be truly enabling.

Developing an enabling outdoor learning environment

An environment which enables, catapults the emphasis towards respectful relationships. There is a dynamic attached to this relationship; that of a 'to and fro' collaboration which meanders between adult initiated, child initiated and partnered play. When the outdoor space is pioneered as an environment promoting success for all children, planning takes on the role of documenting the process of thinking – noting the journey that the outdoors

DOI: 10.4324/9781003505266-3

has for supporting learning. These professional thoughts commence the start of the intended respectful relationship as cited above. Considering both the learning potential and the purpose of the outdoor environment merges both in a potentially dynamic synchronicity. Sandseter et al. (2020) explored the type of outdoor spaces children themselves preferred and which practitioners were able to observe progress in. In their study, Sandseter et al. captured a variety of different outdoor environments through video to aid observation and analysis, including the more traditional playground type species, spaces where nature and equipment were blended and the pure forest school/outdoor classroom environments. Whilst all environments documented levels of interaction and engagement, the most successful environments were those where the children were introduced to the potential of the different resources included in them. Free discovery type play was indeed evident but much of this plateaued without the additional adult support in place. Support primarily occurred through modelling and shared learning conversations and talk.

> For practitioners and facilitators (e.g. landscape architects) of children's outdoor play, an understanding of predictability of how children perceive affordances and actualise them should be basic knowledge.
>
> Van Eyken & Duncan (2020)

Our first contribution in this chapter is by Paul Silver-Wolfe, Educator at Little Wild Tribe, who shares the unique characteristics of this setting. There are valuable insights to how provision is set up, how both adults and children interact in it and the many positive benefits for their children's development.

Paul Silver-Wolfe: my view of Little Wild Tribe: outdoor learning at its best

Little Wild Tribe (LWT) is not just a forest school at a nursery; it is an outdoor learning environment for children aged 6 months until they go to school. We are situated in a country park allowing our children to be outside surrounded by nature. We have a base camp that has a couple of large tents and two wooden buildings to use when the weather is not appropriate to be outside. I work with the older children, aged three to four, and we make use of a wooded area in the park which we walk to and from each day. The nursery is divided into three tribes: the Minis (6 months-2), the Saplings (2-3), and the Woodland (3-5). The age brackets are a rough guide as each child progresses on their own merit depending on how they are developing and able to assess risk and communicate.

LWT has an ethos of holistic learning. Every part of the child's day is carefully thought about and risk assessed to ensure maximum enjoyment and engagement with all aspects of the seven areas of learning. As an educator, it is my goal to get our children confident and resilient to every aspect of learning and development. The environment and nature are very important to each child's development where they gain a huge respect for both flora and fauna and benefit from the calming effect of the greenery, also becoming physically fit from all the walking and climbing (each child walks approximately three miles a day).

Respecting our environment also extends to respecting our children by letting them talk, problem solve and come up with ideas, by making their own decisions using their knowledge and judgement. No is a word rarely heard as we prefer to respect our children's choices, allow them to make mistakes and give explanations for why not to do something.

The woods gives the children a chance to take managed risks with climbing and running around over uneven ground. We use continuous provision (CP) at the woods and base camp. With designated areas for role play, bug hunting, building and digging, art and a stage area to perform on, each day we add to the CP with our own activities.

The EYFS is taught using our own curriculum (called the Cultural Calendar). This gives our educators a starting point for activities to engage the children and progress learning. Our curriculum is divided into months and is a connected curriculum as we include the prime areas in everything we do. A sustained shared thinking approach is applied to activities, where our children collectively problem solve using the CP.

The children learn quickly to understand risks because of being outdoors all the time. There are several factors to take into account each day. The weather, the animals, the plants and the two service roads we cross daily are helping the children to make the correct choices with our guidance. This I believe creates confidence and a resilience to failure.

Maybe the biggest factor for our children's success is the space we give them. Both basecamp and the woods are large areas for the children to spread out. We provide areas to relax and hide and open space to run around or use for large activities. By the time our oldest children are ready for their next adventure of going to school, they have learnt to be friendly, having developed a culture of looking after one another. Their last summer with us is spent learning at a greater depth with more tool use such as saws, hammers, electric drills and screwdrivers. Our older Woodlanders gain a respect for fire as we regularly have a campfire going and facilitate the children building and lighting their own. I also encourage the creation of their own artist masterpieces on the forest floor or to hang in our gallery, allowing each child to use their creativity such as organising the acting-out stories or musical performances on our stage. To enlarge the children's knowledge of the local area, we undertake longer walks to the local library and shops and the castle nearby which seems to build their physical resilience, making for a more enjoyable outing. We will also take these older children further into the park for nature walks to discover and learn about our ecology. One of my favourite activities on these walks is to go litter picking as this gives me the chance to explain why we must keep the environment free of rubbish.

A lot of the positive outcomes for learning outdoors are hard to quantify even though there is a consensus of opinion and lots of research stating that being surrounded by nature improves mental wellbeing and keeps children healthy. The feedback from parents is positive with most children still enjoying being outside in nature and achieving at school.

In this second contribution to this chapter, Thalia Krassa, trainee primary teacher, reinforces the importance of outdoor learning, sharing both UK and international perspectives.

Learning led versus resources led

Just as with the indoor learning environment, the same process of being learning led should also be followed, not least to provide a consistency of approach for the children in the setting/school. Predictability through agreed routines provides an element of calm and balance for children who can then busy themselves in the world of playing without being consumed by uncertain thoughts and feelings. Leading from planned learning as well as anticipating independent spontaneous learning outdoors secures the expectation of ambition – experiences outdoors **will** support development. As shown in both research and practice in Early Years settings/schools, this intention is entirely admirable, forming a significant aspect of intention statements and ethos of establishments. However, what can often differ is the availability of appropriate outdoor spaces and resources to make this a reality. Practitioners want to be able to encourage children to be able to embrace nature, exposing them to various landscapes and afford them the opportunity of interacting with scenery; they completely understand the power of these experiences for their children's holistic development. However, constraints of budget, time, expertise, safety considerations, parental choice, etc. can negatively impact the desire and advancement of the outdoor experience. In these circumstances, the trajectory of learning led, the potential of the environment to promote learning and the role of the adult to strengthen this learning are paramount in working towards a quality experience outdoors. Without this trajectory in place, agreed and followed, the type of environment is somewhat irrelevant and defunct. The most well-resourced nature-based outdoor environment cannot on its own provide optimum learning but a well-thought-out environment which engages, directs and challenges children together with a knowledgeable, enthusiastic and committed Early Years workforce can and does generate desired personal growth and outcomes.

In this second contribution to this chapter, Thalia Krassa, Trainee Primary Teacher, reinforces the importance of outdoor learning, sharing both UK and international perspectives.

Thalia Krassa: learning environment: outdoors

Outdoor learning has been a prominent aspect of early years education for millennia, highlighting the significant role of the outdoors as an invaluable asset and setting in which children acquire knowledge through their senses and engagement with the physical surroundings. The premise behind these techniques was that children effectively address issues via playing and generate learning by exploring and experimenting in their environment. Research suggests that outdoor activities and exposure to nature are crucial for the physical and cognitive growth of children. Additionally, utilising outdoor areas as educational settings can enhance children's well-being and academic progress. Outdoor learning is based on the concept of engaging in educational activities outside of traditional indoor classroom environments. It allows children to explore, play, create, and actively explore, build, and communicate their ideas. A natural outdoor educational and play environment refers to an outside area at an early childhood education institution that is equipped with various characteristics intended to encourage both organised and unorganised exercise, activities, and gaining knowledge. Outdoor learning is a deliberate educational activity that can be conducted both within and outside of a school setting. It involves interactive experiences with multiple resources and items. It can also be conducted in several settings. For instance, urban children may engage in activities such as exploring a town to observe the architectural structures of buildings or analysing the numerical patterns shown on dwellings. It may occur in a playground when an educator brings the children outside to acquire knowledge about the concepts of shadows and light. Outdoor learning has gained popularity in Icelandic classrooms in the past few years. These outdoor classes entail children acquiring knowledge and skills in an outdoor setting, allowing them to engage every sense they have in seeing the real world and nature. Þelamerkur, a school located in North Iceland, has utilised the presence of a local river and woodland to educate children about nature and conduct outdoor maths sessions. The early childhood playing field should serve as a vital educational setting that fosters children's engagement in play, exploration, physical activity, and self-expression through many means. Outdoor education should be accessible to all children, regardless of their age or aptitude. Even young children, regardless of their age, derive advantages from the educational opportunities offered by outdoor learning. It can also have a significant positive impact on children with special needs. Establishing a sensory garden in a preschool environment or outdoor educational space offers children the opportunity to engage in outdoor exploration and learning. An outdoor learning environment that incorporates a diverse range of colours and materials, together with ramps and hiding spots, offers an ideal garden for children with different needs. It provides advantages for every child; therefore it is crucial that the activities are tailored to the particular abilities of each child. In Swedish woodland schools, children are organised into cohorts consisting of peers of the same age, and tasks are chosen according to the aptitude of each cohort. Efforts to foster reverence for the environment should be supported. Preschool educators ought to foster children's inherent inquisitiveness towards their surroundings and utilise it as a means to educate them about the surrounding world. It is important for individuals to remember that nature provides a diverse range of resources and chances for investigation and revelation.

In this next contribution, Natasha Nechat-Murphy, a Teaching Assistant, explores in more detail the aspect of ESE: Environmental and Sustainability Education and how adults can support children to engage in this important area of learning.

Natasha Nechat-Murphy: the numerous benefits of the outdoor environment and its impact on children's development

Bruner and Piaget were pioneers of physical exploration outdoors. They understood that by engaging in practical outdoor experiences, children internalise prior knowledge and develop a solid understanding of fundamental concepts. We must view the outdoor environment as an extension of learning, rather than a separate setting from the indoor classroom. This perspective allows for continuity, consistency, and consolidation of children's learning.

The outdoor environment provides an opportunity to educate children about Environmental and Sustainability Education (ESE). Through ESE, children acquire knowledge and skills that will help them create a more sustainable future. This type of education enhances cognitive, socio-emotional, and behavioural dimensions of learning, while also promoting the achievement of sustainable development goals. For example, over the course of an academic year, children can build upon their existing knowledge of ESE by making their own compost and planting their own flowers. This hands-on experience allows them to understand the benefits of sustainable practices. Children can further develop their knowledge by transforming their outdoor area into a wildlife garden using the flowers, plants, and vegetables they have grown. This collaborative activity not only promotes sustainability but also solidifies their understanding of sustainable development goals. Throughout these activities, children are actively investigating, experiencing, and learning about the natural world. By growing flowers and plants, they can connect with nature and develop a deeper appreciation for the environment.

Children not only gain a deeper understanding of the world around them through the outdoor environment, but they also enhance their physical development, artistic expression, communication skills, social and emotional growth, literacy, and mathematical skills. In the wildlife garden, children can watch plants grow and measure their height with rulers and metre sticks as learning of measurements is developed practically and mathematical concepts are grasped visually. Outdoor spaces also encourage language development through meaningful interactions between children, adults, and peers. By engaging in physical activities, children lay a foundation for language and cognitive growth, which educators can further enhance by introducing new vocabulary. Outdoor environments offer a variety of writing tools and canvases, allowing children to expand their mark-making skills beyond the confines of the indoor classroom.

Scientific inquiry and artistic abilities are enhanced by engaging children in outdoor learning experiences. This not only fosters their connection with sustainability but also stimulates their creativity and critical thinking. By establishing cross-curricular connections, children's natural curiosity and motivation are nurtured, encouraging them to become lifelong learners. Additionally, learning outside allows children to apply their existing knowledge in new and meaningful contexts, whilst promoting adaptability and deeper understanding. It's important for educators to carefully plan learning experiences to ensure a seamless progression of knowledge over time that prioritises depth over breadth. Engaging children in active learning through outdoor sustainability projects empowers them to make a positive impact, while the benefits of being outdoors on their mental health and wellbeing are significant.

Following on from Natasha's insightful contribution, Sandra Beale, Science Communicator to 0-6 and founder of Toddler and Early Years STEM shares personal reflection on how provision outdoors introduces children to the world of STEM.

Sandra Beale: toddler and Early Years STEM (science, technology, art and maths)

The learning environment outside is full of adventure and possibilities. It is the place where life unfolds every second, be it watching the busy insect highways in a pond or watching the bees and butterflies flit from flower to flower, each busy creating invisible networks, or the spiders spinning their intricate sticky webs.

I love taking the STEM sessions outside especially in the autumn and spring so the children can get up close with all the nature around them. I let them use magnifying glasses to look at insects closely, observe the pattern of leaves, watch as the slow snail navigates its way around a stone leaving a slimy trail, or the earthworms wriggle out of sight when their soil is disturbed.

As part of their outdoor discovery, I encourage the children to collect leaves of different sizes and textures and to trace the leaves with the tips of their fingers and feel the differences in each leaf. The children are also encouraged to sit quietly and listen to the bees hum, woodpeckers drum, frogs croak, and the melodious call of birds and appreciate the natural music of outside.

One of the experiments I enjoy doing with the children is an autumnal soup, where each child puts in different leaves, conkers, twigs, and so forth in a big bowl of water and then scoop their creation into smaller bowls.

I often ask the children to observe what happens to pinecones in cold water and how to tell if a leaf is breathing in water. To take the experiment further I let them add food colouring to the water, which they love to do. This is a fun and messy experiment with lots of water and colour and in the process the children are learning and building the foundation to further discoveries and explorations.

Another favourite is creating a river with foil. For this experiment you would need a roll of foil, some pebbles, water and blue food colouring. Let the children decide how to build the river. You could guide them by explaining that a fast-moving river follows the rules of gravity as it flows downwards from a height compared to a river that flows on one level.

Roll out the foil on the grass or outdoor space and turn up the sides so water doesn't spill out, putting a few pebbles around the sides to give a bit of support. You could stack a few books or bricks to give the river a bit of height, then add blue food colouring to a jug of water and let the children pour the jug onto the foil to create their river. To make it more fun, you could suggest a boat race with small paper boats.

The outdoor environment offers endless STEM opportunities!

The next contribution gives an important reminder of the many benefits for children to spend purposeful time in the outdoors, reinforcing the significance of implementing an effective planning and monitoring process.

Jake Balding: embracing nature: the power of an outdoor learning environment

In our world, as early childhood education is recognised as that important first step to a young person's development, the outdoor environment currently stands as a beacon of exploration, discovery and innovation. With this comes endless opportunity as our outdoor learning environments go beyond the boundaries of a standard playground, but rather they serve as a dynamic classroom that links children to nature.

Research shows that a natural outdoor play and learning environment enriches child development through benefitting health, wellbeing and emotional development within our youngest learners (Cooper, 2015). The key to unlocking these huge benefits? Two things: an upkept environment and a natural one. It is through these two benefits that we can truly explore the many great possibilities that come with it.

The developmental opportunities are well documented but the benefits of using an outdoor environment do not stop there. Perhaps one of the biggest achievements with a natural outdoor setting is the ability to cultivate environmental consciousness within the children. As they are allowed to dig in the soil, plant seeds and watch as different wildlife explore these vast environments, an appreciation for the outdoor environment and all that connects it will flourish.

In order to achieve these many great benefits however, the design of the outdoor environment plays a crucial role. A setting cannot just throw resources anywhere and hope that this will provide sufficient benefit to the child, but these such resources must work around the natural aspects of the environment, as it is crucial not to disturb this balance. Any resource placed into the outdoor learning space must serve a purpose, so that it may cater to the inclusive needs of all children (Stine, 1996).

There is a need to constantly be adaptive in the Early Years sector, and practitioners, parents, and carers must always be looking to place the child's best interests at heart. In a world of constant change, with climate concerns on the rise, and the number of children now with access to screens, it is now more important than ever to utilise the outdoor spaces in effective ways (Kiviranta et al., 2024).

Fey Cole, FE Curriculum Manager for the Department of Health, Life and Personal Sciences provides an intriguing reflection piece in the next contribution. Highlighting international outdoor learning practices provides an opportunity to reflect on our own existing or intended practices.

Fey Cole: shaping provision through voluntary governance

I live and work in Northern Ireland where the luscious green spaces come from copious amounts of rain and the seasons are well defined. Wellington boots and muddy puddles are very much our thing! A focus of my work in early years education is on developing outdoor provision and I frequently have the opportunity to visit many exceptional settings across the province who have moved away from static climbing frames and only break times outside, to facilitating the full early years curriculum outdoors. With this approach, the children have autonomy to transition with ease between the indoor and outdoor environment.

My work has taken me on trips to visit settings across the globe and to collaborate with practitioners from other countries. This has challenged my perspectives on outdoor play and led to me having to rethink how the outdoors is utilised when working in small spaces and with extreme temperatures. When visiting Hong Kong, the heat was so extreme that outdoor time had to be limited and when working with colleagues in India, I learnt that the air quality was so poor in certain areas the time outside also had to be restricted.

When visiting early years settings in Madrid, the built-up city environment meant that many of the settings did not have outdoor spaces, so instead practitioners made use of community spaces for children's learning. It was a joy to observe how children not only connected with nature but also connected with people from the local community. Children observed adults making a bench and helped fetch the tools, learning their purpose. Children and adults tended to the beds full of produce together that could be brought back to the nursery and people's homes to use as ingredients in the kitchen. I reflected on how the same could be created within the United Kingdom.

We may not have these same community spaces ourselves, but children can gain a vast amount from getting out to the local allotments or park to visit those taking care of them, or from you dedicating a space in your own play space for community work. In my book on intergenerational practice (Cole, 2023), I have shared case studies from nursery and primary school educators who have connected with grandparents and older residents of their town through sustainable activities linked to children's learning. These have included making up window boxes together, learning new woodwork skills from the adults and sharing stories outdoors. For us to feel we belong, we need to feel connected. By opening our own outdoor space (following the required health and safety procedures) children get to develop meaningful relationships with people they may not normally get to meet, and with the natural world.

We are at a crisis point when it comes to global warming. As Early Years educators we may not have the capacity to change the path governments are following, but we can connect children with the natural environment and teach them an ethics of care, for how we respond to both others and to the environment. If they are role-modelled values that look outwards towards others and society, we can make a difference for the next generation.

In the next contribution, Louise Monange, Director of Nursery operations: The DEN Nursery Group shares how research has led to the development of an outdoor learning environment which has both supported and challenged children.

Louise Monange: the transformative power of outdoor learning in Early Years education

The DEN Nursery Group has strategically aligned its methods and approaches with the latest findings from neuroscience, emphasising the significant benefits of outdoor environments. By incorporating innovative educational models such as Forest Schools and Urban Forest Schools, the DEN Nursery Group provides early years children with a wealth of transformative learning experiences. Rooted in neuroscience, these approaches utilise the natural world to foster holistic development across cognitive, emotional, social, and physical domains. Through outdoor exploration, children can engage deeply with their environment, facilitating a richer and more impactful learning journey.

Neuroscience underscores that children learn best in environments rich in sensory experiences that allow for exploration. The outdoor environment engages all the major eight senses, stimulating neural pathways that improve learning and memory retention. For instance, in Forest Schools, children actively engage with their surroundings, which fosters critical thinking and problem-solving skills. Engaging in activities like climbing and jumping develops balance and spatial awareness, while awareness of body positioning aids coordination and physical development. Activities such as building structures with natural materials or creating art from leaves require planning and adaptability, equipping children with essential cognitive skills vital for their development. This hands-on, experiential learning not only encourages scientific inquiry but also deepens their understanding of ecosystems.

Limited access to open green spaces should not be a deterrent to an exciting learning environment. For example, while access to natural spaces can be limited in urban environments, an Urban Forest School can be created, effectively integrating outdoor learning into city life.

The soothing effects of nature on the developing brain are profound, particularly concerning stress and anxiety reduction. Both Forest and Urban Forest Schools equip children with coping skills through their interactions with the natural world. Engaging in risk-taking activities, such as navigating uneven terrain, enables children to learn about their limits and capabilities in a secure setting, thereby fostering emotional regulation. This connection to nature cultivates emotional resilience, helping children manage challenges with greater ease.

Collaborative outdoor activities promote the development of critical social skills. In both Forest and Urban Forest Schools, children frequently participate in group tasks, such as building shelters or exploring nature trails. Such teamwork requires effective communication, negotiation, and empathy, enhancing social cognition. By working together, children develop a sense of belonging and interconnectedness with both their peers and the broader environment. This collective learning experience reinforces community bonds, promoting a supportive network among students.

The outdoor environment provides an expansive, imaginative canvas for play and creativity. Forest Schools emphasise open-ended play, encouraging children to transform found objects, like sticks and stones, into fantastical elements of their imaginative narratives. This type of self-directed play allows children to express themselves freely and explore their ingenuity.

The integration of outdoor environments into early years education through models such as Forest and Urban Forest Schools illustrates the profound impact that nature can have on children's learning. The outdoor environment plays a pivotal role in shaping a generation of resilient, creative and socially conscious individuals, capable of thriving in an increasingly complex world.

Echoing the views shared by Louise, Simon Airey, Visiting Teacher, provides a personal insight into how the outdoor environment can be used to support both key knowledge and skills, emphasising the flexibility of the outdoors to support, guide and challenge children's thinking.

Simon Airey: using the outside classroom as a visiting teacher

> Providers must provide access to an outdoor play area. If that is not possible, they must ensure that outdoor activities are planned and taken on a daily basis.
>
> (Dfe 2025: 40)

The outdoor classroom can offer a plethora of opportunities and experiences for children. Exploring natural elements such as soil, water, plants, and animals stimulates children's senses and lays the foundation for curiosity, communication and inquiry. For example, if there is a mud kitchen in the outdoor classroom, children can mix different natural materials together, fostering creativity, sensory exploration and social interaction.

Secondly, outdoor spaces facilitate hands-on exploration and active learning, which are central to the EYFS framework. Children have the freedom to engage in open-ended, child-initiated play, allowing them to follow their interests and curiosity. Through activities like building with loose parts, balancing on logs or engaging in imaginative play in natural settings, children develop their creativity, problem-solving skills, and physical coordination. These experiences support the EYFS goal of promoting active learning and critical thinking skills in young children (Dfe 2025: 17).

The outdoor classroom brings concepts to life. For example, rather than discussing the weather in group time, I prefer to take the children outside so that they can directly experience different types of weather. It is imperative that the children experience all weathers and that we adapt what we are wearing accordingly. If it is raining, the communication that can occur is far more rich than sticking symbols of the weather onto a chart.

Risk-taking is something that can occur more frequently in the outside classroom. It is imperative that the children are involved in assessing the risk in the outside classroom for themselves. Sometimes, I would take children outside with clipboards and they would use visual prompts to indicate if something was safe or not. For example, they would see if the floor was too slippery or if something was broken. The ripple effect of this was that they would tell other children in order to highlight risks and work together with an adult or other children in order to mitigate the risks.

The outdoor classroom also enables provocations. Planting fruit and vegetables with the view to making meals with them is a link to a life skill and demonstrates to children the importance of sustainable food practices, environmental stewardship and healthy eating habits. For example, we made vegetable soup and shared this with the children's parents and carers.

The outdoor classroom serves as a valuable environment for co-regulating with children. Engaging in nature-based activities, such as observing flowers or trees, can have a calming effect on children's emotions. Hanscom (2016) says that because being outside creates opportunities for movement, this helps to "develop a strong vestibular system, which supports attention… and also helps regulate emotions in children" (p. 156). By incorporating nature-based experiences into their daily routine, educators can create opportunities for children to manage their emotions and cultivate a sense of inner peace.

This next contribution, by Sam Robinson, Programme Lead and Lecturer in Early Childhood Studies, provides a thoughtful piece for personal reflection.

Sam Robinson: branching out: the endless opportunities of Forest School

As a former Forest School Practitioner, I have experienced first-hand the rich and wonderful opportunities the outdoors environment has to offer in enhancing children's learning and development. The Forest School ethos naturally lends itself to developing a stronger connection to nature, which can reduce stress, increase motivation and boost overall mental health and wellbeing. I observed a number of skills in Forest School that could not be replicated in an indoors classroom environment. When children engage in activities like creating a bug habitat, climbing a tree or building a den, important cognitive skills can be enhanced, such as concentration and problem solving. Everybody can succeed at Forest School, and this is a very powerful message for children to receive, as it builds self-esteem, motivation and a sense of achievement. These experiences are significantly important for children and their holistic development. Another significant benefit of being outdoors is inclusivity. The outdoors caters for all learning styles and needs, which can help children feel empowered and engaged.

I was so inspired by Forest School that I decided to investigate the benefits of forest school as part of my research for my masters studies, titled: Branching out: The findings from a local Forest School Intervention for Primary School aged Children. My research found a clear increase in children's personal, social and emotional development. There were significant increases in children's levels of wellbeing, challenge and engagement. Notably, all the children who took part in the interventions developed respect for themselves, others and the environment. During the sessions, children developed a deeper understanding and awareness of their surroundings. An example of this relates to conversations which would take place between myself and the children about creatures' natural habitats and which areas we would dig.

From my work in Forest School, as well as my research, it is clearly evident to me that all children should have opportunities to play and learn outdoors. Although this need is reflected in Early Years frameworks, it becomes increasingly less prominent once children enter school and are expected to engage in more 'formal learning'. As practitioners, we have the ability to take learning outdoors and make it accessible for all children. By doing this, we can unlock the strengths, interests and potential of children which could not only promote positive outcomes, but also help children feel seen.

Lyndsey Farmer, Vogrie Outdoor ELC, continues this important discussion, exploring the #redjacketpeople community they have developed. This final contribution ensures that the key messages of the importance of outdoor learning included in this chapter are celebrated.

Lyndsey Farmer: #redjacketpeople

Vogrie Outdoor ELC is a fully outdoor setting which caters for a maximum of 56 children in any one day. The setting has the full use of Vogrie Country Park and is a Local Authority ELC within Midlothian Council.

Vogrie provides a learning environment which enables children to explore their capabilities to their full extent. The curriculum is experienced in a natural and authentic way with opportunities to immerse themselves in concepts and skills. For example, when discussing river flow, depth and direction, we go to the river and observe and when safe to do so we will enter the river, allowing children to feel the speed of the water. Our children use their wellies as an indicator for depth along with welly sticks to discuss whether they can enter without getting wet feet. Our environment becomes the resource along with our skilled adults nicknamed the #redjacketpeople who firmly believe in the importance of outdoor learning and the ability to build children's wellbeing in the outdoors and in caring for our environment.

The environment allows our children to develop emergent literacy through discussion, large-scale mark making on the forest floor, and storytelling in spaces that inspire the mind. Using the natural elements of our setting such as fallen trees, slopes and rivers our children use their bodies, building their muscle memory on a daily basis. These movements have been proven to enhance children's ability for literacy skills once in a classroom.

Risk is explored as a solution-focused concept. Instead of a ban on certain risks we explore ways along with our children in which we can overcome the risks to make the experience possible. When assessing risk we follow a benefit-risk outlook, always analysing how the benefit to children's learning and development can outweigh the risks.

The changing seasons provide new provocations, allowing our children to ask questions and discuss their ideas and thoughts around changes to the environment. Most recently, after a couple of strong storms, our children found that their beloved "bag tree" had blown over. It was a huge, towering beach tree and the effects of this coming down were devastating to the surrounding area and to the physical landscape. The children were extremely concerned about how this had happened discussing between themselves and their #redjacketpeople. They wondered if it had been a bear and decided to try pushing it to work out how heavy it was, alas they were unable to move it even an inch. Together with their #redjacketpeople, a weather app and discussion we discovered the effects Storm Isha had on our tree. With further exploration and investigation we discovered that our bag tree had weak roots which were crumbling in our hands. This provided a deep sense of understanding of how Mother Nature interacts with the Vogrie environment but also how trees can become sick with disease meaning they stand less chance of survival during storms.

Our environment, along with the #redjacketpeople, provide learning which ensures children build a special bond with nature for years to come. After being open for 4 years, seeing many children off to school, the #redjacketpeople have a strong awareness of the importance of outdoor learning in building confident and capable learners who are not frightened to challenge their minds through problem solving.

In conclusion

This chapter explores the transformative impact of outdoor learning environments in early years education, emphasising their unique role in fostering children's physical, cognitive and emotional development. It highlights how well-planned outdoor spaces contribute to essential skills like resilience, environmental awareness and holistic growth, reinforcing the importance of practitioner involvement in shaping meaningful experiences. The contributions showcase diverse perspectives—from forest schools to urban play environments—demonstrating how outdoor learning deepens engagement through exploration, risk-taking, and collaborative learning. Through reflective insights and international comparisons, the chapter advocates for the intentional design of outdoor spaces that empower children to connect with nature, engage in creative problem solving and develop a lifelong respect for their surroundings.

Summary of key points

- The role of the adult is crucial in ensuring that learning outdoors is maximised. This includes a secure subject knowledge, a skilful blend of the awareness of the unique characteristic of the outdoors together with the most effective strategies for interaction.
- Learning led rather than resource/activity led shifts the balance towards success.
- Outdoor learning environments provide a natural setting for children to develop a deep respect for the world around them. By engaging in hands-on experiences such as planting, observing wildlife, and exploring natural landscapes, children gain an understanding of sustainability, conservation and their role in protecting the environment for future generations.
- The outdoor space serves as more than just a play area—it is a dynamic environment that fosters cognitive, social and emotional growth. Through active exploration, problem solving and cooperative activities, children refine key skills that contribute to resilience, confidence and their ability to navigate complex challenges both inside and outside the classroom.
- Initiating a new outdoor environment or evaluating a current outdoor environment could involve the whole school/setting community.

References

Cole, F. (2023). *Intergenerational Learning in Schools and Settings: An Educator''s Guide*. Oxen, England: Routledge Publication.

Cooper, A. (2015). Nature and the outdoor learning environment: The forgotten resource in early childhood education. *International Journal of Early Childhood Environmental Education*, 3(1), pp. 85-97, [pdf] Available at: https://files.eric.ed.gov/fulltext/EJ1108430.pdf (Accessed August 22nd 2024).

DfE (2025). Early years foundation stage statutory framework for group and school-based providers. Setting the standards for learning, development and care for children from birth to five. Available at: https://assets.publishing.service.gov.uk/media/687105a381dd8f70f5de3ea9/EYFS_framework_for_group_and_school_based_providers_.pdf (Accessed 21 July 2025, 13 September 2024).

Hanscom, A. J. (2016). *Balanced and Barefoot* - Raincoast Books.

Kiviranta, L., Lindfors, E., Luukka, E., and Rönkkö, M.L. (2024). Outdoor learning in early childhood education: Exploring benefits and challenges. *Educational Research*, Taylor & Francis Group, 66(1), pp. 102-119 [pdf] Available at: https://www.tandfonline.com/doi/pdf/10.1080/00131881.2023.2285762 (Accessed August 21st 2024).

Sandseter, E. B. H., Storli, R., and Sando, O. J. (2020). The dynamic relationship between outdoor environments and children's play. *Education 3-13*, 50(1), pp. 97-110. https://doi.org/10.1080/03004279.2020.1833063

Scollan, A., and Farini, F. (2021). From enabling environments to environments that enable: Notes for theoretical innovation at the intersection between environments, learning and children's agency, *An Leanbh Óg: The OMEP Ireland Journal of Early Childhood Studies*, 14(1), pp. 20-39.

Stine, S. (1996). *Landscapes for Learning: Creating Outdoor Environments for Children and Youth*. New York: John Wiley & Sons. https://www.booktopia.com.au/landscapes-for-learning-sharon-stine/book/9780471162223.html

Van Eyken, J., and Duncan, M. J. (2020). Affordances and outdoor play: A theoretical perspective on children's interaction with natural environments. *Children's Geographies*, 18(6), pp. 705-717.

4 Effective partnership with parents

Poppy Gibson

Introduction

Building effective partnerships with parents in the Early Years means creating a strong, collaborative relationship where educators and parents work together to support a child's holistic development and wellbeing. In order to best support and nurture the learners in our care, an effective partnership between parents and carers and the setting is fundamental. This fourth chapter contemplates the boundary between early years settings and home, drawing on research and reports. In this chapter we share valuable insights from ten experienced professionals. These contributions are from practitioners who have developed their own effective parent partnership process, both on personal and school levels, and provide reflections on the differences these processes have made for their shared support for their children.

Pondering question: how can a true partnership develop which respects and engages all families?

Partnerships are especially important as the people best placed to help the early years setting understand the child are the parents and carers themselves. Meaningful relationships between school and home have been shown to have a positive and significant influence on student achievement (Ashfaq, Sami, Yousaf, 2024) as well as children's holistic development (Fu, Wu and Zhuo, 2024).

How can true partnerships be achieved?

Several strategies will be explored through this chapter, but the themes that run through them seem to be open communication, mutual respect and shared responsibility among all adults involved (Ngadni and Shuang, 2024). There must, therefore, be a focus from settings and school leaders to consider their communication frameworks, the training provided to staff around communication, and the role of community support in enhancing collaboration (Fu, Wu, and Zhuo, 2024).

Building effective partnerships with parents in the early years means creating a strong, collaborative relationship where educators and parents work together to support a child's holistic development and wellbeing (Kambouri et al., 2022). This partnership recognises that parents are the child's first and most important educators and that their involvement is

DOI: 10.4324/9781003505266-4

crucial for a child's success (Vuorinen, 2021). Having a partnership between home and the early years setting can help create a safe space with the child feeling supported and understood, and surrounded by adults that care about them and care for them. This partnership can be especially important for parents of a child with challenging behaviour, as found in a study in Finland (Rautamies et al., 2021).

Rautamies et al. (2021) found that the two most important ways to develop trust were the teacher's relationship with the child, and fair teaching practices. The study also highlighted the value in the teacher's support of the parents as being capable, and the encouragement of the parents as being active parties in the educational partnership (Rautamies et al. 2021). These findings enrich understanding of the development of trust in educational partnership when working with the parents of a child with challenging behaviour.

As you read through this chapter, practical examples of how to foster trust, respect and open communication will be shared from skilled practitioners.

In this first contribution, Julie Taylor, Nursery Class Teacher within a primary school setting, reflects upon the importance of parent partnerships in the crucial early years' stages.

Julie Taylor: the importance of parent partnerships

For as long as I can remember, parent partnerships have always been part of the training process for education professionals, and, having worked in schools for several years now, I can fully understand why this is so important. Becoming a parent and seeing the importance of these relationships from the other side, I believe, made me a better practitioner, and has cemented my approach to building strong relationships with families. A negative interaction with a prospective childminder had me vowing that I would never make a family feel how we were made to feel that day. Early years is the starting block for the rest of school life, so building strong relationships from the off supports a more positive impact when children transition through school and sets the footpath for their lifelong learning journey. As a nursery teacher, I am often the first face of the educational process and I feel it is extremely important to engage not only children, but family members too. This helps make families feel a valued part of the school community and that there is a togetherness in providing the best opportunities to suit their children.

I find it imperative to discover the socioeconomic needs within the local area to allow me to fully understand what families may be facing daily. In the years following COVID, I feel it is fair to say that practitioners are seeing a greater need in the children attending early years settings but also acknowledge the needs of family members have become more prevalent too. Families are facing a much higher degree of poverty, and the strains of everyday life are having a profound impact on parents and carers. Thus, meaning that they may need our support too.

My years of experience have strengthened my acknowledgement that ways of communicating and life in general are ever changing. It is important to understand why you are trying to build positive parent partnerships and to also have strength and courage to try new ways of communicating and making changes where necessary. One of the biggest positive impacts on communication within early years at my school has been an online messaging app which has supported many of our parents who suffer with anxieties which make verbal conversation difficult. Feedback from this has been overwhelming and as a school, we are looking into ways of rolling this out for other year groups. Although technology is fantastic for some, it is also important to recognise and support those families for whom technology is not a favourable option. Getting to know the whole family is one of the privileges of working within the early years. Learning new languages or Makaton to communicate with families, even on the simplest of levels, has built bridges and allowed relationships to flourish. Inviting families into school has enabled skills to be learnt and shared, friendships have blossomed and support networks between families have appeared. Being part of the Early Years feels like belonging to a huge family of individuals who, together, can make a difference to all involved.

Clearly, the value in partnerships is the way that this fosters belonging and opens up the channels for communication. Regular and open communication channels, both formal and informal, are essential. This could include newsletters, emails, phone calls, parent-teacher conferences, and informal conversations. Active listening and respectful dialogue are crucial to understand each other's perspectives and concerns.

Building trust and respect

A foundation of trust and mutual respect is essential for a strong partnership. Educators should value parents' and carers' input and perspectives, while parents should trust the educators' expertise and professionalism.

In this second contribution for the chapter, Dr Paulette Luff, Senior Lecturer in Early Childhood, Education and Care at Anglia Ruskin University, shares a valuable insight into how to build trust as part of an effective relationship.

Paulette Luff: the triangle of trust

When the first child in a family starts at an early years setting, parents will encounter a great deal of unfamiliar terminology. The meaning of the term 'parent partnership' might seem self-evident to practitioners but for parents, explanation might be required. The aspiration for settings to work together with and alongside families should be clarified and also demonstrated through day-to-day ways of working.

A wonderful example of partnership in action comes from the three-to-four-year-olds room in a private day nursery. A three-year-old child started at nursery still in nappies and, once she had settled in to nursery, toilet training began. The approach of the staff was for the parents to let them know what they were doing at home and then to carry on with the same methods at nursery. The parents decided to stop using nappies at all during the day, to give frequent prompts to use the potty, and to accept any 'accidents' calmly, changing wet clothes with gentle reminders to ask for the potty next time. The parents implemented this at home, during a holiday week, and then it was continued both at home and at nursery. The mother was worried and embarrassed by the thought of her child wetting the floors at nursery and causing extra work for staff but the practitioners set her mind at rest. Over the next few weeks, they did a fantastic job supporting the child to use the potty. When the child was dropped off and collected there were quick updates about how she was getting on. When it seemed as though little progress was being made, the nursery staff gave plenty of positive encouragement and told the parents that it was important not to give up. This was great advice, reassuring to the parents, and very soon the child was clean and dry at home and nursery – with only occasional lapses!

This exemplifies the implementation of a triangle of trust (Goldschmied and Selleck, 1996; Elfer et al., 2011) or triangle of care (Hohmann, 2007; Brooker, 2008, 2010) whereby the child, at the apex of the triangle, is supported by parents and practitioners, at each of the bottom vertices, with positive interactions on every side (Luff and Hryniewicz, 2021). A balanced relationship is established with all parties participating to achieve a mutually set goal. The staff listen to the parents and implement their chosen toilet training techniques, thus empowering the parents and providing consistency for the child. When the parents have doubts, and begin to waiver, backup from the practitioners is supportive and leads to the child reaching the developmental milestone of becoming clean and dry. Communicating within this triangle is not always so straightforward, as there can be tensions and conflicts, but persistence from professionals is important. Sadownik and Višnjić Jevtić (2023) argue that respect for and engagement with parents is always in the best interests of the child and upholds the rights of the child to family identity, to life within one's family, and to education (UN, 1989).

In this next contribution, Chris Williams and Angie Barkworth share the experience of using 'Chatta' with families. They outline how regularly celebrating children's achievements, both big and small, strengthens the partnership and reinforces the positive impact of collaboration.

Chris Willams and Angie Barkworth: using 'Chatta' to support engagement with families

Involving families in the early years can be so much more than simply informing them and reporting on events, progress and challenges. At Bricknell Primary School, in Hull, we have wanted to create a partnership to help families build on the work we do at school. We have been using 'Chatta', a simple approach which allows staff and children to create audio-visual storyboards based on the activities the children have been doing and the topics we are covering. It's perfect for supporting language and vocabulary development, interaction and storytelling, and it really does unlock progress for children. The 'Chatta' storyboards help with sequencing and processing skills and are very strong at removing barriers to learning and language use. Chatta has been particularly useful for EAL pupils as they are learning and using vocabulary and have gained the confidence to speak in front of the group as there are no wrong answers when inventing our stories in the classroom.

We held a meeting at school to introduce 'Chatta' to families. Over 60 people came, encouraged by their children who already know how Chatta works and enjoy it. The families use the Chatta story making software to turn everyday events and activities into stories. For example, if they'd visited the park they would sit together and reflect on the trip later, using images and voice recordings to make the story, almost like a talking postcard. Lots of the families share their stories with us at school and we use them to celebrate and retell the children's activities and experiences. The things we, and the families, really value from this partnership are the ways in that it complements the children's early language learning experience at home and at school. Using Chatta is a collaborative experienced based on what matters most in language development. Modelled adult language, interaction, sequencing and storytelling, with lots of opportunities for children's oral rehearsal and composition.

Effective partnership with parents 37

As Early Years practitioners we nurture, question, comment and praise the children focusing on the language we use, the words children hear linked to their activities. Chatta helps us turn every activity into a story to retell with the children, for them to tell to us, their peers and their families. Using the sequences of photos makes it so easy for them to know what they want to say. Sharing these stories with families and encouraging them to let their children explain what they've been doing and learning about at school has been so powerful in expanding the opportunities children have to build their speaking skills and confidence.

We suggest activity ideas regularly, but there are no limits with Chatta and the creativity and imagination so often comes from the children. They make stories about family members, days out, favourite games and toys, instructions to make breakfast – anything! By involving families in creating audio-visual storyboards based on everyday activities, 'Chatta' enhances language and vocabulary development, interaction and storytelling skills.

In this next contribution, Kierna Corr, Head of Nursery, shares a reflection on the value of Froebelian education and building a partnership outdoors.

Kierna Corr: the partnership of outdoor learning

In the past few years I have undertaken some further studies to become a Froebelian educator and this has really helped me to articulate and understand why it is so important to bring families along with us during all that we do during the nursery year. *Unity, Connectedness and Community* is one of Froebel's key principles and as a teacher it is my role to ensure the children in my nursery class are allowed opportunities to be involved in the local community and I need to see the community that already surrounds and influences the child as they come into my class.

In my class I embarked on a whole new approach to learning over 15 years ago when I began to spend more and more time outdoors and develop the playground to be a more natural environment that can offer lots of play opportunities that embrace elements of risk. Time and again, I hear colleagues say things like 'Oh our families wouldn't allow us to do that' when I talk about campfires and climbing trees. I am often puzzled by this statement as we have honestly never had any issues with any of own families embracing our approach and then I realised that the biggest factor in this understanding is that our children are settled in outdoors and dropped off into the playground not the classroom.

During the settling in time, when children are in smaller groups for a shorter time, we, as a staff, have the chance to talk to the family member who is settling the child in about the 'why' of what they are seeing in our setting. We get to explain that children do climb up the slide, can climb on the summer seats or short ladders to look over the fence and can climb the trees, move logs and stumps about, and more and why we feel these are necessary development stages for young children. We can share photos of their child having fun in the rain or climbing on structures in the playground through our class communication app and I can tag the areas of learning being met by the activity so families begin to see all the benefits of their child being allowed to take part in these activities.

When families drop children off into the playground they get to see how excited their child is on a wet day because the water barrel will be full. They get to explore the playground for a while with their child and see the tree their child has been swinging in or climbing in.

By having regular 'stay and play' sessions we get the opportunity to show families how young children learn through play and the value of allowing children to explore a range of activities and resources and we can show them they do not need to buy expensive toys for their child to learn and have fun. Being open, honest and making all communication two way is the key in my opinion to having a good relationship with families.

In this next contribution, Danielle Kelly, Early Years Lecturer, reminds us of respecting and understanding the family background and both educators and family having a shared understanding of the child's growth. This helps them align their expectations and approaches to supporting the child's growth.

Danielle Kelly: sharing child development

Parent partnerships are a key overarching principle to the Early Years Foundation Stage (2024). The principle encourages Early Years practitioners to secure strong partnerships with parents and carers to support children to learn and develop. Therefore, building positive, trustworthy and respectful relationships with parents are crucial. Early years practitioners can work together with parents by sharing information, encouraging them to participate in events and be part of the decision-making process for their child. Working together in partnership with parents and recognising them as first and co-educators can help them to build their confidence in supporting their child's learning. Therefore, by recognising the role of the parent it can support children to find a love for learning, build respectful relationships and boost their self-esteem.

The key to effective partnerships with parents is having effective communication and a sense of trust, value of belonging. You can develop these attributes through the parents' first show-round and settling-in sessions. These opportunities help parents to become familiar with the environment their child will be spending time in and begin to build a sense of trust. As practitioners during these events, we can find out about their family values, culture and aspirations for their child, which can build into your curriculum to support children's learning. This all helps to strengthen partnerships between parents and practitioners. I found that many children have family relatives that lived in different countries and some children celebrated different cultures and festivals. Therefore, I prioritised this in our curriculum to help children learn about the world around them. I invited parents in to read stories in their home language, share photographs, teach children key words and join in with activities to support children's understanding of their culture. This all helped parents and children to develop a sense of belonging within the setting. Children were able to learn about similarities and differences and develop respect for others by Early Years practitioners and their parents working together as key educators in the first stage of their life.

After the COVID-19 pandemic, we furthered our partnerships from handover discussions and online learning platforms to share their child's development. We wanted to support parents more with learning at home. So, I came up with the idea of parent workshops which focused on the areas of learning. This would benefit both parents and children because it would help parents to share ideas and learn strategies to support learning at home. So, I contacted a local speech and language therapist, and we set up our first parent workshop together. Parents attended the session. They learnt strategies to support children's emerging communication and language skills and developed their own friendships. Practitioners and parents developed stronger relationships as they were able to discuss their child in a safe space. This helped us to work together and plan ideas to support their child's individual needs. From this, we introduced home-learning packs with monthly ideas to support children through stories, rhymes and other activities. Parents felt their feelings and ideas were valued and we continued to put on further workshops to continue to support them. After the COVID-19 pandemic, children began to make good progress in their development.

In this next contribution, Sarah Roebuck, Programme Leader in Higher Education, explores how educators need to take control in empowering parents. Effective partnerships must involve openly discussing and addressing any challenges or concerns together, with a focus on finding solutions and supporting the child's wellbeing.

Sarah Roebuck: moving towards parental empowerment

The current published Early Years Foundation Stage (EYFS) Statutory Framework (DfE, 2025) like its predecessors has continued to emphasise partnership working with parents and/or carers promoting the concept that 'children benefit from a strong partnership between practitioners and parents and/or carers' (DfE 2023: 7). Although the EYFS 'seeks to provide this' there is no guidance within on how to achieve the desired practitioner/parental partnership. The keyperson is expected to 'build a relationship' with parents as part of their role; however, accompanying verbs associated with parents within the EYFS, including share, discuss, agree and inform, can lead to overwhelming feelings for practitioners and confusion on how to achieve true partnerships.

As a nursery practitioner and keyperson, through social learning principles, I was involved in building partnerships with parents through activities such as child settling-in time, daily keyperson chats, newsletters, parents evening, weekend bear, concerts and the annual summer fair. It was not until I became a nursery manager and was able to truly reflect and act within practice that I realised to make a difference to children's outcomes that the partnership must develop into parental involvement leading to parental empowerment. I had the privilege of managing nurseries in disadvantaged areas where each family was unique; therefore each needed to be celebrated. I began utilising the parents' personal and cultural knowledge within the setting to enrich practice and encourage involvement. On a weekly basis, parents within the setting were cooking cultural dishes for children and parents to sample, reading stories to children in their mother tongue, participating in show and tell, and parents accompanied the setting on visits to local landmarks and bug hunted with us in the woods just to name a few. Whilst parents were involved and having fun it ensured a sense of belonging which secured partnerships and led to parents communicating their concerns and needs whilst practitioners listened. It also ensured that any barriers to education that parents may have experienced were identified including the perceived imbalance of power between practitioners and parents.

Once I had facilitated the partnerships to this stage, practitioners were then confident in organising weekly parental activities and I could turn my attention to parental empowerment and the home learning environment. I invited parents to participate in weekly activities within the setting with their children to demonstrate how children learn and provide opportunities to deepen their understanding. My intention was to provide an understanding of their child's needs through demonstration and role modelling with the hopes of continuing in the home. The first activity was to demonstrate how to make gloop involving children and demonstrating appropriate language whilst incorporating the learning requirements of the EYFS. Parents were given a takeaway pack including corn flour, making instructions and laminated resources that were stage appropriate for their child. Parents started sending photos of their families making gloop together, some of which was enhanced through listening to their child's interests. With the support of my team, we had surpassed the EYFS vision of partnership working, we had achieved parental empowerment!

Building relationships and partnerships with parents does not need to be overwhelming or confusing. It does, however, require committed leaders to be invested in this aspect of practice who recognise the benefits for children and are prepared to invest in individual families, role model activities and ultimately to reflect and act for inclusive environments.

In the following case study, Catherine Hitchcock, Headteacher, outlines the excellent work their school does in building a strong partnership before children even begin attending the school. They show how all practitioners value and respect parents' knowledge and expertise, recognising them as their child's first and most important teachers.

Catherine Hitchcock: effective partnership with parents

At Donhead Prep School, we continue to evolve our EYFS parental engagement to strengthen home school partnerships. It is crucial for EYFS pupils that the partnership between the school and home is established long before the child steps foot in the door. As part of our admissions process at Donhead we offer opportunities for prospective preschool and reception families to engage with our school such as open days, guided tours, and community social events like our Christmas and Summer Fairs.

In the term before the child joins us at Donhead, we host more formalised events to develop home school EYFS partnerships: a 'stay & play' for preschool parents and children to join and for reception a taster morning for the children and a social coffee morning for the parents on the same day. These sessions not only prepare the children for the start of their educational journey at Donhead but they help with familiarisation of the site and provide social and informal connections on site amongst parents. We have designated staff that visit every feeder nursery to Donhead and ensure that we see each individual child in their setting prior to joining us in early years. We find these relationships with the nurseries and day care settings very important for transition support and communication. In addition, we conduct a curriculum evening for new parents, which is a formal occasion in the evening, when classroom teachers in preschool and reception deliver a curriculum information session about the term ahead. This session equips parents with essential information, ensuring a collaborative approach to their child's early education.

Once the term has started at Donhead, the EYFS team prioritise clear communication channels and continued partnership development. This is done via a range of formalised meetings with parents, daily in-person chats at the classroom door at drop-off and pick up, the use of a computerised software package to ensure daily communication, termly 'Sharing our Learning' sessions and a weekly parent newsletter. A strong partnership from the very beginning allows for a comprehensive understanding of children's needs, both academically and socially. At Donhead we know that parents and the Early Years team can work together to address challenges and celebrate achievements.

At Donhead, parents in EYFS are involved in the school and are encouraged to provide regular feedback. Parents are asked to join the Parent Forum, which meets termly with the SLT, and add their voice to the shaping of the school. As a reflective school, we use this feedback to adjust and improve partnership efforts. We request for parents to volunteer their time as 'Parent Readers' and visit the school to contribute to class talks, for example on religion and culture or within an assembly, for instance people who help us. This helps us to create an inclusive atmosphere where all parents feel valued and encourage diversity and cultural interactions. The Parent Forum has allowed EYFS parents to feel more connected to the school and empowered, knowing their input is valued. We have seen that increased satisfaction from this dialogue has led to more active participation in school initiatives such as volunteering for the Friends of Donhead, our PTA organisation.

We are proud, at Donhead, of the wide range of support we provide for parents both in terms of curriculum and pastoral support. We offer workshops for parents of children in reception and preschool, for example phonics workshop, child development, learning strategies and emotional regulation. We share resources weekly that help parents support their children's education and development at home so that we can have a shared vision for the child.

In this next contribution, Courtney McAllister, Postgraduate Researcher, highlights the need for a two-way process of knowledge sharing between home and the early years setting.

Courtney McAllister: two-way communication and collaboration

Effective partnerships with parents in early childhood education and care (ECEC) are core to the importance of early educators working with families. The Early Years Foundation Stage Statutory Framework (DfE, 2025:7) highlights the benefit to children of strong partnerships between educators and parents/carers, and what providers must do following the learning and development requirements of the statutory framework. From this, guiding early educators to building the skills and confidence to work in partnership with parents, and designing this to be embedded in everyday practice, can enhance engagement between both to highlight key issues and topics relating to children's learning and development.

Supporting effective partnerships can begin to be established from a strong foundation of the key person approach. Early educators should then discuss updates with parents/carers on their child's development and any progress made. These discussions should influence current practice, give ideas and assess any emerging learning and development needs to foster children's individual care needs. Although there is no requirement to keep written records for ongoing assessment (DfE, 2025:18), early educators understanding children's interests and what they know and can do, is key to the interactions they have with children to ensure they act on their own day-to-day interactions and consider the observations that parents/carers share, to create meaningful learning opportunities.

With many ways to build effective partnerships with parents, it is essential that both early educators and parents/carers invest time to recognise and establish that engagement and communication is a two-way process, to ascertain a meaningful professional relationship.

This supports the deepening of understanding children's individual needs and development, to establish context in how high-quality interactions can enhance approaches and practice to meet individual needs. Ideally, having an effective parental partnership is desired, however, there can be limitations of developing these partnerships and overcoming barriers to making this 'effective' which can have an impact on children and their development.

The explorations of adverse impacts upon poverty, income and employment, educational services and support and health, results in further inequalities which can then make partnerships with parents disproportionate. It would then be to establish what providers envision as fundamental to their parental partnerships, and how early educators will help achieve this, and as a result, the impact in how they can build effective parental partnerships to build quality experiences for children and their learning and development.

The early educator can be a good source of support and could make up for parents/carers inconsistencies to their children's individual learning and development (Solvason et al., 2021), however, with limited research and inconsistencies in policy across the U.K, there remains further work to do for guidance on how effective partnerships should be achieved. Considering this, providers establishing strong foundations through key person approaches, effective communication and considering the views of both parents/carers and children to promote and value the context of individual families into their settings can be a key component to engage and build upon, for future effective parental partnerships.

Case Study:

Child: Nancy-Jayne
Parent: Jayne

First impressions from the start!

Jayne was looking for a secure and safe Early Years setting, where communication, safeguarding and good progress in development was at the heart of her decision. During the initial and the early enrolment process, Jayne happily reported:

- *Welcoming reception to first call of enquiry and introduction to the management team, who would be first contacts of the enquiry.*
- *Substantial information about the nursery and base rooms, including fees and the structure of funding that can be accessed.*
- *Settling sessions to meet keyworker and develop parental partnerships from the very start was established before first day.*
- *Application used as extra communication with parents, in a multifunctional way, such as direct messaging, newsfeed posts and learning journey developments.*

Jayne reports the importance of safeguarding and policies, and this was embedded from the start with passwords for collection, no photos without consent and using a bell-entry system which was part of the initial introduction to the Early Years setting.

Effective partnership with parents 43

> Jayne discusses the importance of Nancy-Jayne and her keyworker, where there were always efforts made to show the developments Nancy-Jayne made, taking part in handover discussions at the end of the day, and opportunities to share information directly at the beginning of the day. In the instance that Nancy-Jayne's keyworker was not available, the Early Years setting had a buddy keyworker system in place to ensure continuity in Nancy-Jayne's development and in sharing key information, was central to partnerships.
>
> Jayne reflects on the experience and the importance of building meaningful relationships from the start when choosing an Early Years setting for children. Although the amenities are key to suit a family's needs such as affordability, access of funding and its application, including opening and closing times for familiess that may commute, securing effective parental partnerships from the start is key. This played an integral part in decision making and how the setting can be a consistent good source of support for children and their families.

This chapter ends with a final contribution from Steve Mackay, Deputy Headteacher, which reminds us how effective partnerships can be built from the very second the school gates open.

Steve Mackay: the primary school journey for the whole family

As children embark into the formal compulsory education system it is a pivotal opportunity to forge positive relationships with all stakeholders. The benefits of such will ensure the entire school community gains positively. I have always maintained that successful education may occur when the educators, children and parents all work in unison. If this is left to chance it is not entirely a successful inclusive approach. You find that the 'needy' or the 'loud' or those who had a positive experience with their own education are the individuals relationships are forged with. As a positive primary school, we have worked hard to establish great relationships with all of our parents with huge success. As we open the school gates, greeting the children and families, there are always a number of children desperate to enter and race in eagerly! During this ten-minute window each morning, we are approachable, friendly, available to discuss issues in order to hopefully 'nip them in the bud' and, by our own interactions, hopefully show that we are human! Reflecting upon this, I was looking at how this can impact the children long before they enter our early years setting. The trigger for this was a toddler in a pushchair who called over to me at the start and close of each day saying 'hi' and my name. I realised that over time an effective partnership had grown, not only with the parents but with a future pupil. Quite naturally I realised that through body language, smiles and saying 'hello' there were many 2-4-year-olds where strong connections with future schooling had already been established. Once our new intakes were all registered the pre-school visits began… albeit the children are young and 'outgrowing' their nursery places there was a sense of this big step in their lives. Some exhibited excitement, some quite nervous and some naturally shy. I have found visiting, talking to the children and engaging with their play or discussing their art also forms a connection – a face to recognise when visiting their 'big school'! Children make comments showing their understanding of connections. Clearly the information gleaned from such visits assists us enormously in beginning to understand the family framework and needs of the individuals. Schools have tried and tested routes for their intake and are passionate about these. It is always important to think ahead and reflect upon what is offered to see where improvements can be made. I was conscious that children all of a sudden were coming into school, separated from their parents (whilst attending a meeting), and felt we were missing an opportunity to help both the children and parents, many totally new to the school, to gain a sense of belonging and uniformity and be welcomed into our school family. To this end we created a morning where children and families were invited to a play session. Parents were present to informally meet all the staff and each other. One parent, new to the area from London, was concerned they did not know anyone. I connected them to the parents of the boy their son was playing with. Staff, children and parents all interacted well, felt welcomed and experienced the environment. This really helped them to feel more settled as they attended the more formal sessions and started school. Over time, potentially, this should reduce separation issues and impact positively with their mental health. We maintain our partnership with parents throughout their primary journey. EYFS begin with home visits plus have the daily personal contact at the start and end of the day. This gradually diminishes as the children progress through their growth at school. Although this is great preparation for secondary education we value our close contact with parents.

In conclusion

This chapter examines the crucial role of building effective partnerships with parents in early years education, highlighting the impact of collaboration on children's holistic development and well-being. Drawing from research and practitioner insights, it explores how trust, open communication, and mutual respect create meaningful relationships between families and educators. Contributions emphasise practical approaches, including digital tools for engagement, outdoor learning partnerships and culturally inclusive practices. The overarching theme is that fostering strong parent-educator relationships enhances children's confidence, development and long-term success by creating a supportive, community-driven learning experience.

Summary of key points

- Invest time in connection: partnerships must be built on trust and authentic connection and respect.
- Value communication: learning new languages or Makaton to communicate with families, even on the simplest of levels, can build bridges and allow relationships to flourish.
- Celebrate successes: regularly celebrating children's achievements, both big and small, strengthens the partnership and reinforces the positive impact of collaboration.
- Get involved: parents and carers must be actively involved in their child's learning journey. This could include participating in school events, volunteering, attending workshops and contributing to the classroom environment.
- Shared understanding of child development: educators and parents should have a shared understanding of early childhood development principles and milestones. This helps them align their expectations and approaches to supporting the child's growth.

References

Ashfaq, O., Sami, A., and Yousaf, H. (2024). Parent-teacher collaboration and its effect on student's achievement at pre-school level. *Pakistan Social Sciences Review*, 8(2), pp. 386-399.

Brooker, L. (2008). Just like having a best friend. In T. Papatheodorou and J. Moyles (Eds.) *Learning Together: Relational Pedagogy*. London: Sage.

Brooker, L. (2010). Constructing the triangle of care: Power and professionalism in practitioner/parent relationships. *British Journal of Educational Studies*, 58(2), pp. 181-196.

DfE (2025). Early years foundation stage statutory framework for group and school-based providers. Setting the standards for learning, development and care for children from birth to five. Available at: https://assets.publishing.service.gov.uk/media/687105a381dd8f70f5de3ea9/EYFS_framework_for_group_and_school_based_providers_.pdf (accessed 21 July 2025, 13 September 2024).

DfE (Department for Education). (2023). *Statutory framework for the Early Years Foundation Stage: Setting the standards for Learning, Development and Care for Children from Birth to Five*. London: Department for Education. Available at: EYFS Framework – September 2023 PDF (Accessed: 13 September 2025).

DfE (Department for Education). (2024). *Early Years Foundation Stage*. Statutory framework for the Early Years foundation stage for group and school providers (https://publishing.service.gov.uk).

Elfer, P., Goldschmied, E., and Selleck, D.Y. (2011). *Key Persons in the Early Years*, (2nd edn). London: Routledge.

Fu, Y., Wu, C., and Zhuo, L. (2024). Parent-school collaboration as a foundation for holistic child development. *Journal of Roi Kaensarn Academi*, 9(11), pp. 1821-1830.

Goldschmied, E., and Selleck, D. (1996). *Communication between Babies in Their First Year*, video and booklet, London: National Children's Bureau.

Hohmann, U. (2007). Rights, expertise and negotiation in care and education, *Early Years: An International Journal of Research and Development*, 27(1), pp. 33-46.

Kambouri, M., Wilson, T., Pieridou, M., Quinn, S.F., and Liu, J. (2022). Making partnerships work: Proposing a model to support parent-practitioner partnerships in the Early Years. *Early Childhood Education Journal*, 50(4), pp. 639-661. https://doi.org/10.1007/s10643-021-01181-6

Luff, P., and Hryniewicz, L. (2021). Models of partnership with parents in early childhood settings in England. In L. Hyrniewicz and P. Luff (Eds.) *Partnership with Parents in Early Childhood Settings: Insights from Five Countries*. London: Routledge.

Ngadni, I., and Shuang, C.Y. (2024). The Role of Preschool Teachers, Parents, and Principals in Facilitating Home-School Partnership in Early Childhood Education. *International Journal of Academic Research in Business and Social Sciences*, 14(8), pp. 338-353.

Rautamies, E., Vähäsantanen, K., Poikonen, P.L., and Laakso, M.L. (2021). Trust in the educational partnership narrated by parents of a child with challenging behaviour. *Early Years*, 41(4), pp. 414-427.

Sadownik, A.R., and Višnjić Jevtić, A. (2023). *(Re)theorizing More-then-parental Involvement in Early Childhood Education and Care*. International Perspectives on Early Childhood Education and Development, Volume 40. Cham, Switzerland: Springer.

Solvason, C., Hodgkins, A., and Watson, N. (2021). 'Preparing students for the "emotion work" of Early Years practice', *NZ International Research in Early Childhood Education Journal*, 23(1), pp. 14-23. Available at: https://oece.nz/members/research/nzirece-journal-2021/emotional-practice/ (Accessed: 13 September 2025).

United Nations [UN] (1989). Convention on the Rights of the Child. Available at: https://downloads.unicef.org.uk/wp-content/uploads/2010/05/UNCRC_PRESS200910web.pdf?_ga=2.78590034.795419542.1582.74737-1972.78648.1582.74737 (Accessed 27 January 2024).

Vuorinen, T. (2021). 'It's in my interest to collaborate...'-parents' views of the process of interacting and building relationships with preschool practitioners in Sweden. *Early Child Development and Care*, 191(16), pp. 2532-2544.

5 Prime area

Physical development

Poppy Gibson

Introduction

In this fifth chapter, all aspects of physical development, including the development of gross and fine motor skills and physical literacy skills will be discussed, including the progression of key knowledge and skills. This chapter shares examples of how practitioners have included quality-first teaching opportunities to support this prime area. Nine experienced contributors from all sectors of EYFS share valuable case studies and reflections on physical development.

Pondering question: how can we improve the physical skills of all children so they become independent in their choices?

Physical development is a cornerstone of early childhood development, encompassing the growth and refinement of a child's gross and fine motor skills. These skills are fundamental to a child's ability to explore their environment, interact with others and achieve developmental milestones. Moreover, the development of physical skills lays the groundwork for physical literacy, which is crucial for a healthy and active life.

Physical inactivity has become increasingly prevalent among young children in early childhood education and care settings. One promising way to intervene and promote physical activity in these settings is to develop children's physical literacy. Where most children spend their weekdays in early childhood settings in the care of early childhood educators, the educators are viewed as 'change agents' and become responsible for developing children's physical literacy. Thus, early childhood educators must possess adequate skills, knowledge and practices to promote such development (Barratt et al., 2024).

Why should physical development be prioritised for children?

Physical literacy is the foundation for lifelong participation in physical activity. It is defined as the motivation, confidence, physical competence, knowledge and understanding to value and take responsibility for engagement in physical activities for life.

Developing physical skills in early childhood is crucial for several reasons:

- Overall health and wellbeing: physical activity promotes physical health, reduces the risk of obesity and chronic diseases, and improves cardiovascular fitness.

DOI: 10.4324/9781003505266-5

- Cognitive development: physical activity is linked to improved cognitive function, including attention, memory and problem-solving skills.
- Social and emotional development: physical activity provides opportunities for social interaction, cooperation and developing self-confidence and self-esteem.
- Academic achievement: children with strong physical skills are more likely to be engaged in learning and have better academic outcomes.
- Life skills: physical skills are essential for daily living activities, such as self-care, mobility and participating in recreational activities.
- Long-term participation in physical activity: developing physical literacy in early childhood increases the likelihood of children becoming active and healthy adults.

Additionally, research into behavioural studies and neuroscience suggests that motor and cognitive development are intrinsically intertwined (Zhou and Tolmie, 2024).

In this first contribution, Dr Jackie Musgrave, Associate Head of School: The Open University gives a useful overview of the landscape of children's health.

Dr Jackie Musgrave: health-related conditions

For many children, there are specific considerations that need to be kept in mind when planning opportunities aimed at supporting their physical development and encouraging them to take part in physical activity. This section gives a brief overview of some of the health-related conditions that require additional consideration when planning physical activities, for example, children with chronic health conditions, special educational needs and complex medical needs. It is critically important that such children have opportunities to take part in activities that promote good levels of physical activity as outlined in the UK Chief Medical Officers' Physical Activity Guidelines (2019) for all children (Musgrave 2024); however, the presence of such conditions can be perceived as barriers to be included in physical activity.

Up to 20% of children have a chronic—that is, ongoing—health condition, such as diabetes mellitus, asthma or sickle cell anaemia. Chronic health conditions can't be cured, instead the typical symptoms that are unique to each condition can be minimised, usually by medication or managing the child's environment. For children with diabetes, there must be a careful balance of carbohydrate intake, accurate calculation of insulin dosage and awareness and monitoring of how much physical activity a child is doing. If this balance is not checked, blood sugar levels can peak or drop, which can have negative effects on the child's health, both in the short and long term.

In the case of asthma, physical activity, especially outdoors on cold days, can provoke typical symptoms such as wheezing and cough, and potentially this can provoke an asthma attack. Sickle cell anaemia symptoms can be provoked by trauma to joints. Not surprisingly, parents and practitioners can be very cautious about encouraging children with chronic conditions to take part in physical activity because of the risk of provoking associated symptoms.

Undoubtedly, children with chronic health conditions do require additional consideration to plan appropriate physical activity opportunities. There can be a tension between providing such opportunities so that children feel included and can benefit from taking part in activities whilst at the same time, there is a need to reduce unnecessary risks that may provoke the symptoms of their health condition.

Children with special educational needs are likely to require additional planning. Children with attention deficit hyperactivity disorder are likely to gain benefits from taking part in physical activity. Children with autism may benefit from additional time to process instructions so that they can be included in activities (The National Autistic Society, 2016).

Children with complex medical needs frequently have reduced or restricted mobility which can, as reported by Sense (2015), be perceived as a barrier to taking part in physical activities. To provide practitioners with guidance about how to maximize physical activity for children with complex medical needs, a toolkit was produced (see link in the following).

Key to successful provision of physical activity for all children is good communication with parents and where appropriate, other professionals, such as physiotherapists or specialist nurses. Writing carefully thought through education and health care plans that are regularly updated and available to all are central to ensuring that the unique needs of children are identified. Gaining knowledge about the possible effects of health conditions and understanding the uniqueness of their impact on children helps planning effectively so that they can be included in activities that will benefit their physical and mental health and wellbeing, both in childhood and across the lifespan.

Questions to consider:

- How can you develop your knowledge and understanding about the health-related conditions that affect the children in your setting?
- How can you plan appropriate physical activities for children with health-related conditions?
- How can you work with parents and other professionals to plan appropriate physical activities for children with health-related conditions?

In this second contribution, Janine Ryan, freelance Early Years Consultant, stresses the importance of physical activity and growth.

Janine Ryan: the importance of physical activity and growth

Physical activity is important for the healthy growth and development of children and should take place every day (NHS, 2022). Children under five who can walk should be physically active for 180 minutes (3 hours) a day (NHS, 2022). It has been reported that only 9% of children aged 2–4 years in England meet the physical activity recommendations (NCSEM, 2022). Research suggests that physical activity may be beneficial for cardiovascular disease risk factors, weight status, fundamental motor skills, psychosocial wellbeing, cognitive development and school readiness (NCSEM, 2022). Evidence from the Education Endowment Foundation concurs that children who take part in physical development interventions make around five additional months' progress in cognitive outcomes (EEF, 2023). Gross motor skills provide the foundation for developing healthy bodies and social and emotional wellbeing. Fine motor control and manipulation help with hand-eye co-ordination which is later linked to early literacy (DfE, 2021).

Children need to learn how to keep themselves healthy, which involves understanding the need for sleep and rest, as well as being active and maintaining a healthy diet. Children need to be able to manage appropriate risk and know their own limitations. Physical play is a perfect way for children to learn how to keep themselves safe.

Physical development is subdivided into three sets of skills:

- locomotor skills, for example running and jumping
- stability skills, for example twisting and balancing
- manipulation skills, such as throwing and catching.

(Ofsted, 2022a)

The brain undergoes a rapid period of development from birth to age 3, at which point it is 80% developed. Physical activity plays a key role in supporting the brain's developing architecture through the construction of neural pathways created through repeating movements, for example reaching for a toy or grasping an object or learning to move. Developing confidence, enjoyment and competence in performing movement skills has a positive effect on children's emotional wellbeing impacting on a child's self-concept, self-esteem, behaviour and emotional and social competence. Physical development also supports children's play and increasing independence and self-care (DfE, 2021). Some emerging research also suggests links between physical activity and improved language, attention and self-regulation (NCSEM, 2022).

Children need to develop their balance, postural control and co-ordination through the vestibular sense. Core strength is vital for a child's ability to keep their position and move from the centre of their body outwards (DfE, 2021). If this is not well developed a child will struggle with gross and fine motor movements and have difficulty keeping their stability and balance. Children need to be able to detect movement and respond to it by maintaining balance. They also need to develop control and coordination of their body in relation to the space around them; this is known as proprioception. They learn whole body control through self-discovery and develop bilateral co-ordination through cross lateral linkage, which means the two sides of the brain are able to process information effectively (Early Education, 2024). This results in a child being able to use both sides of their body in an alternate, coordinated way. Developing core strength and co-ordination is fundamental to a child's ability to communicate, learn language and eventually read and write. Control over the whole body is required to successfully execute fine motor skills, for example using small tools and handling delicate materials (DfE, 2021).

Gross motor movements are made with arms, legs and torso. Babies are preprogrammed to move and intrinsically motivated to do so. Muscular strength develops over time from early movements a pre-mobile baby makes in their attempts to crawl to a pre-schooler running and jumping. By using their whole bodies children become increasingly confident, agile and flexible.

As confidence develops children can take safe risks and challenge themselves physically as they become increasingly well-coordinated. Confidence and coordination in gross motor skills are essential for children in developing their fine motor skills. Fine motor skills are the small movements made with hands and fingers and feet and toes. They involve the complex coordination of muscles, joints and nerves and require body awareness, planning, coordination, muscle strength and precision. Hand, wrist and finger movements are important when picking up objects. Fine movements with the foot, ankle and toes are also necessary for sports, like dancing and kicking a ball. Developing both gross and fine motor skills supports the promotion of physical, social and cognitive development.

Babies should be encouraged to be active throughout the day in a variety of ways. Encourage them to be physically active by reaching and grasping, pulling and pushing, moving their head, body and limbs during daily routines and during supervised floor play. Include at least 30 minutes of tummy time spread throughout the day when they're awake. Toddlers should be physically active every day for at least 180 minutes (3 hours). This should be spread throughout the day, including opportunities to play outdoors, and include standing up, moving around, rolling and playing, as well as more energetic activity like skipping, hopping, running and jumping. Active play, such as using a climbing frame, riding a bike, playing in water, chasing games and ball games is ideal for this age group.

Pre-schoolers should spend at least 180 minutes (3 hours) a day doing a variety of physical activities spread throughout the day, including active and outdoor play. This should include at least 60 minutes (1 hour) of moderate-to-vigorous intensity physical activity (NHS, 2022).

Preschool aged children continue to develop their movement through balancing, riding (scooters, trikes and bikes) and ball skills, going up steps or climbing apparatus, using alternate feet. They skip, hop, stand on one leg and can hold a pose for a game like musical statues. They use large-muscle movements to wave flags and streamers, paint and make marks.

Encourage 3–4-year-olds to transfer physical skills learnt in one context to another one, so that children continue to practise and develop their knowledge. Children might first learn to hammer in pegs to mark their forest school boundary, using a mallet. Then, they are ready to learn how to use hammers and nails on the woodwork bench. Encourage children to paint, chalk or make marks with water on large vertical surfaces. Use walls as well as easels to stimulate large shoulder and arm movements, preferably standing as this supports the development of core strength. Encourage children to 'cross the mid-line' of their bodies—this means that when they draw a single line from left to right they do not pass the paintbrush from one hand to another. This helps to connect one side of the brain to the other and supports future letter formation (Centre for Movement, 2020). Use sequences and patterns of movements with music and rhythm. Provide a range of hand tools for a range of purposes, for example trowels, spades, scissors and pencils. Allow them to be independent getting dressed or undressed, for instance changing their shoes or putting their coats on and fastening them.

As with all areas of learning, the role the environment plays is fundamental and must be carefully considered. Developing an enabling environment with appropriate opportunities for children to develop their physical skills needs to be provided both through the core provision and also carefully planned enhancements and resources which stretch and challenge children and are changed and adapted in accordance with their developmental stage. The EEF (2024) has provided evidence to suggest that gross and fine motor skills can be taught by practitioners explicitly teaching by using verbal prompts such as giving feedback, cues, explanations and suggestions or physical prompts such as modelling and demonstrating. There is no doubt that a skilled practitioner can encourage and extend learning through thoughtful interactions. Sharing games, finger rhymes and books that support physical movement are enjoyable experiences for children and adults too.

In this next contribution, Nick Robinson, from Nick Robinson Sports Coaching continues exploring the fundamentals of high quality physical development, emphasising their **FUN** aspect.

Nick Robinson: physical development

The fundamentals for our early years children are the foundations for a physical healthy active lifestyle in the future years of their life. Being physically active from the early years has an impact with motor skills, fine and gross, cognitive skills, memory, listening, growing and structuring the brain. With a fast-paced lifestyle and modern technology, our early years children can lose valuable physical development hours which can impact motor skills in the crucial developmental years. Children who may have been crawling, climbing, tumbling, rolling, jumping, picking up objects are now reliant on iPads, phones and computers for entertainment and development.

Developing and improving ABCs—agility, balance and co-ordination—are crucial for our early years children to support brain structure; physical exercise plays a huge part in the wellbeing and positive mental health in all children and adults, if our early years children are exposed in a positive environment then our children will enjoy a physical lifestyle. Children are happiest moving, running, crawling, jumping, skipping, dancing and being creative with no pressure, no competition and no rewards. Our children thrive with a physically active healthy lifestyle without pressure and many children unfortunately quit sport because of external pressures and lack of confidence.

Entering competitive environments too early can have a negative impact for our early years children; once playfulness is lost then the fun is lost. The role of practitioners of sport and physical development is to create positive experiences with exercise without pressure, allowing our children to experience creativity, being independent and developing motor skills, learning how our bodies move, problem solving and dealing with setback and disappointment. The aims for practitioners for our early years children is to support our children holistically and to help and guide them to develop self-esteem, confidence and resilience.

Children within the same year group can be on a different journey path; children in the same school year group may have been born in September and children born in July. Children born in September may have been crawling, walking, jumping, skipping and using motor skills many months before the same year group children; to compare the development stage of these children would be like comparing apples and pears. Meeting the needs of the children at different development stages can have a positive impact, as children who are given the opportunity to participate in exercise and sport have an advantage to develop physically and cognitively. Schools delivering physical education to early years children can make a huge positive impact if the adults can meet the needs of the children.

Physical education and positive experiences with energy can help to structure a child's brain. Using exercise and movement when crossing the midline can develop neural pathways and connect the right and left side of the brain, balance and co-ordination can support emotional regulation and physical development can help to build positive self-esteem, resilience and confidence. The positive impact of a practitioner, coach or PE teacher in the early years of children's physical development can make a difference to the rest of their lives. Every child deserves that opportunity.

Improving our children's physical development and active lifestyles must become a priority to support children holistically in their lives. A consideration would be to educate and improve the knowledge of our early years practitioners to support the needs and development of our children at their developmental stage. Replace a PE curriculum with a program of activities specifically for our early years children to support development in gross and fine motor skills: consistent repetition of the same physical movements, working continuously on co-ordination and balance, with very low levels of competing against opponents and only competing against themselves to be the best they can be. Relate physical movement with associations for children: animal movements, superhero movements, reading books; and physical movements can be linked with actions—trees moving in the wind and climbing a ladder would be an example of imagination and movement. Giving children lots of choices to experiment with safe exciting equipment supports children to become independent and make positive choices. We can encourage creative physical movement every day with our children; the most important factor is the make the journey FUN.

In this next contribution, Emalee Caton, Early Years PANCo Lead Tutor, National Day Nurseries Association and Reception Class Teacher, shares with us some top tips on integrating physical education into your Early Years setting.

Emalee Caton: why is physical development so important and how can you make it happen for children?

Young children were born to move! Physical activity is essential for their brain development, helping form crucial connections that aid growth. With 90% of a child's brain developed by age five, it's vital to provide environments that foster both movement and learning. However, only about 10% of children meet the Chief Medical Officer's (2019) recommendation of 3 hours of physical activity per day. For me, this doesn't have to mean structured, adult-led activities; it simply means avoiding long periods of sitting. In the classroom, for instance, children don't always need chairs for activities. Many tasks can be done standing up, such as arts and crafts, cooking or playing with playdough, sand and water.

Physical development plays a key role in lots of other areas of learning, so ensuring children reach their full physical potential helps them thrive in all aspects of life. For example, if a child has difficulty keeping up with their peers physically, it can make socialising and forming friendships challenging. Being coordinated enough to feed themselves fosters independence, as does the ability to dress and undress. Having a good physical activity 'diet' also contributes to a child's overall health and well-being. Regular activity helps lower blood pressure, maintain healthy body weight, improve sleep, enhance concentration and boost mental wellbeing. Establishing these good habits early on lays the foundation for a healthy, active adulthood.

As we know, children love fun and games. In order to entice young children to take part in physical activity, it must be fun. It will be even more fun if you, as the adult, are prepared to play with them and join in. Playing a game of tag, completing challenging obstacle courses or competing in running races are all brilliant ways to get children active during the day and they will absolutely love you for it. I love nothing more than a game of 'stuck in the mud'—you can hear the joy and delight in their voices. Alternatively, you could play some music for dancing,

Prime area: Physical development 53

relax with yoga, or go on a nature walk that engages all the senses. Outdoor play offers a stimulating environment, where children can fully explore and be surrounded by the wonder that is nature. The outdoors gives children the opportunity to move freely and in any way they like, for example, climbing, rolling down hills, racing, swinging, galloping - the list is endless.

It's essential to educate and support parents in understanding the value of ensuring their children get the recommended amount of physical activity. With the right guidance, they can discover the many benefits and find fun, creative ways to keep their children active beyond nursery or school. Having a qualified Physical Activity and Nutrition Coordinator (PANCo) in your setting demonstrates a strong commitment to the wellbeing of children, staff, and families. PANCo learners are equipped with the knowledge and skills to promote the importance of a nutritious diet alongside daily physical activity. They share this knowledge with staff and families, ensuring that the benefits of a healthy, active lifestyle reach everyone involved.

In short, we need to get children moving more. Too many children are living a sedentary lifestyle which has a hugely negative impact on their general health and wellbeing throughout their lifetime.

The next contribution provides a useful overview of the developmental stages involved in physical development. Helen Battelley, from the National Early Years Active Start Partnership (NEYASP) expertly presents a case for physical development to be at the core of any Early Years experience.

Helen Battelley: the science of early childhood physical development and movement play

Early childhood is a period of rapid growth, where physical development plays a crucial role in shaping a child's future health, cognitive abilities and emotional wellbeing. From the moment babies begin to move, they are building the foundation for all future motor skills, cognitive development and social interactions.

Building motor skills: toddlerhood and preschool years

As children move into toddlerhood, they begin to refine their motor skills through play. Running, jumping, climbing and balancing are all part of this stage, where kids gain greater control over their bodies. These fundamental movement skills are crucial—they form the basis for more complex physical activities and sports as children grow.

During the preschool years, movement play becomes more coordinated and deliberate. Whether it is throwing a ball, hopping on one foot or navigating an obstacle course, these activities enhance muscle strength, joint stability and overall coordination. Repetition and practice are key, helping children to fine-tune their motor skills while also improving cognitive functions like memory, attention and problem solving (Roscoe et al., 2024; Adolph and Hoch, 2019).

Movement in babies and infants

Movement starts early, with even the smallest actions—like kicking, grasping and rolling—playing a vital role in a baby's development (Reed and Parish, 2021). These movements help strengthen muscles, develop coordination, and lay the groundwork for more complex motor skills like crawling, standing and walking (Duncombe and Preedy, 2021). As babies move, their brains rapidly develop, forming neural connections that enhance sensory-motor integration, essential for later learning and cognitive development.

Cognitive and social benefits of movement play

Movement is not just about physical health—it also boosts brain power. Active play stimulates the brain, improving cognitive abilities like attention and problem solving. Moreover, it fosters social skills (Madan and Singhal, 2012; Loon and Bell, 2016). When children engage in group play, they learn to communicate, cooperate and navigate social interactions (Bruce, 2021). This kind of play also helps with emotional regulation, teaching children how to manage stress and express emotions constructively (Ball, 2019).

The long-term impact of early physical development

In the UK's Physical Activity and Health Report (2022), Baroness Frances D'Souza wrote 'Without effective, co-ordinated measures led by Government, we run the risk that the next generation of adults will be the least healthy in living memory'.

The skills learned through movement in early childhood have lasting benefits (Hall et al., 2018; Zhang et al., 2019; Battelley, 2021). Children who develop strong motor skills early on are more likely to remain physically active throughout their lives, which is linked to better overall health, lower risks of obesity and improved mental health (Brolin et al., 2018). Moreover, early movement experiences build confidence, enhance self-esteem and foster a lifelong love of physical activity.

Conclusion

In early childhood, movement is much more than just play—it is a vital part of development that shapes a child's future. By encouraging diverse and engaging physical activities, we support not only their physical growth but also their cognitive, emotional and social development. These early experiences lay the foundation for a lifetime of healthy, active living. Experts in Early Years Physical Development have called for a renewed focus on play-based approaches as these may best support children's physical development and physical activity. As an article in the Lancet (Kolehmainen, et al., 2023) suggests, 'Advancing the rights of all children to participate in physical activity requires inclusive, equally ambitious, expectations for all'.

The next contribution by Jane Dorrian, Early Years Lecturer: The Open University, presents a pedagogical example of physical development, highlighting the incidental experiences which can be incorporated into everyday practice.

Jane Dorrian: recognising the value of incidental physical activity

It's tidying up time at the end of a busy morning and a pile of bits and bobs is growing next to the bin—torn sheets of newspaper, a snapped pencil, some leaves that have blown in from outside, all the usual rubbish... or is it? If we look through a child's eyes we might see the newspapers as streamers to run around with, imagine the pencil as a magic wand to flourish, think of autumn and throw the leaves in the air to dodge them as they fall; rather than seeing rubbish they are seeing provocations to move. One of the challenges that has been associated with supporting physical development is the idea that it requires specific resources or expertise or that it is directly related to organised sports but that's not the case, it is just about getting children active. The 'rubbish' mentioned above invites children to run, change direction, bend, stretch, reach, grasp, twist and engage in lots of other movements without any specialist equipment or knowledge from the practitioner, all we need to do is recognise the physical activity opportunity that is afforded.

Recognising the value of these incidental physical activity moments is a positive point to remember when we think about the UK Chief Medical Officer's guidelines (2019) that recommend children aged 1 to 5 years should have at least 180 minutes of activity every day. When faced with that target there can be a temptation to think that we need to deliver a structured session of planned and targeted movement activity so we can show we are hitting the goal, and whilst it is important to have those sessions it is also helpful to think of all the 5-minute unplanned opportunities that our everyday practice and resources provide. A sheet of newspaper can be scrunched into a ball to throw and catch, twisted into rope to jump over, used as a hiding place for someone curled up small; it has given us three different 5-minute activities with a range of fine and gross motor movements, with no need for preparation or equipment.

Recognising and valuing the range of movement and activity that happens incidentally is also a helpful and reassuring message to share with parents who can also assume that physical activity means getting involved in organised sports. This connection can be really problematic, with parents worrying about being able to afford session fees and kit, finding it difficult to organise travel and transport arrangements and dealing with their child's experiences in a competitive environment. As practitioners we have an important role in supporting children to explore sports and organised activities, but it is always good to remind ourselves that opportunities to support physical development are around us all the time, we just need to see them.

In this next contribution, Vicky Cook, EYFS Lead, encourages us to consider how we can take a creative approach when planning physical development for our learners.

Vicky Cook: a creative approach to the development of physical skills

Many of our children have limited opportunities to develop their physical skills beyond our setting and as a result our children need multiple occasions to develop these skills. As an inner-city school with limited outside space, we have had to think creatively to prioritise physical provision.

We are passionate about giving our children resources which combine purchased and free equipment, and this is very evident in our outdoor physical provision. To meet the needs of our pupils we designed a large section of our outdoor space specifically for physical development and have purchased a secured fallen tree with ropes tied to climb alongside free tractor tyres and car tyres, logs, cable reels and sections of decking for the children to use. This area gives opportunities for children to move the equipment independently and create their own trails and obstacle courses which has impacted on their gross motor skills both in moving the resources and in negotiating their creations.

We designed our setting-specific curriculum around the development of gross motor skills through the riding of bikes. We considered the progression of skills from our youngest learners using a balance bike up to our older learners using pedal bikes, and our bikes are a mixture of purchased educational bikes and gifted bikes children would usually ride at home. We have bikes available all the time and encourage their progression through the bikes as part of our child-initiated play. Watching our children use the bikes, we have further enhanced this with skateboard ramps and cones to provide opportunities for children to negotiate objects which has further developed their core stability.

Enhancing other areas with opportunities to develop physical skills has also been very successful for our children. An example of this in practice is the addition of a small step ladder to our builders' yard so that children can build towers that are taller than them, often having to stabilise themselves as they reach to add the last brick or cardboard box. Adding long-handled spades to the sand pit encourages our children to stand up to dig, both balancing and building strength whilst creating. We also have a 'cleaning wall' with a range of brushes the children can use to tidy the environment—they particularly love sweeping up sand and leaves! Another popular area is within our indoor creative area where we have attached a large piece of boarding from floor to ceiling and peg shower curtains to this for painting (easily removable and washable too!). The children have access to a step ladder to climb, or can paint from the floor, encouraging them to strengthen their shoulders and arm strength whilst developing their creativity.

When we enhance the provision focusing on our children's interests, we consider how opportunities can further develop their physical skills. Particularly effective examples have included a car wash created from pallets and blue material where the children cleaned their bikes and large cars using long handled brushes and sponges—lots of very wet but highly engaged children developing their physical skills! Another success was the obstacle course we created linked to their interest in the 'floor is lava' game. We created the obstacle course using a range of materials such as guttering, tyres, cones, cable reels and planks which the children really enjoyed trying to balance on.

Our primary aim is to foster an environment where each child can enhance their physical skills with confidence and independently access resources to support this. Using carefully considered planning, varied resources and supportive interactions, we strive to nurture their physical development, irrespective of their initial skill level or background.

Natalie Weir, PhD Researcher: University of Derby, gives a valuable insight into whether there is more to metrics when we think about physical activity. This contribution prompts reflections on current provision and challenges further teaching and learning ideas.

Natalie Weir: moving beyond metrics: A holistic approach to physical development

What the theory tells us

Research has consistently shown that healthy physical activity (PA) in early childhood is known to enhance cognition, improve physical, mental and cardiometabolic health and prevent harmful weight gain (Jones et al., 2020). Gross motor skill development and PA are also positively associated with a child's development of physical literacy (PL) (Hulteen et al., 2018).

PL is an important concept that involves the development of physical competence, confidence and motivation for PA that enables children to move with ease and confidence in a variety of settings (Whitehead, 2010). It is our relationship with movement and PA throughout life (Physical Literacy Consensus Statement for England, 2023) and reflects the importance of engaging in different types of movement opportunities for a positive and meaningful relationship with PA.

What is actually happening

Physical development is cited as one of the three prime areas of learning and development in the Early Years Statutory Framework (DfE 2025:10) and includes gross motor skills and fine motor skills as two of the 17 Early Learning Goals (ELGs). These goals are designed to ensure children develop essential physical capabilities, which theoretically support their overall health, wellbeing and readiness for future learning. ELG data from 2022/23 show that physical development had the highest percentage of children meeting expected levels. gross motor skills, in particular, topped the charts, suggesting that children are thriving in this area.

However, this optimistic data presents a paradox around whether metrics are truly reflective of children's overall physical health and development. Inequalities exist in UK preschool children's fundamental movement skills (FMS) ability (Foulkes et al., 2015) and only 10% of 2–4-year-old children in England are meeting the Chief Medical Officer's PA guidelines (Roscoe et al., 2019). Research by Duncombe and Preedy (2021) show that in the 10 years between 2007 and 2017, the percentage of children starting school with or at risk of having a movement difficulty (32.17%) almost doubled. This trend of poor motor development and inactivity will have significant implications for health and wellbeing, such as delayed motor development; adverse effects on cardiovascular, bone and mental health; reduced cognitive function and social interaction and an increased risk of obesity (Ofsted, 2022b).

What we should be doing differently

Physical development is a cornerstone of early childhood education, underpinning many aspects of a child's growth and learning—but to truly set our children up for lifelong health and happiness, it's crucial to broaden our approach in the early years. Practitioners should consider integrating a more holistic view of physical development, one that goes beyond the EYFS framework's current scope. Environments (indoor and out), role modelling and a balance of child-initiated and adult-led PA are vital. This should include opportunities for active play (e.g. free and loose parts) as well as regular opportunities for direct motor skill development (often referred to as physical education (PE) sessions). Interventions delivered to preschool children encompassing locomotor skills such as running and jumping, object manipulation including throwing and catching and stability skills such as bending and stretching are extremely effective (Roscoe et al., 2024).

Thus, focus, education, raised awareness and value by policymakers, as well as practical interventions delivered to early years children, are essential not only to develop the

Table 5.1 Definitions of key physical development terms

Key term	Explanation
Physical Activity (PA)	Body movements of varying intensities that require energy expenditure
PA recommendations	The UK Chief Medical Officer's guidelines for children aged 5 years and under state that children need to reduce their sedentary behaviour and should achieve at least 180 minutes of PA every day, with 60 minutes of this categorised as moderate-to-vigorous physical activity. This includes physical activities spread throughout the day, including active and outdoor play–the more the better
Physical Literacy (PL)	Our relationship with movement and physical activity throughout life
Early Years Foundation Stage (EYFS)	An educational framework used in the UK to guide the learning, development and care of children from birth to the age of 5
Physical Development (PD)	One of the three prime areas for learning and development within the statutory EYFS framework
Fine Motor Skills	Control of small muscles, used for hand, finger, lip, tongue and eye movements
Gross Motor Skills	Control of larger muscles for actions like jumping, biking, skiing and dancing
Fundamental Motor Skills (FMS)	Core skills that involve different body parts such as feet, legs, trunk, head, arms and hands that form the basis for more complex movements
Motor Control (MC)	The process of initiating, directing and grading purposeful voluntary movement
Physical Education (PE)	Planned, progressive learning that takes place in curriculum timetabled time which enables children and young people to engage in a range of sport and physical activities

abilities and skills needed to engage in PA but also to introduce them to the fun and joy of movement. This will contribute to PL development and foster a positive relationship with movement that can last throughout a person's life. Ultimately, the responsibility lies with us to ensure our early years children have every opportunity to move, grow and thrive (Table 5.1).

In the final contribution of this chapter, Helen Battelley shares another valuable guide to elevating early childhood physical development and considers barriers to this as well as offering a range of solutions to positively impact physical development for the youngest children.

Helen Battelley: united for a healthy start: elevating early childhood physical development

In March 2023, the National Early Years Active Start Partnership (NEYASP) was launched to address critical issues surrounding physical development (PD) and the increasing inactivity among young children, particularly in the aftermath of the COVID-19 pandemic. This initiative brings together a range of organisations and experts in Early Years (EY) physical development, sport and movement play, aiming to create a unified approach to tackle these challenges effectively.

The significance of early childhood physical development

Early childhood is a vital stage for physical development, forming the bedrock for a child's future health, wellbeing, and life outcomes. Physical activity during these early years is essential not only for physical health but also for cognitive development, social skills and emotional wellbeing. Despite its importance, recent research highlights a concerning decline in physical activity levels among young children.

Since 2011, the Chief Medical Officer for England has recommended that children between the ages of 1 and 5 should engage in at least 180 minutes of varied physical activity each day. However, current data indicates that only 20% of young children meet this target, a worrying statistic that underscores the need for immediate action to address this growing public health issue.

Physical proficiency developed during childhood plays a crucial role in fostering children's engagement and confidence, promoting positive physical activity and health-related behaviours that can last well into adulthood. Early childhood is a critical developmental stage for both the brain and body, during which adults can significantly influence children's physical growth and wellbeing.

NEYASP: a collaborative effort

The creation of NEYASP marks a pivotal step in fostering a more coordinated effort to improve Early Years physical development. By uniting the often-fragmented Early Years sector, NEYASP provides a collective voice advocating for stronger policies and practices. This collaboration aims to create lasting improvements by aligning efforts across the sector.

Helen Battelley, chair of NEYASP, stresses the urgency: 'The decline in access to play and movement opportunities is alarming. We cannot address this issue in isolation. We believe that working together as a collective voice is a more effective approach.'

Guiding principles for early years physical activity

In partnership with Loughborough University, NEYASP commissioned a review of Early Years physical activity, resulting in seven guiding principles designed to support physical activity and reduce sedentary behaviour in young children:

1. Practitioner Training: equip Early Years practitioners with the necessary knowledge, understanding, and confidence to foster physical activity and limit sedentary behaviour.
2. Supportive Environment: create environments that prioritize physical activity, including policies, play equipment, outdoor spaces and regular opportunities for movement.
3. Balanced Activities: offer a mix of child-initiated and adult-led physical activities to engage young children in diverse ways.
4. Structured Physical Activity: provide activities that develop essential movement skills and support physical development.
5. Integrated Routines: incorporate physical activity into daily routines, enhancing learning and development across various areas.

6. Parental Involvement: engage parents to raise their awareness and knowledge of physical activity, encouraging them to continue active play at home.
7. Multi-Component Interventions: implement comprehensive approaches that promote physical activity and support children's development holistically.

Reversing the decline in physical activity

Recent studies reveal a significant decline in physical activity among young children, which can negatively affect their long-term health, wellbeing and life outcomes. NEYASP emphasises the need for strategic, long-term interventions to reverse this trend and promote physical activity from an early age.

This persistent issue has prompted leaders like Baroness Frances D'Souza, who, in the Department of Health and Social Care UK's Physical Activity and Health Report (2022), warned, 'Without effective, co-ordinated measures led by Government, we run the risk that the next generation of adults will be the least healthy in living memory.'

The role of parents and caregivers

Parents and caregivers are essential in promoting physical activity for young children. NEYASP recognises the importance of involving parents in their initiatives and equipping them with tools to support their children's physical development in the home. By fostering active play, parents can help establish lifelong healthy habits in their children.

The impact of COVID-19 on early childhood physical activity

The COVID-19 pandemic has had a profound effect on children's physical activity, with lockdowns and social distancing restricting active play opportunities. As we transition to a post-pandemic world, it is crucial to address the long-term impacts of reduced physical activity and ensure that children can return to regular, joyful physical play.

NEYASP's initiatives aim to mitigate the pandemic's effects and restore active play as a vital part of daily life for young children.

The COVID-19 pandemic has had a severe impact on young children's movement skills, with the effects still being felt today. Only 9% of children aged 2-4 years meet the recommended daily physical activity levels (British Heart Foundation Research Centre, 2018). Research by La Valle et al. (2022) further highlights the pandemic's impact on early childhood education and care in England, noting that many young children faced difficulties adapting to new environments and socializing with peers due to increased time indoors and sedentary behaviour ultimately impeding their access to physical development.

A call to action

NEYASP urges all Early Years stakeholders to join the partnership and contribute to a united effort to support young children's physical development. By working together, sharing resources and advocating for stronger policies, the sector can create a sustainable approach to ensuring that every child benefits from early physical activity.

Helen Battelley concludes: 'The establishment of NEYASP is a significant milestone in enhancing early years physical development. We invite all organisations, practitioners, and parents to join us in this crucial mission to ensure that every child has the opportunity to thrive through active play and physical development.'

In response to these challenges, experts in early years physical development are advocating for a renewed focus on play-based approaches. These methods may be most effective in supporting children's physical growth and increasing their physical activity levels. As noted in *The Lancet*, Kolehmainen et al. (2023) assert, 'Advancing the rights of all children to participate in physical activity requires inclusive, equally ambitious, expectations for all.'

NEYASP is committed to addressing the challenges of physical development and inactivity in young children. By uniting the early years sector, advocating for evidence-based policies, and raising public awareness, NEYASP seeks to create a future where every child can reap the benefits of physical activity and grow up healthy, active and ready to succeed.

In conclusion

This chapter explores the critical role of physical development in early childhood, emphasising the importance of both gross and fine motor skills in shaping a child's overall wellbeing, cognitive abilities and social engagement. It discusses the concept of physical literacy—how motivation, confidence and competence in movement contribute to lifelong participation in physical activities. The chapter features contributions from experts who highlight the significance of practitioner involvement, recognising educators as change agents in promoting physical literacy and encouraging active, playful experiences. The overarching message is that movement should be embedded in daily routines, ensuring all children have opportunities to develop essential physical skills that support their independence, resilience and holistic growth.

Summary of key points

- **Importance of physical activity for children**: physical activity is essential for the healthy growth and development of children. It helps to develop their motor skills, cognitive function and social skills. Children under five years old should be physically active for at least 180 minutes (3 hours) a day.
- **Challenges to physical activity for children with health conditions**: children with chronic health conditions, special educational needs or complex medical needs may face challenges to participating in physical activity. However, it is important to find ways to include them in physical activities, as the benefits are still significant.
- **Strategies for promoting physical activity in children**: there are a number of strategies that can be used to promote physical activity in children. These include providing opportunities for both structured and unstructured play, creating a stimulating environment and educating parents and caregivers about the importance of physical activity.
- **The role of early childhood practitioners**: early childhood practitioners play an important role in promoting physical development in children. They can do this by creating a safe and supportive environment, providing opportunities for physical activity and modelling healthy behaviours.
- **Benefits of physical activity throughout life**: the benefits of physical activity extend far beyond childhood. Regular physical activity can help to improve mental health, reduce the risk of chronic diseases and maintain a healthy weight.

References

Adolph, K.E. and Hoch, J.E. (2019). Motor development: Embodied, embedded, enculturated, and enabling, *Annual Review of Psychology*, 70, pp. 141-164. https://doi.org/10.1146/annurev-psych-010418-102836

Ball, J. (2019). *Supporting Physical Development in the Early Years*. London: Routledge.

Barratt, J., Dudley, D., Stylianou, M., and Cairney, J. (2024). A conceptual model of an effective early childhood physical literacy pedagogue. *Journal of Early Childhood Research*, 22(3), pp. 381-394.

Battelley, H. (2021). *50 Fantastic Ideas for Songs and Rhymes*. London: Bloomsbury Education.

British Heart Foundation Research Centre (2018). *Cardiovascular Disease Statistics 2018*. London: British Heart Foundation. Available at: https://www.bhf.org.uk/what-we-do/our-research/heart-statistics/heart-statistics-publications/cardiovascular-disease-statistics-2018 (Accessed: 13 September 2025).

Brolin, K., Cronin, D.S., Panzer, M.B., Vezin, P., Yoganandan, N., Reed, M.P., Beillas, P. and Gayzik, F.S. (2018). Human body modeling and validation with biomechanics experiments, *IRCOBI Workshop Series*. Available at: https://ircobi.org/wordpress/downloads/ircobi-hbm-2018.pdf (Accessed: 13 September 2025).

Bruce, T. (2021). *Early Childhood Education* (5th edn). London: Hodder Education.

Centre for Movement (2020). Available at: https://www.centreofmovement.com.au/what-is-midline-and-why-is-crossing-the-midline-important-for-your-childs-brain-development/

Chief Medical Officer (2019). Available at: https://assets.publishing.service.gov.uk/media/620a8add8fa8f549097b864a/physical-activity-for-early-years-birth-to-5.pdf (Accessed 20 September 2024).

Department of Health and Social Care (2022). Guidance: Physical activity guidelines: disabled children and disabled young people. Available format: https://www.gov.uk/government/publications/physical-activity-guidelines-disabled-children-and-disabled-young-people (Accessed 14 April 2023).

DfE (2021). *Help for Early Years: Areas of Learning*. Available at: https://help-for-early-years-providers.education.gov.uk/areas-of-learning

DfE (2025). Early years foundation stage statutory framework for group and school-based providers. Setting the standards for learning, development and care for children from birth to five. Available at: https://assets.publishing.service.gov.uk/media/687105a381dd8f70f5de3ea9/EYFS_framework_for_group_and_school_based_providers_.pdf (Accessed 21 July 2025).

Duncombe, R., and Preedy, P. (2021). Physical development in the early years: Exploring its importance and the adequacy of current provision in the United Kingdom. *Education 3-13*, 49(8), 920-934. https://doi.org/10.1080/03004279.2020.1817963

EEF (2023). Early years toolkit: Physical development approaches.

EEF (2024). Early years: Approaches and practices to support physical development Early Education: https://early-education.org.uk/physical-development-early-childhood/

Foulkes, J.D., Knowles, Z., Fairclough, S.J., Stratton, G., O'Dwyer, M., Ridgers, N.D., and Foweather, L. (2015) Fundamental movement skills of preschool children in Northwest England. *Perceptual and Motor Skills*, 121, 260-283. https://doi.org/10.2466/10.25.pms.121c14x0

Hall, A.C., Butterworth, J., Winsor, J., Kramer, J., Nye-Lengerman, K. and Timmons, J. (2018). Building an evidence-based, holistic approach to advancing integrated employment, *Research and Practice for Persons with Severe Disabilities*, 43(3), pp. 207-218. https://doi.org/10.1177/1540796918787503

Hulteen, R.M., Morgan, P.J., Barnett, L.M., Stodden, D.F. and Lubans, D.R. (2018). Development of foundational movement skills: a conceptual model for physical activity across the lifespan. *Sports Medicine*, 48(7), pp. 1533-1544.

Jones, D., Innerd, A., Giles, E.L., and Azevedo, L.B. (2020). Association between fundamental motor skills and physical activity in the early years: A systematic review and meta-analysis. *The Journal of Sport and Health Science*, 9(6), pp. 542-552. https://doi.org/10.1016/j.jshs.2020.03.001

Kolehmainen, P., Jiang, M., Vaisanen, E., Huttunen, M., Ylä-Herttuala, S., Meri, S., Österlund, P. and Julkunen, I. (2023). COVID-19 adenovirus vector vaccine induces higher interferon and pro-inflammatory responses than mRNA vaccines in human PBMCs, macrophages and moDCs, *Vaccine*, 41(26), pp. 3813-3823. https://doi.org/10.1016/j.vaccine.2023.04.049

La Valle, I., Lewis, J., Crawford, C., Paull, G., Lloyd, E., Ott, E. et al. (2022). *Implications of COVID for Early Childhood Education and Care in England*. London: Centre for Evidence and Implementation. Available at: https://www.familyandchildcaretrust.org/sites/default/files/Resource%20Library/Implications%20of%20Covid%20for%20ECEC%20in%20England%20-%20June%202022_0.pdf (Accessed: 13 September 2025).

Loon, M. and Bell, R. (2016). *Professional Practice in Learning and Development: How to Design and Deliver Plans for the Workplace*. London: Kogan Page.

Madan, C.R. and Singhal, A. (2012). 'Using actions to enhance memory: Effects of enactment, gestures, and exercise on human memory. *Frontiers in Psychology*, 3, Article 507. https://doi.org/10.3389/fpsyg.2012.00507

Musgrave, J. (ed). (2024). *Little Minds Matter: Promoting Physical Development and Activity in Early Childhood*. Abingdon: Routledge.

NCSEM (2022). Early years East Midlands. Available at: Early years – NCSEM-EM.

NHS (2022). Physical activity guidelines for children (under 5 years). Available at: Physical activity guidelines for children (under 5 years) – NHS.

Ofsted. (2022a). Research and analysis, Research review series: PE. Available at Research review series: PE - GOV.UK; https://www.gov.uk/government/publications/research-review-series-pe/research-review-series-pe

Ofsted. (2022b). Ofsted: Education recovery in early years. Available at: https://www.gov.uk/government/publications/education-recovery-in-early-years-providers-summer-2022

Physical Literacy Consensus Statement for England. (2023). Available at: https://www.sportengland.org/news-and-inspiration/physical-literacy-consensus-statement-england-published

Reed, M. and Parish, N. (2021). *Physical Development in the Early Years: A Whole Setting Approach*. London: Early Education.

Roscoe, C.M.P., James, R.S., and Duncan, M.J. (2019). Accelerometer-based physical activity levels, fundamental movement skills and weight status in British preschool children from a deprived area. *European Journal of Pediatrics*, 178, 1043-1052. https://doi.org/10.1007/s00431-019-03390-z.

Roscoe, C.M.P., Taylor, N., Weir, N., Flynn, R.J., and Pringle, A. (2024). Impact and implementation of an early years fundamental motor skills intervention for children 4-5 years. *Children*, 11(4), p. 416. https://doi.org/10.3390/children11040416

Sense. (2015). Making the case for play. Making the case for play: Findings of the Sense Public Inquiry 2015 - Sense

The National Autistic Society. (2016). Autism, sport and physical activity. Available at: Autism-sport-physical-activity.pdf (https://thirdlight.com/)

UK Chief Medical Officers. (2019). UK Chief Medical Officers' Physical Activity Guidelines. Available at: Physical activity guidelines: UK Chief Medical Officers' report - GOV.UK (https://www.gov.uk/) (Accessed 9 April 2024).

Whitehead, M. (Eds.) (2010). *Physical Literacy: Throughout the Life Course*. London, UK: Routledge.

Zhang, B., Kan, L., Dong, A., Zhang, J., Bai, Z., Xie, Y. et al. (2019). The effects of action observation training on improving upper limb motor functions in people with stroke: A systematic review and meta-analysis, *PloS One*, 14(8), p. e0221166. https://doi.org/10.1371/journal.pone.0221166

Zhou, Y., and Tolmie, A. (2024). Associations between gross and fine motor skills, physical activity, executive function, and academic achievement: Longitudinal findings from the UK millennium Cohort Study. *Brain Sciences*, 14(2), p. 121.

6 Prime area
Personal, social, emotional development

Poppy Gibson

Introduction

Personal, social, and emotional development (PSED) refers to the growth of a child's ability to understand and manage their emotions, interact effectively with others and develop a positive sense of self. PSED in the early years is crucial because it lays the foundation for children's future success. In this chapter, we include ten contributions from practitioners who have developed a series of activities which support the development of key PSED skills.

Pondering question: what should be included in a curriculum which both nurtures and supports?

The area of personal, social and emotional development is one of the prime areas in the Early Years Foundation Stage (Holman, 2024). Helping children understand their emotions is valuable when we see the early years as the building blocks towards adulthood (Soni, 2014). PSED refers to the growth of a child's ability to understand and manage their emotions, interact effectively with others and develop a positive sense of self. It is a crucial aspect of early childhood development, laying the foundation for future success in relationships, learning, and overall wellbeing.

The significance of PSED in a child's development

PSED is fundamental to a child's overall development for several reasons. Children who are emotionally and socially secure are more likely to be engaged in learning, have better concentration and demonstrate greater academic achievement. Strong PSED skills are essential for positive mental health (Mahoney et al., 2021). Children who can manage their emotions, build healthy relationships and cope with challenges are less likely to experience anxiety, depression and other mental health problems. PSED also helps children develop the social skills they need to interact effectively with others, build friendships and participate in social situations. By prioritising PSED in the Early Years, educators can provide children with the essential foundation they need to thrive (Alam, 2022).

Prime area: Personal, social, emotional development

The crucial role of the adult in creating and supporting PSED skills

Johnson (2023) highlights that especially in the early years, the roles of adults in emotional regulation is key; this expands from just being the parent or carer or primary caregiver, to then the key person in nurseries and day care setting, the teacher and support staff at school and the role of multi-professional teams.

In this first contribution, Sophie Smith-Tong, Mental Health and Wellbeing Lead and Founder of Mindfulness for Learning, shares information on mindfulness and the successful mindfulness sessions they have been running in their EYFS setting.

Sophie Smith-Tong: mindfulness in the EYFS

Mindfulness is the act of being present. This process, one of bringing the focus back to a chosen anchor (quite often the breath), is a learned skill. Once practised, mindfulness enables us to develop the ability to respond rather than react; vital for all children who are consistently met with challenging interactions that require less reactivity and more contemplation.

Where I work, as the reception teacher and mental health and wellbeing lead, we deliver daily mindfulness sessions from our Baby Room right up to Year 6. Yes! You hear that right, our 6-month-old babies are familiar with breathing techniques and it is magical. When I deliver staff training on Mindfulness in the Early Years Foundation Stage the most common response from educators is, 'I have tried it but they just won't keep still or focus for that long'.

You would be right in thinking babies and children in their early years cannot sit still for that long, developmentally most are not ready and it is misguided to think that mindfulness is about physical stillness or forcing the body or mind into doing things it isn't ready or wanting to do—in fact this is the opposite of what mindfulness is trying to cultivate which is acceptance; embracing what is. This is inclusive of a child noticing that the body wants to fidget, stick their finger in their nose or stick their tongue out to touch their chin as they explore the sensation. It is also accepting of the fact that their mind may want to wander, ask questions, call out or make a humming noise. Mindfulness for little ones may not look or sound how you imagine or meet your desired expectations of 'zen' but my response to this is—get rid of your expectations! Learn to be mindful, enjoy and accept the unpredictable ride of mini mindfulness and you will all reap the personal, social and emotional benefits. Attempt to be curious and interested in the varied responses you receive from young children; mindfulness will not always be a sight of beauty in the early years but believe that the work is being done on the inside.

Mindfulness in our setting (which is a Children's Centre and Primary School) looks different in every room. In the Baby Room it's the daily gathering of all adults and babies with the adults very much modelling the act of taking time to breathe. In the Toddler Room it's the daily gathering of children to name feelings and focus on being with these feelings through the act of breath. In Nursery it's exploring how this feels physically through a variety of breathing techniques and in Reception thinking about our responses and exploring more nuanced emotions through story, messages and puppetry. The one constant in our mindfulness sessions from the baby room to year 1 is the use of our puppet, Mindful Mo©. An approach designed by us at Mindfulness for learning, Mindful Mo© is able to explore breathing and emotional intelligence in a way that is safe, flexible and tailored to each individual and cohort. Mo is tangible, a symbol, a physical way that all of the children can recognise the abstract space carved out for self-reflection.

So, if you are unsure as to whether it is possible to practice mindfulness in the Early Years, then let me confirm: it really is, and not only is it possible, it's beautiful.

The second contribution in this chapter explores the absolute significance of being trauma informed, in order to effectively support PSED. Claire Plews, HE Counselling Curriculum Coordinator: University Centre Weston, EdD researcher University of Bristol, presents the case for a cohesive sequential framework to support all children.

Claire Plews: creating continuity—trauma-informed practices throughout the learning journey

Governmental focus on mental health support in education has increased, particularly after the COVID-19 pandemic. This attention aims to address the ongoing decline in children's mental wellbeing, which can significantly impact their lifelong health (Izett et al., 2021). Early intervention and preventative strategies in early years are therefore crucial.

The 2021-22 UK government spending review allocated £79 million to expand mental health support for 345,000 more children and young people in school settings (DfE, 2023). However, with 9 million children in the UK, schools and early years settings are regularly charged with filling this gap, often without adequate resources or training (Golberstein et al., 2020).

My doctoral research, which employed creative, co-designed methods to explore adolescent perceptions of mental health provision in education, revealed a concerning trend. Participants reported that for them the education system not only failed to support their mental health but actually contributed to their struggles during their formative years. The young people in the study indicated that they viewed secondary education as less nurturing and more restrictive than earlier schooling, hindering self-development and identity formation (Plews, 2024). The pandemic provided a temporary respite from these challenges and highlighted this issue for the young people in the study.

This finding underscores the importance of early years settings, but it is concerning that the nurturing focus often diminishes as children progress through the school system. Maintaining nurturing and child-centred provision is crucial for children's emotional wellbeing and shouldn't be limited to the early years. This implies a significant shift needed in the current educational system however, which often favours behavioural methods focused on obedience, control and punishment, viewing 'disruptive' and 'challenging' behaviours as manipulative or attention seeking (Vericat Rocha & Ruitenberg, 2019).

Trauma informed practice

While child-centred practices are needed throughout all stages of education, pedagogical research and my observations from two decades of working in mental health also suggest that fostering trauma-informed emotional regulation and distress tolerance strategies from early years onwards can safeguard against adult anxiety and mental health issues (Lathan, 2024).

This approach enables practitioners to recognise trauma's emotional and behavioural manifestations while developing a child's self-regulation and coping skills (Milot et al., 2015). However, although trauma-informed approaches to education and early years care are not a new phenomenon, the importance of viewing children who have experienced trauma as whole individuals, not just as subjects of intervention or victims is especially highlighted. We should be cautious of diagnostic criteria overshadowing the uniqueness of each child. Instead, we should consider children in the present, not just as future adults, and aim to address the systemic inequalities that impact their development (Vericat Rocha & Ruitenberg, 2019).

These recommendations have significant implications for both policymakers and Early Years practitioners, requiring a thorough review of current practices and policies to ensure alignment with trauma-informed principles *throughout* the educational journey. This approach aims to create a cohesive framework that supports children's emotional wellbeing and development across all stages of education, emphasising the importance of continuing the good work laid down in early years settings.

The next contribution, by Lily Sheikh, Early Years practitioner, shares the importance of developing a collaborative approach to nurturing a respectful understanding of gender in the EYFS.

Lily Sheikh: challenging gender stereotypes in PSED

Some may argue that actively teaching about gender in the EYFS is too young, however it's quite the opposite. This is where beliefs start to form, making it crucial to educate children to think critically and question others' views. Early Years practitioners can smoothly integrate discussions about gender stereotyping into PSED, which focuses on nurturing children's positive self-image, relationships and respect for others. Actively challenging gender stereotypes from a young age helps towards creating a more inclusive society (UNICEF, 2022).

One effective way to encourage self-expression is to provide experiences that challenge stereotypical norms. For example, ensuring everyone is represented, particularly in areas where they're not typically seen, such as women in STEM (Science, Technology, Engineering, and Mathematics). This can be achieved by displaying photos of both female and male scientists. By doing so, children grow up without questioning why an individual is in a particular job based on their gender, rather than their ability. Providing opportunities for children to explore different roles and responsibilities traditionally associated with different genders helps them understand that these roles can be fluid and not fixed. This can also be demonstrated in the toys and costumes we provide for them and how we interact in that context; it is important that we don't actively encourage or dissuade a child to or away from an activity based on what their gender stereotypically likes, rather it is important to make sure that children receive equal opportunities to participate in everything (Barea & Marín, 2020). Reflecting on my own school experience, nursing was commonly seen as a woman's job while men were more often depicted as doctors. However, there has been noticeable change over the past decade. It's crucial to emphasize the importance of fostering critical thinking skills. In my current setting, the children I work with demonstrate strong critical thinking abilities; they tend to question statements of gender rather than jumping to assumptions. This is a result of how they are being taught.

A method to help children recognise and challenge stereotypes is by engaging in active discussions with them, either through group discussions, children's literature or games. These discussions should aim to stimulate their interest and enable them to articulate their emotions, allowing them to express themselves without feeling constrained by gender expectations. Addressing any misconceptions that arise in an early years setting is crucial (Aina & Cameron, 2011). Children are greatly influenced by their peers, and if one child expresses a stereotype, others may mimic and internalize those views (Vygotsky, 1978). It's important to approach these discussions in a way that doesn't belittle the child but rather educates them. By fostering an environment where children feel empowered to question and learn, we can help them develop a more inclusive understanding of gender.

Strong collaboration and partnerships with parents are essential in creating a gender-neutral atmosphere in early years education. Children absorb their parents' views, so effective partnership ensures consistency in learning and development experiences at home and in the setting. This collaboration also helps identify concerns early and allows parents to reinforce learning at home.

Michelle Yeung, Year 1 teacher at Sha Tin Junior School, shares, in this next contribution, how children are supported to understand emotions, rehearse and strengthen the skill of self-regulation and become more independent in their thoughts and views.

Michelle Yeung: building a child's knowledge for life

In the past, children were expected to be seen and not heard. In the past, children were expected to behave with no exceptions. Fast forward to the present day, there is immense pressure on children to thrive academically, socially and emotionally. These three aspects of achievements must coincide with one another. Most notably, academic excellence and sociability cannot be achieved if a child's emotional well-being is not at an optimal level. When a child is feeling happy and safe, it is only then that they are able to acquire knowledge and engage in social situations. It is unrealistic to expect anyone to be in a constant state of happiness; accepting all forms of emotion is the first step to the development of emotional wellbeing.

The most basic emotions young toddlers may feel are happy, sad and scared. As they develop and are exposed to different life experiences, their range of emotions may include excitement, surprise and shyness amongst others. Helping children identify their emotions is the first step to emotional development. Once children are able to identify their feelings, the next step will be to teach children strategies to regulate their emotions.

In my class of 4- to 5-year-olds, my very first lesson in teaching emotions is by showing children a variety of facial expressions. The children will be given a mirror and I will ask them to try to replicate the facial expressions they see. Most importantly, children will not be given names of these emotions, rather, we will have a discussion about situations where a person may show this type of expression. This exercise will help the children to better identify their emotions by relating them to their past experiences rather than being limited by the confines of emotion names. The second lesson will be to give names to some basic feelings; our school uses The Zones of Regulation as a tool for students to identify their emotions. The Zones of Regulation groups emotions into the blue zone, the green zone, the yellow zone and the red zone. The blue are the sad, tired and sick feelings. The green are the happy and calm feelings. The yellow are the silly and excited feelings where you feel you start to lose control. The red are the angry and explosive feelings. The key is for the children to understand that all feelings are valid and it is okay to be in all four zones, while the green zone is where the best learning can take place. However, children should understand that while it is okay to be in all four zones, it is not healthy to be stuck in the blue or red zone for prolonged periods of time. This is where the lessons on emotional regulation will begin.

Basic regulation techniques I introduce to my students are five-finger breathing, squeezing playdough, hugging a toy, doing jumping jacks, going for a walk or talking to a teacher. While they may seem like simple tasks, it takes a lot of reminders and practice before the children are able to self-regulate without the teacher's support; especially with those big explosive feelings. On the children's journey to becoming emotionally literate, my students do a self-emotion check-in daily when they come into the classroom. I have magnets for them to place their names onto the colour zone they are feeling that morning. During our morning routines, I will check in and have a chat with those students who have put themselves in the blue or red zones and we will work together to see if we can find a strategy for them to get themselves back into the green zone before the afternoon. This is a rigorous journey for educators and young learners but it is a valuable journey worth taking.

This knowledge that educators can instil in their students is the knowledge they can hold for their lifetime, across disciplines, across cultures and across situations.

In this next contribution, Melanie Yates-Boothby, EYFS Lead, SENCO and Nursery Teacher, shares a personal account of how PSED is planned for, implemented and evaluated.

Melanie Yates-Boothby: relationships make our nursery a nice place to be

We are in a critical moment in time following the COVID-19 pandemic when almost half of parents reported children's worsening social-emotional skills (Cattan et al., 2023) and NHS (2023) reported 1 in 5 children had a probable mental health disorder.

Our school is an inclusive setting with increasing numbers of children with special educational needs, therefore it is important to us to promote their unique strengths, understand their difficulties and ensure our children feel valued and their views respected. My nursery classroom mantra reflects the ethos underpinning our social and emotional learning environment. 'Together, we make *our nursery* a nice place to be'.

At the core of our provision for social and emotional development is relationships. The most important thing we can do to promote learning is to form genuine caring relationships first, particularly for children who may present with challenging behaviour. The student-teacher relationship is like a model for children of how we treat others. Losh, Eisenhower and Blacher (2022) assert the quality of these relationships significantly contributes to pupil engagement, potentially serving as a key protective factor for classroom success for children with autism. This is also true for neurotypical pupils as of course engagement cannot occur in the absence of quality relationships.

From Day 1 we model kindness and respect in our interactions. I believe the relationships we form and how we speak to the children in our care each day become their inner voice. This inner voice will become their values, which in turn have the potential to change the world for the better. We are positive in our daily interactions and routines (and I don't mean in an ingenuine tokenistic way because they can smell it a mile off). We are also mindful of those little moments when we can model appreciation and thank our children, 'Thank you for tidying up those toys and making our nursery a nice place to be'; 'That's great sharing! When we take turns and share like that, we make our nursery such a nice place to be!'

We are mindful. Education is sometimes in such a rush; there is a constant temptation to rush to finish an activity, rush to tidy up, rush to wash our hands; rush to learn to read before we can even listen and understand what someone is saying. We *plan time* for mindfulness activities, to help our children develop an appreciation of the world and people around us. We teach children how to eat mindfully, see and talk about the world and its beauty with awe and wonder, and if someone snatches a toy you were playing with it is a problem we can solve together with support and understanding. It isn't always about implementing an off-the-shelf, all-singing and dancing social and emotional scheme of learning, it is about working in collaboration with our children through play, to meet their individual needs wherever they are and equipping them with the tools to be self-regulated and emotionally ready for learning.

We know that settled and emotionally ready children are ready to learn, flourish and grow. Let's make our settings a nice place to be!

In the following contribution, Lousie Turnbull, Programme Leader for Early Years provision, advocates for all practitioners to participate in high-quality professional development focused on PSED, highlighting the sustained impact of this for themselves and their children.

Louise Turnbull: mental health and emotional quotient within PSED and the early years curriculum

PSED is a prime area in the Early Years foundation stage, looking at three different aspects which include self-confidence and awareness, managing feelings and behaviours and making relationships. This is an area which links most closely to a child's mental health and can influence mental ill-health. The Mental Health of Children and Young People Survey reports that '5.5% of 2-4-year-old children experience a mental health disorder. This rises to one in eight children and young people aged between 5 and 19, with emotional disorders reported as most prevalent' (NHS Digital, 2018, cited in Seaman and Giles, 2019, p. 66).

Since the pandemic, PSED has been the area in which many practitioners have felt that children have regressed in comparison to the other six areas of development. PSED involves self-regulation and being able to manage self are two aspects which filter into mental health and wellbeing. This involves how children see themselves and understand emotional quotient, which is an immense part of our future lives and something that there can be a distinct lack of as we grow older. The importance of good emotional wellbeing is something that is carried through life, supporting children to be able to make positive relationships and have a positive sense of themselves, as well as being able to be resilient and have the coping strategies to be able to navigate through life.

Early years practitioners seem to have a more diverse knowledge of personal, social and emotional development due to the EYFS. However, there is a distinct lack of mental health training and support in place, especially for Early Years educators who predominantly have the difficult task of supporting children with their feelings and behaviours in the crucial stages of their lives. Although educators have indicated a good knowledge of PSED, children and young people are still requiring more support with their wellbeing.

In early years educator training, mental health and wellbeing is embedded within the core units, looking at the health and wellbeing of children, but with no specific mention of mental health. This means that it is dependent on the knowledge and confidence of the tutor teaching as to how in depth they would go into mental health and linking this to PSED. It would be beneficial to integrate this as part of the teaching and learning for practitioners and primary teachers, by acknowledging the need for it in early years and teaching of children. This can be carried out by those students who access placement and in future, careers in early years and primary teaching. Also, the importance of having mental health first aid as a mandatory aspect in early years along with physical first aid to ensure that the personal, social and emotional needs of children can be met from the earliest age to support the growth and development of being able to reiterate and manage our feelings as children, but also as we grow.

The next contribution introduces the notion of 'covid gilet' and its meaning within EYFS. Lucy Fox, Early Years Leader, effectively explains how this phrase has cemented a shared vision of what both adults and children mean to progress and flourish.

Lucy Fox: COVID gilet

When I first began discussing this year's cohort with our head, the phrase 'COVID gilet' kept cropping up – particularly when talking about policies and key messages/journeys for the upcoming year. The meaning behind the phrase was simple: our ethos and values remain the same; what we want for our children remains the same; the expectations and outcomes we desire both in terms of delivery and end goals remain the same. And yet, we must not lose sight of the unprecedented year we were about the embark upon with our 2024/2025 Reception cohort. For this reason, a 'COVID gilet' was important for us; a lens which we could look through with our new children and their unique early years in mind.

As an EYFS team, we have had to rewire our thinking this year in many ways. Remembering heartbreaking facts such as the knowledge that our children have had to learn basic facial expressions and emotions by looking at eyes only has been vital when making adaptions to fit the needs of every child. And if there was ever a year to say that 'every child is different and therefore needs their own unique journey towards KS1', it is this one.

Building awareness of the upcoming challenges both within the team and across the wider school network has been an important first step in welcoming our lockdown babies. Only when we are all truly aware of the challenges that these children have faced in their development, and the mystery surrounding the impact that this may have on their early education, can we face our academic year with an openness and willingness to adapt as is necessary and to be innovative and not afraid of change when it is needed.

The second most important step we have taken as a school this year is the acknowledgement of our 2024/2025 parents and the impact that having their children in a national lockdown may have had on them. As we all know, our relationship with parents and/or carers within the EYFS and the extent to which we can engage with their child's development can play a huge role in how successfully that child moves through the first few years of their school lives.

What we know about these parents is that they had no access to anti-natal groups or classes, regular health visitor checks, community baby and toddler groups and many more things that us with older children took for granted when our babies were born.

Parental mental health was largely left unchecked, babies were denied access to wider social situations and new mothers were largely left on their own. Throw in the fear of a global pandemic which is killing thousands every day and it's no wonder we as practitioners are seeing a very different style of parenting this year.

For this reason, developing strong relationships with our parents has been more important than ever. So far, we have developed a number of strategies:

- We have a no-opt-out approach to our daily app, on which we regularly communicate with parents about day-to-day school life and the individual journey of their child. We also weave our app through our teaching, bringing our parents and wider family network into the classroom with us.
- Our classroom displays have been changed this year. Each child has their own individual display square on which their own personal learning journey can be documented. Each square contains a picture of the child at school and one at home, again weaving the two together as places of happiness and safety.
- We have worked hard to develop several plans to bring parents into our classrooms and to spend time with them and their children together. So far, our parents have loved this and have really valued the chances we have given to come and see their children thriving in school, whether this has been a casual drop-in session or a more prescribed and planned event.

As I said at the start, this year is an unprecedented year. We don't know the impact that lockdown had the educational journey of these children yet. What we do know though is that by approaching the year with an open mind and a willingness to adapt along the way, we are giving them the best chance at success and that is all that matters.

The next contribution written by Hannah Baker, Co-CEO at Partnership for Children, invites thoughts on the power of using storytelling as a tool to enhance learning in PSED.

Hannah Baker: storytelling as a powerful tool for social and emotional learning

Social and emotional learning (SEL) is a crucial part of personal, social and emotional development, and includes improving self-confidence and self-awareness, managing feelings and behaviour, and making and managing relationships.

The evidence shows us children who take part in SEL interventions make around three additional months' progress in early years settings and reception classes and can have a positive impact on young children's social interactions and attitudes to learning, and on aspects of early learning across the curriculum. Importantly, although all children benefit, children from disadvantaged backgrounds have, on average, weaker SEL skills at all ages and therefore, a focus on SEL is important for closing the disadvantage gap (Education Endowment Foundation Early Years Toolkit, 2023).

However, effective, nurturing and supportive SEL relies on embedding strategies within everyday practice rather than a one off or separate area of focus. A wonderful way to do this is through storytelling.

Stories have always been a key part of our social and emotional learning programmes at Partnership for Children. Books with relatable characters who face age-appropriate challenges allow children to connect with the narrative on a personal level. Remember, books should be seen as both mirrors and windows (Bishop, 1990)—mirrors to help children see themselves and windows to introduce them to the lives of others so ensure books represent diverse cultures, ethnicities, family structures, abilities and perspectives. Look for books with expressive illustrations that clearly depict the characters' emotions through facial expressions and body language. This helps children identify emotions and understand nonverbal cues, which are crucial for building empathy and social awareness.

Once you have a carefully selected SEL library, how can books be shared with children with a focus on developing their PSED skills? Stories create a shared experience for children, promoting social interactions and dialogue. Practitioners can engage children in interactive storytelling by asking questions, encouraging predictions and discussing characters' feelings and actions. Adding discussions after the story with open-ended questions encourages children to think deeply about the characters' emotions and actions. Questions like 'How did the character feel?' or 'What would you do in that situation?' promote critical thinking and emotional literacy.

Daily storytelling can be extended and embedded throughout continuous provision through weekly or fortnightly role play. Bandura's social learning theory (1971) shows us that children learn behaviours through observation and imitation. Creating a role play area, story sacks, small world provision or puppet play resources based on a story about emotions can be a powerful way to bring the book's themes to life and support children's understanding of their own emotions. This hands-on approach allows children to practice social interactions and explore emotional responses, reinforcing the behaviours observed in the story.

The integration of storytelling into early childhood education provides a powerful tool for fostering social and emotional learning and ensuring a nurturing and supportive curriculum where all children are supported to develop skills for life through the magic of books.

The penultimate contribution in this chapter, heightens the importance of planning for an environment which supports and challenges PSED learning. Anne Rogers, an Early Years Consultant, includes a range of activities and experiences which can be used alongside children when playing together.

Anne Rogers: developing an environment to support PSED

As children progress through different ages and stages of development, we must monitor their progress not only physically and academically but also observe how they are coping and feeling.

Mental health awareness is about being aware of how someone is feeling and what impact this is having on their day-to-day life and development. Young children can be susceptible to having mental health issues for many reasons, including:

- A predisposed genetic condition
- Situations that they live through

'All children deserve the care and support they need to have the best start in life. Children learn and develop at a faster rate from birth to five years old than at any other time in their lives, so their experiences in Early Years have a major impact on their future life chances' (Dfe 2025: 7).

Wellbeing means being confident, happy and healthy and focuses on developing as a person. Children's relationships and interactions with their families and communities contribute significantly to their sense of wellbeing. They need to feel valued, respected, empowered, cared for and included. They also need to respect themselves, others and their environment. Children feel positive about themselves when adults value them for who they are and when they provide warm and supportive relationships with them. This will help children to become resilient and resourceful and learn to cope with change. Being allowed to express themselves creatively will help enhance wellbeing.

> Children with mental health issues may become:
> Withdrawn
> Clingy
> Aggressive towards peers
> Fussy eaters
> Act out of character.
> Strategies to help and support children include:
> Reassure the child that they are loved and that things will get better
> Provide activities that will support their needs
> Provide a safe and secure environment
> Put routines in place so the child knows what will happen next.

Research shows that yoga is beneficial in many ways to young children not only physically but mentally too. Make a routine of animal poses to accompany a short story and get the children to act out the poses and do the stretches.

Provide a place of their own within the setting to put their belongings such as a drawer or a basket. Make a personal booklet and gather pictures of their families and places and people important to them for them to look at.

Give them opportunities towards independence such as helping them to learn how to dress themselves and offer lots of praise and recognition and positive encouragement.

It is important to explain things that are happening to children in an age- and stage-appropriate way. Keep routines as close to normal as possible as it will help them to keep on track. Observing changes in behaviour is vital and further advice can be sought from other professionals should there be any concerns.

Children thrive within environments that support their individual and diverse development needs and enabling environments offer children security, comfort, choice, engagement and opportunity.

Children's learning is best supported when they have opportunities which allow for movement and action, creativity and imagination, independence and collaboration.

The final contribution in this chapter, by Sarag Guscott, Higher Education Practice Tutor and Lecturer at Inspire Education Group, celebrates the implementation of sensory aware strategies, highlighting their impact for children's PSED development.

Sarah Guscott: sensory-aware strategies for enhancing personal, social and emotional development in early years

PSED is a cornerstone of early childhood education, providing the foundation upon which children build their self-awareness, relationships and emotional regulation. To nurture and support PSED effectively, a curriculum must integrate an understanding of sensory processing—how children perceive and respond to sensory input—because it is intrinsically linked to their ability to manage emotions, interact socially and navigate their environment.

Sensory processing, encompassing the eight sensory systems (sight, hearing, taste, smell, touch, proprioception, vestibular and interoception), plays a critical role in PSED. These systems influence how children experience the world, interact with others and regulate their emotions (Ayres, 2005). In the wake of the COVID-19 pandemic, children's sensory needs have become even more pronounced, with many exhibiting heightened sensitivities and challenges in social situations (EEF, 2021). A PSED curriculum that is mindful of sensory processing can help address these challenges, creating a supportive environment that fosters emotional wellbeing and social competence.

Key components to include in a sensory-aware PSED curriculum:

1. Sensory-Sensitive Emotional Regulation: to help children manage their emotions, the curriculum should include sensory-based strategies. For example, a 'calm box' containing items like stress balls, textured fabrics and scented playdough can be provided for children to use when they feel overwhelmed. This allows children to self-soothe using sensory input, facilitating better emotional regulation.
2. Sensory-Informed Social Skills Development: group activities can be designed with sensory considerations to make social interactions more accessible for children with different sensory profiles. For instance, instead of traditional circle time, a practitioner might arrange the group in a loose, semi-circle where children can have a bit more personal space, reducing sensory overload. Additionally, activities that incorporate movement, such as a 'follow the leader' game with varying speeds, can help children practice social skills like taking turns and following directions in a way that feels engaging and manageable.
3. Building Resilience Through Sensory Integration: sensory play is a powerful tool for building resilience. Activities like 'heavy work' tasks, where children push, pull, or carry weighted objects, can help them develop proprioceptive awareness and self-regulation skills. This not only supports their sensory needs but also helps them build the resilience needed to cope with stress and frustration.

76 Early Years Essentials

4. Mindfulness and Sensory Awareness: mindfulness practices that engage multiple senses can be particularly effective for PSED. For example, a practitioner might guide children through a 'sensory walk' where they focus on the different sounds, textures and smells in their environment. This helps children stay grounded and develop a greater awareness of their sensory experiences, which is crucial for emotional regulation and social interaction (Porges, 2011).
5. Collaborative Sensory Strategies: collaboration with families and specialists is key. For instance, creating a 'sensory profile' for each child, developed in consultation with parents and occupational therapists, can ensure that the sensory needs of each child are understood and supported both at home and in the educational setting.

(Kranowitz, 2005)

An illustrative example comes from a practitioner who introduced 'sensory storytime' sessions. These sessions involve reading stories while incorporating sensory elements like textured props, scents and sounds that align with the narrative. This approach not only makes the story more engaging but also supports children's sensory needs, helping them to better focus, participate and connect with the content emotionally.

In summary, integrating sensory processing into the PSED curriculum is essential for creating environments that nurture and support the diverse needs of children, particularly in a post-pandemic world. By recognising and accommodating the sensory dimensions of PSED, educators can foster personal, social and emotional growth in ways that are both inclusive and effective.

In conclusion

This chapter delves into personal, social and emotional development (PSED) as a fundamental aspect of early childhood education, championing its role in shaping emotional intelligence, resilience and relationships. It presents insights from practitioners who advocate for mindfulness, trauma-informed approaches, gender inclusivity and emotional regulation strategies to support children's holistic growth. Contributions highlight the importance of fostering secure attachments, self-awareness and collaborative learning environments, underscoring how PSED influences lifelong wellbeing and educational success. The chapter also explores practical interventions, including sensory-aware strategies, storytelling and engaging classroom dynamics, to nurture positive identity formation and emotional literacy in young learners.

Summary of key points

- Children who develop strong social skills are better able to form and maintain healthy relationships with peers, family and teachers. This leads to greater happiness and wellbeing.
- Children who can manage their emotions and focus their attention are better able to learn and succeed academically. PSED skills help children develop self-discipline and resilience, both essential for school readiness.
- Children who learn to understand and manage their emotions are better equipped to cope with stress and adversity. This helps prevent mental health problems later in life.

- Children who feel good about themselves and their abilities are more likely to take risks, try new things and persevere through challenges.
- Investing in PSED early on has a ripple effect throughout a child's life, leading to greater success in school, work and personal relationships.

References

Aina, O.E. and Cameron, P.A. (2011). Why does gender matter? Counteracting stereotypes with young children. *Dimensions of Early Childhood*, *39*(3), pp. 11-19.

Alam, A. (2022). Positive psychology goes to school: Conceptualizing students' happiness in 21st century schools while 'minding the mind!'are we there yet? evidence-backed, school-based positive psychology interventions. *ECS Transactions*, *107*(1), pp. 11199.

Ayres, A.J. (2005). *Sensory Integration and the Child: Understanding Hidden Sensory Challenges*. Torrence, CA: Western Psychological Services.

Bandura, A. (1971). Social learning theory. New York: General Learning Press.

Barea, E.M.G., and Marín, Y.R. (2020). Gender stereotypes in childhood. *Pedagogia Social*, (36), pp. 125-138.

Bishop, R.S. (1990). Mirrors, windows, and sliding glass doors. *Perspectives: Choosing and Using Books for the Classroom*, *6*(3), pp. ix-xi. Columbus, OH: Ohio State University, College of Education.

Cattan, S., Farquharson, C., Krutikova, S., McKendrick, A., and Sevilla, A., (2023). 'Almost half of children saw their social and emotional skills worsen during the pandemic – and economic turbulence played a role'. Published on 1 August (2023). Available [online] at: https://ifs.org.uk/news/almost-half-children-saw-their-social-and-emotional-skills-worsen-during-pandemic-and-economic (Accessed 1st September 2024).

Department for Education, DfE (2023). School pupils and their characteristics, 2022/23, Schools, pupils and their characteristics, Academic year 2022/23 – Explore education statistics – GOV.UK (https://explore-education-statistics.service.gov.uk/)

Dfe (2025). Early years foundation stage statutory framework for group and school-based providers. Setting the standards for learning, development and care for children from birth to five. Available at: https://assets.publishing.service.gov.uk/media/687105a381dd8f70f5de3ea9/EYFS_framework_for_group_and_school_based_providers_.pdf (Accessed 21 July 2025).

Education Endowment Foundation (2023). *Early Years Toolkit*. London: Education Endowment Foundation. Available at: EEF Early Years Toolkit (Accessed: 13 September 2025).

Education Endowment Foundation (EEF) (2021). *Best Evidence on Impact of COVID-19 on Early Years*. EEF.

Golberstein, E., Wen, H., and Miller, B.F. (2020). Coronavirus disease 2019 (covid-19) and mental health for children and adolescents. *JAMA Paediatrics*, *174*(9), pp. 819-820

Holman, K. (2024). The social and emotional development of children aged birth to three. In *Early Childhood Studies: A Student's Guide*. London: SAGE, p. 33.

Izett, E. et al. (2021). Prevention of mental health difficulties for children aged 0-3 years: A review. *Frontiers in Psychology*, *11*. Available at: https://doi.org/10.3389/fpsyg.2020.500361.

Johnson, T. (2023). The social and emotional needs of children. In C. Hayes (ed.) *The Early Years Handbook for Students and Practitioners* (2nd edn). London: Routledge, (pp. 270-285).

Kranowitz, C.S. (2005). *The Out-of-Sync Child: Recognising and Coping with Sensory Processing Disorder*. New York, NY: Perigee Trade.

Lathan, S. (2024). *Creating a Trauma-Informed Classroom*. St. Albans: Critical Publishing.

Losh, A., Eisenhower, A., and Blacher, J. (2022). Impact of student-teacher relationship quality on classroom behavioral engagement for young students on the autism spectrum. *Research in Autism Spectrum Disorders*, *98*, 102027. Available at: https://doi.org/10.1016/j.rasd.2022.102027 (Accessed 23rd December 2023).

Mahoney, J.L., Weissberg, R.P., Greenberg, M.T., Dusenbury, L., Jagers, R.J., Niemi, K., Schlinger, M., Schlund, J., Shriver, T.P., VanAusdal, K. and Yoder, N., (2021). Systemic social and emotional learning: Promoting educational success for all preschool to high school students. *American Psychologist*, *76*(7), p. 1128.

Milot T, St-Laurent D, and Éthier, L.S. (2015). Intervening with severely and chronically neglected children and their families: The contribution of trauma-informed approaches. *Child Abuse Review* 25(2), pp. 89-101.

NHS (2023). Mental Health of Children and Young People in England, 2023 - wave 4 follow up to the 2017 survey. Available [online] at: https://digital.nhs.uk/data-and-information/publications/statistical/mental-health-of-children-and-young-people-in-england/2023-wave-4-follow-up# [Accessed 1st September 2024]

NHS Digital. (2018). *Mental Health of Children and Young People in England, 2017: Summary of key findings*. London: NHS Digital.

Plews, C. (2024). 'I was trapped in a cycle and had no choice': School mental health provision: Casting a spurious veil over the real issues. In *FORUM* (Vol. 66, No. 1, pp. 52–64). London: Lawrence and Wishart.

Porges, S.W. (2011). *The Polyvagal Theory: Neurophysiological Foundations of Emotions, Attachment, Communication, and Self-Regulation*. New York, NY: W.W. Norton & Company.

Seaman, H. and Giles, P. (2019). Supporting children's social and emotional well-being in the early years: an exploration of practitioners' perceptions. *Early Child Development and Care* [Online] *191*(6) July, n.p. Available from https://doi.org/10.1080/03004430.2019.1649668 [Accessed 27 August 24]

Soni, A. (2014). Personal, social and emotional development (PSED). In J. Moyles, J. Payler, and J. Gergeson (eds.) *Early Years Foundations: Critical Issues*. Maidenhead: McGraw-Hill/Open University Press, pp. 88–97.

UNICEF (2022). *Tackling Gender Inequality from the Early Years. Strategies for Building a Gender-Transformative Pre-Primary Education System*. Available at: https://www.unicef.org/reports/tackling-gender-inequality-early-years [Accessed 19 March 2024]

Vericat Rocha, Á.M. & Ruitenberg, C.W. (2019). Trauma-informed practices in early childhood education: Contributions, limitations and ethical considerations. *Global Studies of Childhood*, 9(2), pp. 132–144. Available at: https://doi.org/10.1177/2043610619846319

Vygotsky, L. (1978). Interaction between learning and development. *Readings on the Development of Children*, *23*(3), pp. 34–41.

7 Prime area

Communication and language development

Jayne Carter

Introduction

Anecdotal reflections from Early Years practitioners have highlighted the increase of children experiencing speech, language and communication difficulties as they join early years settings. Further discussions note that there are a multitude of identified difficulties including lack of vocabulary, delays in listening and attention skills, articulation of specific sounds and comprehension needs. There is also a significant rise in children needing additional support for social communication including using language through play and the understanding of how language can facilitate collaboration. The thought-provoking submissions we have included in this chapter highlight the range of impressive strategies and approaches practitioners have needed to implement into their provision to meet this increasing need for their children.

Pondering question: how can we ensure that all children become confident and competent communicators?

The National Literacy Trust present stark statistics which serve to highlight the ongoing crisis. In their latest policy report 'Creating confident communicators: How the government can help every child find their voice' (2024) they highlight the plight of children in the early years.

'Yet, last year, the statistics were bleak:

- almost a third (31%) of five-year-olds started primary school without the language, communication and literacy skills they need to thrive
- this statistic rises to almost half (47%) of children from disadvantaged communities'

Data such as this, whilst difficult to read, surely evokes further reflection as to what can be done to improve these statistics and move society towards a place where communication or oracy is prioritised. Despite numerous interventions, programmes and approaches being implemented both at a national level (Every Child a Talker for example) and at a local level bespoke to individual community needs, there is still an evident need to improve children's speech, language communication skills.

In this report, The National Literacy Trust advocates for significant parliamentary changes, urging the government to act swiftly and with purpose. Their proposals are purposefully ambitious in light of their findings, with a focus on improvement for all but specifically for children within a disadvantaged group. A priority stated is the collaboration of all agencies who provide support for children in the early years as well as their families. This collaboration needs to move from a simple information transfer approach to one where an integrated framework is planned.

> However, the extent to which this reform translates to sustainable improvements in children's outcomes will ultimately depend on the quality of system leadership and the capacity of local and central government to facilitate closer coordination.
>
> (page 20)

A strategic improvement plan is imperative to move this model towards true integration. It is an absolute necessity to the success of this policy change that leaders are equipped with sufficient knowledge of early years, specifically early language research models, as well as the skills to be able to evoke and sustain a new multi-agency framework.

Oracy as a thread for improvement in CLLD?

The Oracy Education Commission in their report 'We need to talk' (2024) adds even more fuel towards a strategic overview of the proposed communication model suggested by The National Literacy Trust. The statement from their chair, Geoff Barton, goes as far as to propose that oracy should be 'the fourth R', campaigning that oracy becomes a 'key part of every teacher's repertoire, whichever age groups they work with, or subjects they teach' (page 5). With this in place, all children's skills in learning **to** talk and learning **through** talk as well as learning **about** talk provide a foundation of both knowledge and skills for children to exploit as they navigate through the increasing demands of the curriculum. The report moves from intentions to proposed implementation by offering precise recommendations for jurisdictive leaders to commit to. These include key additions to initial teacher training and other practitioner qualification boards; namely the thread of oracy to drive all professional development modules and accreditation paperwork. Practitioners need to see how this oracy thread claims its place as a pivotal mechanism underpinning all areas of the curriculum so it has status as an area in its own right as well as a conduit in promoting learning in the wider curriculum.

Another fundamental modification is the permission and freedom for school/setting leaders to plan a curriculum with more flexibility, one which champions communication, oracy, talk as the fundamental vehicle for social and educational change. Where schools have pioneered this approach, the tenacity and determination of the whole team, particularly the senior leadership team, often feel that they need to justify that this is the 'correct' approach for their school community. Enhancing the autonomy of a school to design a curriculum which is visionary, sustaining and clearly focused on increasing all children's life chances needs the backing of the system which advocates curriculum expectations.

Engaging families in the CLLD curriculum

In all evaluation reports, guidance documents and supportive case studies currently presented, the role of the family seems to play a significant part in improving children's early language skills. Adding the extensive information shared from practitioners and teachers to this comprehensive bank of resources, a creative model of engaging families goes somewhere to achieve the intention of true collaboration. There is no doubt that a commitment to both the child and their family from the school/setting accelerates this collaboration, although, like the proposals for strategic change in communication already described, this approach is ultimately down to the dedication, enthusiasm and resilience of the staff team, rather than carrying out any expected rule included in statutory documents. Essex Research School presented their findings and reflections of effective parental engagement, using the early years as a model for consideration. In their pre-recorded webinar 'Lessons learnt from early years on how to engage parents with their children's learning' they proposed designing a range of invitations to parents, to capture both their desired way of accessing key information as well as being accommodating and flexible to ensure engagement. From this webinar, my reflections were, somewhat ironically, about how a similar approach to communication for children could support family involvement too. Providing opportunities to access key knowledge in a range of contexts as I would plan for the children could also be a model for our parents. For example, sending information home via a newsletter, then followed up as a text alert could capture interest. Including the views of families (as I would for the children) could also strengthen engagement. Can we find out what is worrying them or what they want more information about? Sourcing this vital intelligence not only gives the message that family members are indeed part of the school/setting but rapidly increases the chances of attendance at meetings and further engagement.

Supporting parents specifically in knowing more about communication and how to support their children's language skills can indeed take advantage of this suggested design model. Sending ideas home for aspects such as shared reading, top tips for chatting together or play based activities can contribute to the desired collaboration. The EEF in their blog 'Making use of TRUST Talk' (2021) offers a structure to consider as part of a wider parental engagement strategy, with the focus on communication and language. This model uses reading as a tool to place other effective adult-child interactions on. It presents in a concise mini-chunked format advice about what to say when sharing a book together. A framework such as this could be the motivation for further meetings or modelled sessions which parents could attend to increase their knowledge and confidence even further.

As accented by the EEF in their Early Years Toolkit,

> Parental engagement approaches have, on average, a positive impact of five months' additional progress. It is crucial to consider how to engage with all parents to avoid widening attainment gaps.
>
> What is apparent is the necessity for all adults to engage and commit to a CLLD curriculum which not only supports children's current development, but provides a framework for future success.

In this first contribution, Laura Wulcock, a Nursery Teacher at Latchford St James CE Primary School, shares how children are supported in developing their own communication and language skills. There is a real emphasis on how all the adults work together to create a shared understanding of best practice.

Lauren Wilcock: communication and language development in our school-based nursery

Communication and language are weaker areas on entry in our nursery due to a range of factors, including English as an Additional Language (EAL) and being situated in a highly deprived and low-income electoral ward in England. We have adopted a range of strategies to support our children to develop their communication and language skills to provide them with the best start to their education journey. Our practitioners model language daily in a range of contexts through play, talk and conversations, singing rhymes and reading stories. Reading to our children plays a vital role in exposing language to our children. Our literacy sessions focus on one key book for approximately 2 weeks to allow the children to become familiar with the story, begin to join in with repeated refrains and retell key events from the story. We have a range of high-quality supporting books in the reading area that children can access independently or share with their peers and practitioners. In addition, we add puppets to the reading area to support the children with retelling their favourite stories. For example, the children loved using the three pigs and the wolf puppets to retell the story 'The Three Little Pigs', using repeated refrains from the story 'I'll huff, and I'll puff, and I'll blow your house down'. Furthermore, we have incorporated daily story time to introduce a wide range of vocabulary in a variety of topics and work in partnership with our parents providing reading books weekly to share at home.

Additionally, we assess our children's vocabulary and understanding upon entry to allow us to improve their communication skills within play with their peers and adults and within group sessions. Our children begin learning vocabulary in short interventions with our speech and language support assistant by identifying pictures or real objects and then applying this knowledge to short games, such as 'Find the pair' or 'Kim's Game'. Once the children become confident with the vocabulary, they begin to use phrases and sentences to communicate their needs with others or to initiate, direct and elaborate ideas within their play. For example, English is Child A's second language and following our interventions, they are now beginning to use phrases to direct their play with their peers, 'I know what to do. One minute. Finished'. We have a language-rich environment to promote communication and language, including family pictures in the home corner to spark conversations. For example, Child B 'look, that's me and my mummy and my daddy and my sister'. Child C replies 'I have a sister too, look that's me, my mummy, my daddy and my baby sister'. We continuously enhance and develop our learning environment to promote communication and language skills and provide a range of open-ended resources for the children to explore freely.

In this second contribution, Jess Gosling, Phase Leader Early Years with Year 1, British Nursery School of Wilanow, Poland provides an international perspective on how the curriculum is planned to ensure that all children become confident communicators.

Jess Gosling: developing language and communication skills in very young learners

When I begin to teach a class, my priority is to develop communication and language skills for all children. All other areas of the EYFS Framework (DfE 2025: 9) pivot on CLLD. For example, a child needs the language to explain how they feel (PSED) or must describe the processes of creating their constructions (EAD).

I sing nursery rhymes daily, to encourage understanding of rhyme as well as memorisation of language structures. I model these first with images or video and usually include puppets. Not only does this add to the enjoyment, but it also helps the students connect the lyrics to a visual. I have witnessed many students sing (including multilingual learners) before they can have a basic conversation.

In addition, I develop a Content and Language Integrated Learning (CLIL) curriculum. For each activity, I create sentence stems, alongside key vocabulary. This language will be individualised for each student, depending on their needs. These are often experiences, such as food tasting, shopping or acting out a story, so the children are fully involved and immersed in using the language for purpose.

Following the experience, we have small group discussions, sharing the language and taking turns to listen to one another, building up back-and-forth conversations. I encourage the most confident speakers to begin so that the language is modelled many times before a less confident speaker contributes. After a child presents their idea, I release them, to reduce the group size. That way, those less confident students have just one other student or the teacher to communicate with. In my conversations with less confident or able speakers, I model supporting sentences or repeat back phrases/full sentences to develop their language.

I also use literacy to develop language. I begin the year with simple language-based texts. As the children build fluidity within their language skills, I then progress the level of the text to repetitive stories. Next, I use stories with clear plots including causes and consequences. This gradual development of story content and language scaffolds the students' ability to recount stories in the same way. In small groups we recall known stories together using story language. I also provide wordless books for home readers and encourage parents to focus on developing story detailed language.

When the students are confident using story language, I develop their communication skills further by introducing 'Helicopter Stories'. The children tell their own stories to an adult, who scribes. The stories begin in a basic, organic way and then we build in structure with mapping and guidance with examples. The quietest students contribute eventually, as the excitement of story creation and acting with friends is infectious. We also explore stories to a greater depth through Greg Bottrill's 'Drawing Club' (2022), whereby students draw a character or aspect of a story shared, using their imagination. The student can communicate in detail what they are drawing and why, as well as describing intricate parts of their images.

This next contribution provides a very useful insight to how children with English as an additional language are supported to develop confidence in both home language (s) and English, accentuating the importance of planning with intention.

Vicky Cook: the learning environment—the motivation to communicate

In our setting, many children begin with limited language and we have a high proportion of EAL learners, often starting with no English. As a result of this we prioritise the development of communication and language throughout our provision.

To encourage communication, our children have to be inspired and motivated to interact—our environment and resourcing is fundamental to this. We have designed our environment around small, zoned areas, both those familiar to children such as our home area where children can use their own experience to interact and develop confidence, and those to spark curiosity and interest, such as the hidden sensory area with light table and unusual objects. We thought creatively about the use of space; for example turning storage sheds outside into a Builders' Yard with den building equipment. Here our children create secret spaces to interact and use a suitcase to make a transportable fairy garden. We value a mixture of purchased and free resources, initially creating talking spaces by securing pallets together to make pallet dens. We found these very effective, just placing one unusual object in them or two bean bags and a telephone, inspired communication.

When designing our setting we considered areas which would prioritise the need for children to interact; for example our floor pallet equipped with a microphone, clothes and instruments becomes a stage for our performers. Skilful modelling by the practitioners is vital to areas beyond the everyday experience of our children. Working closely 'in role' has had a significant impact on the children's communication in areas such as this.

Opportunities for awe and wonder throughout our environment are prioritised and have a high impact on the motivation to communicate. Areas have been developed to foster this such as our small allotment where children can see new plants grow and eat their produce. Our regular fire pit activities where children are able to toast and eat their food—the wonder expressed by our children when the paper first catches light and the smoke billows around them is a spark for further talk. Planning visits and visitors beyond our children's everyday experience have resulted in inspiration to communicate and opportunities for practitioners to introduce new vocabulary. Taking advantage of unplanned opportunities are also key to inspiring talk, the snow falling around them or the opportunity to jump in puddles both excites them and encourages communication.

Careful planning of additional resources added to provision specifically to promote talk have had a significant impact on the desire for our children to communicate. We always have sound buttons and recordable microphones throughout our setting, both for adults to leave messages for the children, or giving the children the chance to use them to record messages for their friends. We use telephone receivers with tubes attached between them for children to talk to each-other—we often have children laughing when voices mysteriously come through the phone! We use a range of old telephones just placed together on a side with other provocations such as a clipboard; these often inspire so many conversations.

Opportunities which have specifically impacted on communication for our EAL learners include hearing their home language using talking pens, bilingual books recorded onto CDs and practitioners learning some simple words in the language they can use. I can happily say sit down in at least six different languages now and this has given our EAL learners the confidence to talk to us.

Ultimately, our goal is to create an environment where every child feels empowered to communicate effectively and confidently. Through intentional design, diverse resources, and skilled interactions, we strive to support the holistic development of all children, regardless of their starting point or background and have seen the positive impact of this in the accelerated progress our children make.

In the next contribution, Hannah Robinson and Kelly Thompson draw on their wealth of experience as EYFS practitioners, explaining passionately how their intention of a collaborative approach to communication and language development has positively impacted their children and families.

Hannah Robinson and Kelly Thompson: fostering language development in a diverse school context

Within education, language development stands as a cornerstone for academic success and social integration. Over the many years of research one constant finding remains: – the level of learning and development children reach is dependent on them acquiring language in the earliest years of life (Al-Harbi, 2020). However, in a diverse school such as Park Academy, which has significantly high levels of need, such development can pose significant challenges. This case study delves into the landscape of language development within a school characterised by elevated levels of diversity and complexity. With a particular focus on interactions, the study explores how educators navigate the convergence of various factors.

Park Academy welcomes pupils from diverse linguistic and cultural backgrounds. Upon entry, a significant proportion of students face substantial hurdles, including language barriers compounded by limited exposure to English prior to enrolment. Many arrive days before their first day of school, adding an additional layer of challenge for both students and educators alike. Currently, 80% of the Reception cohort are EAL learners. A growing number of students present with speech and language difficulties, necessitating specialised support to foster effective communication skills. Compounding these factors is the high mobility rate among students, leading to disruptions in continuity and consistency within the learning environment. A considerable proportion of students lack preschool experience, further exacerbating the developmental gap in language acquisition.

The school has implemented a comprehensive approach to promote language development, focusing on fostering high-quality interactions within the learning environment.

Ensuring staff have a deep understanding of the multifaceted nature of language development within our school has been paramount. Professional development for the early years staff has centred around ensuring the team are equipped with the necessary skills to facilitate language-rich interactions. Timetables have been adjusted to afford educators dedicated time for meaningful engagement with students and the school recognises that staff who wonder and listen during interactions and talk just at the right moment are vital to enhance children's learning. Both the indoor and outdoor environments have been carefully considered to ensure they are 'inspirational environments that changes and include quirky objects and things that lie outside the ordinary' (Bottrill, 2022).

The school places a strong emphasis on building positive relationships between staff and pupils. Home-school links are actively nurtured through parent workshops, online learning journals and stay-and-play sessions, fostering a supportive environment for language development beyond the school gates.

Daily routines incorporate opportunities for language-rich activities such as songs, rhymes and 'snack and chat' sessions. Additionally, the school provides frequent, daily opportunities for shared reading and ensures a diverse range of meaningful, interest-led activities that promote active, hands-on learning and real-life experiences, enriching the language development journey for all students.

The implemented strategies have had a profound impact on student's language development for all, not just those with a significant language gap. Children have made significant strides in language proficiency and have developed essential communication and social skills necessary for thriving within and beyond the classroom. Students have the ability to express their wants and needs effectively, fostering greater autonomy and confidence in communication. Students have honed their ability to articulate thoughts and ideas coherently, enhancing both their expressive and receptive language skills and laying a solid foundation effective life-long communication.

The next contribution incorporates the excellent pedagogical ideas already shared and builds upon them further, offering even more ideas for reflection. Janine Ryan, an Early Years Consultant, provides a very useful development overview and reminds us of the importance of understanding this to then consider how to use it in our own settings.

Janine Ryan: becoming a confident and competent communicator

Communication and language skills lay a foundation for future academic success and over all wellbeing (Voice21). They are crucial for thinking and learning in school and enable children to access the curriculum. Children's communication and language skills develop through a series of identifiable stages outlined in the Early Years Foundation Stage framework: listening and attention, understanding and speaking (DfE, 2025: 12).

Research on the impacts of COVID have reported a decline in language and communication skills in young children (The National Literacy Trust, 2024). In addition, it is well reported that children from socioeconomically disadvantaged backgrounds are most at risk (EEF, 2017).

Babies are pre-programmed to communicate and from the very earliest age they learn to express their needs to their primary caregiver. This is initially in the form of crying, meeting their need for food, comfort, or to indicate boredom, tiredness or loneliness. When a responsive, caring adult meets these needs a baby feels secure, safe and loved. These early communications and responses support the development of neural pathways which lead to effective brain development and promote secure attachments. As babies develop their speech they start to coo, gurgle and babble and eventually use single words as they express themselves. There are rapid gains in vocabulary from two words to simple sentences, which tends to happen between the age of 2 and 3, when there is an explosion of expressive language from 50 words to 1000. Children develop the ability to structure longer sentences to clarify ideas and events and their language becomes quite complex.

Children require the means, reasons and opportunities (Money and Thurman, 1994) to develop their language to communicate and become confident, competent communicators.

Babies: the 'serve and return' approach demonstrates how an adult can support the development of communication (Harvard University, 2024). They understand by pointing or gesturing they can communicate their needs. Babies enjoy singing, music and toys that make sounds and start to listen and respond to a simple instruction. In practice blowing bubbles can capture a baby's attention, and help them to start to understand turn-taking and about the back and forth of communication and interaction to support the idea of a conversation.

As they blow, they develop the muscles in their mouths needed to pronounce different sounds. Sharing Communication Boxes full of objects of significance, photos, books or favourite toys provide props that encourage children to engage in meaningful interactions which helps to develop important relationships.

Toddlers: at this age children start to understand single words in context—'cup', 'milk', 'mummy' and frequently used words such as 'all gone' and 'bye-bye'. They can follow simple instructions and recognise and point to objects if asked about them. They start to develop conversation and engage in pretend play. Provide lots of opportunities for children to re-enact their experiences from home. Share books, songs and nursery rhymes to introduce new language. Keep instructions simple, don't overcomplicate things. Introducing a listening treasure box, filled with interesting noises, for instance foil, pots and pans or musical instruments will engage children in active listening, listening to individual noises. Establishing turn taking as they explore different sounds is important as it forms a key part of the communication process.

Young children: can attend for longer periods and can start to pay attention to more than one thing at a time. They understand a question or instruction that has two parts, such as: 'Get your coat and wait at the door'. They start to understand 'why' questions. Share story books through dialogic and interactive reading (EEF, 2024); evidence indicates this approach improves children's language and communication. Provide opportunities to re-enact books through role play and enhancements to continuous provision. Ensure there are plenty of communication friendly spaces for children to practise their talk (Jarmen, 2007). Story Scribing provides an opportunity to support the exploration of early language by scaffolding children's learning and writing down exactly what children say. This can be in the form of creating picture books or older children may transcribe more elaborate stories. Sensitive narration of children's play provides opportunities for children to hear language and develop understanding and is helpful for complex concepts like for example 'tomorrow'.

The ECAT strategies and resources provide a bank of useful strategies to support effective speech, language and communication: https://resources.leicestershire.gov.uk/education-and-children/early-years/early-years-foundation-stage-eyfs/learning-development-and-assessment/every-child-a-talker-ecat/strategies-and-resources

Rachel Summerscales, the founder of Honest Childhood, explores the importance of planning for how vocabulary can be taught, highlighting the role of this within the whole CLLD provision.

Rachel Summerscales: growing children's vocabulary

Children need adults to provide choices in provision that give them opportunities and motivations to develop their vocabulary. Sometimes these choices are led by adults through explicit teaching such as modelling, or implicit where children can choose the resources they wish to engage with across the learning environment. Expanding children's vocabulary therefore requires careful consideration and planning before an activity or resource is available for children to engage with if adults are to maximise the learning opportunities.

A starting point and key aspect of developing children's language is how adults discover what words children already know. This often happens in conversation, that sensitive back-and-forth interaction and questioning that aims to build the bank of words children use and understand.

It's here that adults watch, listen and learn what words children use automatically and those which may need direct teaching. For example, a child is playing with the dogs pretending to be a vet. You overhear the child repeatedly saying 'dog' despite there being distinct differences and types of dogs. It is here that you would be curious, and sensitively engage in conversation to determine if the child knows other words to distinguish between the types of dogs, such as puppy, dalmatian, poodle or if the child is able to categorise on physical features such as small dog or fluffy dog. Having a realistic selection of resources in areas of provision that naturally stimulate vocabulary use is imperative.

Using a stimulus, such as a real-life object, provides children with a concrete understanding of what you are talking about. Vocabulary is acquired when children hear new words repeatedly and understand their meaning in a variety of contexts before using those new words in their own talk without support. Providing real-life resources and realistic experiences wherever possible helps children to transfer new vocabulary to other contexts where they may experience that real-life object again and apply their learning. It is in these provision opportunities that you can directly teach new words.

Engaging children in activities that involve observation of real-life objects is one approach you could take to understand children's levels of language whilst simultaneously introducing specific new words. For example, a painting activity that encourages children to observe key features of a plant opens the opportunity for the adult to model vocabulary accurately. Commenting, explaining, showing and naming are all key elements of high-quality teaching in the early years that can easily be put into practice in this type of activity such as:

- Using different levels of questioning to give opportunities for children to use the new words such as 'Tell me about you drawing', 'What have you drawn there' and 'How are you going to draw your...?'.
- Explaining and showing provides information to support understanding of chosen tools or resources such as the size of the paintbrush for specific parts of the plant, 'you could use the small paintbrush for fine details of the leaves and stem'.
- Naming and labelling provide the key words associated with the plant, expanding vocabulary and levelling up children's language, such as using these key words to identify parts of a plant based on what you know about children's current levels of language such as, some children may need to learn 'leaf' and 'flower' whereas others may need to learn more complex language such as 'seed' or 'petal'. Repetition is key to children developing their vocabulary and is more effective when adults carefully craft learning experiences to suit the levels of language of children in their care.

Introducing new words in adult-led activities should be thoughtfully planned for and sensitively woven into everyday conversations to enable children to successfully adopt new words.

The next contribution provides a very interesting account of how the Australian Early Development Census can be used to ensure that CLLD development remains a priority in the Early Years. Fran Myers-Baird, an Early Childhood Project Advisor, presents a concise explanation of this data collection tool.

Fran Myers-Baird: place-based pedagogy and language development

The Australian Early Development Census [AEDC] is a nationwide population-level census of early childhood development, captured every three years on children entering their first year of full-time school. This collection provides Australian society with an overview of children's development, across five domains including language/cognitive skills and communication skills. Results are then reported at school, community, state and national levels, enabling better targeting of resources to increase the wellbeing of children and their families.

This dataset is not a measure of the quality of teaching but presents an opportunity to evaluate the systems and programs in place to support children from birth. It is an opportunity for educators to extract from pedagogy, holistic reflections and ethical, professional observations of each child to reflect upon future practice. Further to this, Grieshaber et al. (2023) has explored how the data is captured and its potential fidelity.

When this data is implemented using a strength-based approach to shift educators' metacognition and biases, the AEDC can transform and empower children, families and communities.

The nationally approved learning framework was developed to reflect contemporary research and guide educators' curriculum decision-making when developing, delivering and evaluating quality programs and practice across early childhood services. Belonging, Being and Becoming: The Early Years Learning Framework for Australia (V2.0) describes place-based pedagogy as educators' knowledge of the context that will influence how plans and practices are implemented, contributing to the quality of how each child's learning, development and wellbeing is supported (Australian Government Department of Education, 2022).

During the 2021 AEDC collection, language and cognitive skills had the greatest significant difference across Queensland. Significant difference, in this case, means a level of certainty that the change did not occur by chance.

The AEDC was then used to inform place-based pedagogy, to ensure programs and practices reflect the local context through responsive and inclusive planning to improve the holistic development of children and young people within the service. For example, an early childhood service used the language and cognitive data as a research tool to inform pedagogical practice. Educators then reviewed the service from a child's perspective, reflected upon research and multiple perspectives to recreate an authentic and purposeful language-rich environment. Additionally, educators incorporated intentional opportunities that involved children developing skills in explaining, listening and questioning. For example, using oral storytelling with young children, aiming to foster a deep therapeutic, emotional connection and understanding of the world (Perrow, 2012).

Cross (2011) highlights the importance of educators recognizing, understanding, considering and drawing upon children's past experiences. Educators can make informed curriculum decision-making using this data in combination with an understanding of children's culture, knowledge, abilities and interests. In saying this, datasets can provide educators with an opportunity to provoke, question and evaluate their pedagogical practice. This dataset does not replace the importance of the partnership between educators and the child, their family and their community or represent cultural specificity.

The final contribution in this chapter explores selective mutism. Diana Wilson, a Headteacher and former head of Early Years provides a comprehensive and very supportive overview of how current provision for CLLD can be adapted to ensure children in the Early Years with selective mutism are still supported.

Diana Wilson: selective Mutism

Social or pragmatic language skills develop as early as 0-3 months, when caregivers start to socially interact with the infant who responds back by cooing, eye contact, smiling and other responses to familiar faces (Doll, 2021). Children for whom opportunity for language development and social care is insufficient during early years of their development could potentially develop speech anxiety disorders. Selective mutism (SM) is one of the speech or social language anxiety disorders common amongst children and even adults. It is more than just a child choosing not to talk (Nathanson, 2024; Doll, 2021; NHS, 2022). Children with SM demonstrate anxiety from places, situations, people and activities that prevent them from expressing even basic needs such as toileting, pain and need for food. Consistent failure to speak in social situations where there is an expectation, such as in a classroom, is a common indicator of SM which needs attention (Vogel et al., 2022; Doll, 2021; NHS, 2022; Driessen et al., 2020). This section apprises strategies to create a pressure-free environment for children with SM.

Children deficit in social language skills are at a disadvantage of potential negative long-term consequences. If not treated early, these can have adverse effect on mental, social and emotional functioning which subsequently impact academic performance. Early identifications and interventions have beneficial prognosis to recovering from this condition. The need for speech therapists is now ever rising for provision of therapeutic procedures in school and/or as necessary. It is also important to note that therapeutic procedure is low-paced process, however, decrease in anxiety is visible after successful implementation of achievable strategies (Ludlow et al., 2023; Boneff, 2021; Muris and Ollendick, 2021; Oerbeck et al., 2018; Muris and Ollendick, 2015).

Some dos and don'ts

Observations during early years play an important role for planning interventions and provision for support to children with SM. A whole school approach of concern and awareness is crucial in providing support to children with SM.

Children with SM do not enjoy being the centre of attention, therefore direct questioning and eye contact need to be avoided. Furthermore, making a big deal from their lack of speech only increases their levels of anxiety as they want to talk but their high levels of anxiety make it harder for them to speak. Therefore, assuring the child that they can have fun and enjoy activities without talking reduces their anxiety to making new connections with more individuals at school and at home.

The following is an adapted list of resources for daily checks as provided by the speech and language pathologist Emily R. Doll. Incorporating some of the resources from the list below can be helpful.

1. Feeling rating charts
2. Talking ladders
3. Find-a-friend bingo

4. Playdate log
5. Talking goals
6. Talking questions
7. Scavenger hunt of different types
8. Talking maps

Smooth transition for children with selective mutism

Transitioning time in the academic year could be scary and increase anxiety in children with SM. Nathanson (2024) discusses a range of strategies both school and parents can make use of to help children with SM feel comfortable about the new environment. First and foremost is planning for transition prior to the new academic year; meeting the new teacher in the child's current classroom setting is highly advisable. This allows the child to slowly make the next move with reduced anxiety and getting familiarised with the new teacher; their voice, style of teaching and other attributes. In addition to this, talking positively at home and in the current classroom about transition is ideal for building social comfort and readiness.

Finally, sharing with staff written information and talking to them through what you know about the child is ensuring safeguarding and child protection against vulnerabilities.

In conclusion

This chapter explores the critical role of Communication and Language Development (CLLD) in early childhood, addressing growing concerns about speech, language and communication delays in young learners. It highlights national reports advocating for systemic improvements, particularly for disadvantaged children, and promotes oracy as a foundational skill across the curriculum. Contributions from educators offer insights into fostering communication skills through storytelling, interactive reading, purposeful play and targeted interventions for EAL learners and children with selective mutism. The overarching message is clear: early years settings must embed communication as a vital thread, ensuring children develop confidence and competence in language that supports their lifelong learning and social development.

Summary of key points

- A secure understanding of the trajectory involved in learning to communicate is fundamental to the support then provided. Communication is far more than simply talking.
- It's important to provide planned explicit opportunities for communication to teach children the skills involved in becoming a communicator.
- A purposely planned environment is also significant in ensuring that children have a reason to communicate.
- Early intervention is crucial in identifying potential delays or gaps in understanding and application. A short intensive additional support either on an individual basis or in small groups can provide sufficient boost for children to accelerate their learning in speech, language and communication.
- Developing a consistent approach to supporting speech, language and communication is crucial. This consistency includes both practitioner knowledge and confidence in knowing which interaction or resource will support and scaffold.

References

Al-Harbi, S.S. (2020). Language development and acquisition in early childhood. *Journal of Education and Learning* (EduLearn), *14*(1), February 2020, pp. 69-73 ISSN: 2089-9823. https://doi.org/10.11591/edulearn.v14i1.14209

Australian Government Department of Education. (2022). *Belonging, Being and Becoming: The Early Years Learning Framework for Australia (V2.0)*. Canberra, ACT: Australian Government Department of Education for the Ministerial Council.

Boneff, K. (2021). *Parental Influences in Selective Mutism: The Intergenerational Transmission of Anxiety Symptoms and Outcomes of a Parent-Focused Intervention*, Eastern Michigan University. [Master's thesis].

Bottrill, G. (2022). *Can I Go and Play Now?: Rethinking the Early Years*. London, England: Corwin Ltd.

Cross, B. (2011). Children's views of their lives and well-being. *Children & Society*, *25*(6), pp. 409-419.

DfE (2025). Early years foundation stage statutory framework for group and school-based providers. Setting the standards for learning, development and care for children from birth to five. Available at: https://assets.publishing.service.gov.uk/media/687105a381dd8f70f5de3ea9/EYFS_framework_for_group_and_school_based_providers_.pdf (accessed 21 July 2025).

Doll, E.R. (2021). *Treating Selective Mutism as a Speech-Language Pathologist*. San Diego, CA: Plural Publishing.

Driessen, J., Blom, J.D., Muris, P., Blashfield, R.K., and Molendijk, M.L. (2020). Anxiety in children with selective mutism: A meta-analysis. *Child Psychiatry and Human Development*, *51*, pp. 330-341.

Education Endowment Foundation (2021). EEF Blog: Making use of TRUST Talk https://educationendowmentfoundation.org.uk/news/eef-blog-how-to-make-use-of-trust-talk-to-support-shared-reading-at-home

Education Endowment Foundation (2024). Approaches for supporting communication and development. https://educationendowmentfoundation.org.uk/early-years-evidence-store/communication-and-language?approach=interactive-reading

Education Endowment Foundation (EEF). (2017). *Early Years Toolkit: Parental Engagement*. London: Education Endowment Foundation. Available at: https://educationendowmentfoundation.org.uk/education-evidence/early-years-toolkit/parental-engagement (Accessed: 13 September 2025).

Grieshaber, S., Sumsion, J., and Cheeseman, S. (2023). Pedagogical documentation in early childhood education: Making children's learning visible, *Contemporary Issues in Early Childhood*, *24*(1), pp. 5-18.

Harvard University (2024). Center on the developing child. Available at: https://developingchild.harvard.edu/science/key-concepts/serve-and-return/

Jarmen, E. (2007). All about...communication friendly spaces. Available at: https://www.nurseryworld.co.uk/content/features/all-aboutcommunication-friendly-spaces

Ludlow, A.K., Osborne, C., and Keville, S. (2023). Selective Mutism in children with and without an autism spectrum disorder: The role of sensory avoidance in mediating symptoms of social anxiety. *Journal of Autism and Developmental Disorders*, *53*(10), pp. 3891-3900.

Money, D. and Thurman, S. (1994). Means, reasons and opportunities. Available at: https://library.sheffieldchildrens.nhs.uk/the-means-reasons-and-opportunities-model-of-communication/

Muris, P. and Ollendick, T.H. (2015). Children who are anxious in silence: A review on selective mutism, the new anxiety disorder in DSM-5. *Clinical Child and Family Psychology Review*, *18*(2), pp. 151-169.

Muris, P. and Ollendick, T.H. (2021). Current challenges in the diagnosis and management of selective mutism in children. *Psychology Research and Behavior Management*, *14*, pp. 159-167.

Nathanson, L. (2024). Selective Mutism: Supporting transitions in Early Years settings, *Early Years TV* [online video]. Published: 7 June 2024. Available at: Early Years TV episode with Lucy Nathanson (Accessed: 13 September 2025).

NHS (2022). *Mental Health of Children and Young People in England, 2022 - Wave 3 Follow-Up to the 2017 Survey*. London: NHS Digital. Available at: https://digital.nhs.uk/data-and-information/publications/statistical/mental-health-of-children-and-young-people-in-england/2022-wave-3-follow-up (Accessed: 13 September 2025).

Oerbeck, B., Overgaard, K.R., Stein, M.B., Pripp, A.H., and Kristensen, H. (2018). Treatment of selective mutism: A 5-year follow-up study. *European Child and Adolescent Psychiatry*, *27*(8), pp. 997-1009.

Oracy Education Commission (2024). *We need to talk: The report of the Commission on the Future of Oracy Education in England*

Perrow, S. (2012). *Therapeutic Storytelling 101 Healing Stories for Children*. Stroud, Gloucestershire, UK: Hawthorn Press.

The National Literacy Trust (2024). *Creating Confident Communicators: How the Government can Help Every Child Find their Voice*. London: National Literacy Trust. Available at: National Literacy Trust oracy report (Accessed: 13 September 2025).

Vogel, F., Reichert, J., and Schwenck, C. (2022). Silence and related symptoms in children and adolescents: A network approach to selective mutism. *BMC Psychology*, 10, pp. 1-15.

8 Specific area
Literacy

Jayne Carter

Introduction

The range of contributors in both this chapter and others, especially those exploring communication, self-regulation and the involvement of parents in children's learning, have all contributed to the focus of this particular chapter; literacy. We cannot add any more depth to their already useful and thought-provoking essays. We would, instead, like to use their submissions as inspiration to explore the link between becoming an effective early years reader and an equally effective early years writer, considering if and how each discipline is mutually supportive. Our hope is that you are then able to add the contributor's thoughts and descriptions as a framework for personal reflection and challenge of your own research rich practice.

Pondering question: how can we ensure that all aspects of the literacy curriculum are planned to ensure children build on prior learning?

It is always remarkably interesting to us that often teaching and learning in reading and writing are presented as discrete curricula; highlighting the specific research and effective provision for each individual discipline. Given the focus on the development of a holistic ethos in the early years and the connection encouraged between the prime and specific aspects in conjunction with the characteristics framework, would a similar focus for reading and writing be helpful too? The link between reading and writing seems a natural integration, not only to provide extra opportunities for children to practise key skills included in both disciplines but also to fully capture the mutually responsive set of skills included in both aspects.

Key learning from research

When reading about developing effective readers and writers in the early years, the range of research, evaluation studies and models have predominantly shared Scarborough's Reading Rope (2001) and Sedita's Writing Rope (2024). As separate models, they both offer rich reflections and guidance for practitioners, skilfully bringing together the interconnected aspects involved in each discipline. I have used both with new teachers and more experienced teachers as well as in a variety of training and network sessions. I love the opportunity to discuss these with colleagues, guiding us all towards using the models as a tool for auditing current practice and mapping next steps for improvement. The Reading Rope organises the skills and processes of becoming an effective reader into eight components, represented as strands in a rope. These components are grouped into two categories: word recognition and language comprehension. Word recognition is the ability to decode words accurately and fluently in text; phonological awareness, phonics and sight word recognition are the skills which contribute to word recognition. Scarborough includes background and vocabulary knowledge, language structures (including syntax), verbal reasoning (including the ability to make inferences) and literacy knowledge (including knowledge of print concepts and genres) under language structure.

In the EYFS, these elements of becoming a competent and confident reader are presented in the EYFS statutory framework (2025) as:

> Reading consists of two dimensions: language comprehension and word reading. Language comprehension (necessary for both reading and writing) starts from birth. It only develops when adults talk with children about the world around them and the books (stories and non-fiction) they read with them, and enjoy rhymes, poems and songs together. Skilled word reading, taught later, involves both the speedy working out of the pronunciation of unfamiliar printed words (decoding) and the speedy recognition of familiar printed words.
>
> (DfE 2025: 10)

Connections between literacy: providing a sequenced and supportive framework

Note the connection between reading and writing in this expectation; namely language comprehension. This link is there to shape provision as a criteria which you would anticipate being part of any early years curriculum. Using language as the connector, provides practitioners with clear direction, planned to maximise learning for both reading and writing, starting the journey of thinking about both disciplines as a partnership.

Sedina's writing rope follows a similar design to Scarborough's, presenting the significant elements when learning to write proficiently again as strands of a rope interconnected together. There are five strands included in this model: the first is transcription, which includes spelling and handwriting. The second is writing craft, which includes word choice, awareness of task, audience and purpose and use of literary devices. Next is text structure, which includes an understanding and use of form for the main types of text (narrative, informational, opinion/argument), paragraph structure, patterns of organisation (description, sequence, cause/effect, compare/contrast, problem/solution), and linking words that make connections between parts of text. The fourth strand is syntax, which focuses on an understanding of grammar and sentence elaboration. The final strand is critical thinking which includes knowledge of the writing process such as strategies for generating ideas and gathering information before writing.

When returning to the EYFS statutory framework, there is a pertinent reminder of the nature of an early years writer. Once again, the significance of language is highlighted, providing the bridge for children to develop both their reading and writing skills.

96 Early Years Essentials

'Writing involves transcription (spelling and handwriting) and composition (articulating ideas and structuring them in speech, before writing).' DfE (2025: 10)

Implementing research and pedagogy: insights for impact

As previously mentioned, both separate 'ropes' have been shared during consultancy discussions. One particular network meeting prompted me to start exploring possible connections between reading and writing for myself. During a conversation about developing early years literacy overviews for our group of schools, childminders and settings, practitioner exchanges naturally steered towards exploring provision. I started by looking at the reading rope and posed the simple question 'would these also apply to learning to write?' The beginnings of a research project! This very small-scale exploration started a discussion which was certainly useful at the time and for this professional network. Together, we were able to start plotting similarities and discrete characteristics to move us towards a deeper understanding of reading and writing and reading/writing. Unanimously we all agreed that language could be the vehicle to loop the two disciplines together.

Sedina, in the blog *Connecting the Ropes: Integrating Reading and Writing Instruction* (2024), explored this in a much more robust and sustaining way.

The strands from each 'rope' are explored with a focus of connectivity and mutual support.

This diagram shows these identified features clearly (Figure 8.1).

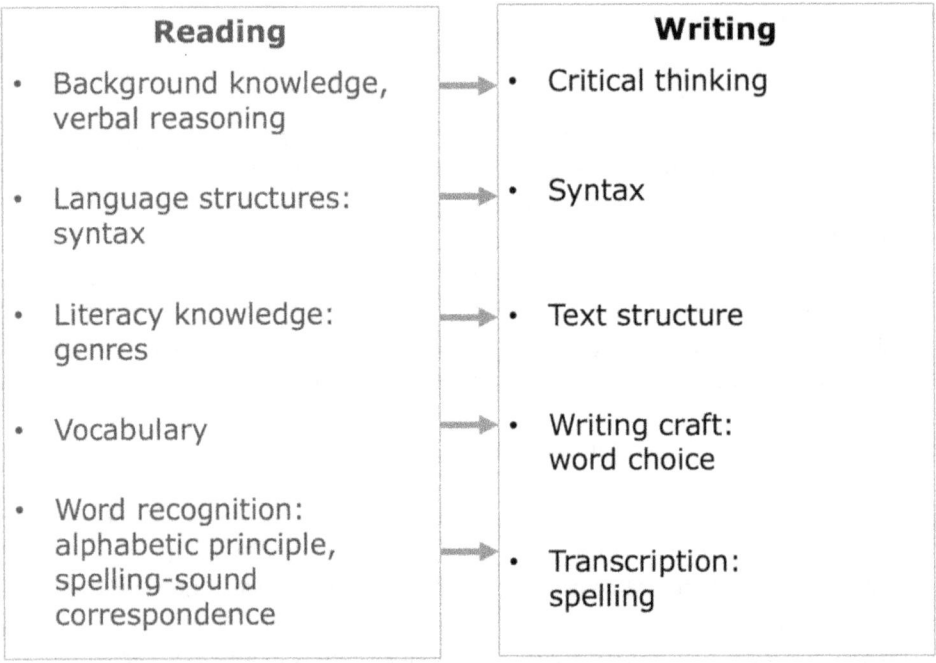

Figure 8.1 https://keystoliteracy.com/blog/connecting-the-ropes-integrating-reading-writing-instruction/

Taking my initial small-scale beginnings of action research on this connective study, I have been inspired to consider Sedina's expert views and consider this model specifically for early years.

Sedina continues in her blog explaining the reasons for the chosen links. I hope to add to this by offering my own views and ideas, intended to guide all adults in early years in considering their open literacy provision.

Background knowledge, verbal reasoning/critical thinking

Sedina states categorically, 'Proficiency with skills related to these components is essential for both reading comprehension and writing. They represent the most challenging, high levels of thinking.' The skill of inference is a driving force included in these aspects. Inference calls on a learner to engage their bank of background knowledge and prior experience, developing groups of key vocabulary as part of these memories. The storage and retrieval system as part of this process is also an essential component of strengthening reading and writing development. Having a thorough knowledge of a range of contexts which are stored as knowledge and language enables the learner to draw on these when either making sense of read text or when deciding on a focus for writing.

For early years teaching and learning, the importance of developing background knowledge cannot be overestimated, especially as some of our children would benefit from an enhanced collection of lived experiences to use to build more imaginative experiences for themselves. Taking the time to pre-empt what may be missing from some children's life repertoire before ether sharing a text or embarking on shared writing provides an experience which is accessible to all children; one which removes barriers and promotes personal achievement. The 2023 EEF guidance 'Early Literacy' consolidates this importance. One of their primary recommendations is the awareness and implementation of executive functioning skills. They express executive functioning as including working memory and speed of retrieval from memory. They define working memory as 'an executive function that describes our ability to temporarily hold and manipulate information in our mind. It acts as a mental notepad that helps us complete tasks and solve problems.' Providing a rich tapestry of events, contexts and situations certainly grows knowledge and if skilfully modelled, helps learners to match vocabulary to these situations. My view is that teaching executive functioning skills as part of this direction propels knowledge from known facts to applied knowledge. Using again strategies embedded into the acquisition of speech, language and communication skills could be useful here. Visual tools such as mind mapping and, pictorial diagrams as well as word/object tools offer the learner a framework to be able to manipulate (as the EEF explain) the information so it can be worked/used to its most proficient level.

Syntax

Both 'ropes' have strands devoted to syntax, providing an accessible connection between reading and writing and providing the practitioner with a further opportunity to strengthen their subject knowledge and pedagogy of both as discrete banks as well as how they can support each other. Within the early years, we strive to support all children's syntactic awareness, so they are able to understand how a sentence is constructed. The intention is that when reading learners are able to use their comprehension skills to ascertain meaning and nurture their love of the text, whist in writing, understanding not only what a sentence 'looks like' but also how they can independently follow the rules of syntax to construct their own recognisable sentences.

Text structure

Text structure refers to how a piece of text is built. For reading, an understanding of text structure provides clues to making meaning. Knowing how different texts are structured also improves writing. One of the five strands in the writing rope is devoted to text structure at multiple levels. Where reading and writing blend is the expectation that learners understand and are able to apply knowledge about how a text 'flows', which subsequently aids them towards demonstrating this expertise through their writing. Being exposed to structures in a variety of written and also auditory text, in conjunction with deliberate spotlight given by the practitioner, equips the learner with the tools they need to accelerate both their reading and writing skills. Another component of text structure is understanding how text is organised, including description/explanation, sequence, cause/effect, compare/contrast and problem solution. Awareness of these patterns while reading supports comprehension, and awareness of these patterns enables learners to select the best options for presenting what they want to say in their writing. Transition words and phrases are the final component of text structure identified in the writing rope. When reading, if learners are able to notice and store transitions such as first, next, last or however, their comprehension skills continue to improve. The knowledge and skills of transitions they have encountered and assimilated serve them well when moving their thoughts, opinions and reflections into their chosen written form. In the early years there is a priority of sharing the concepts of 'beginning, middle, end' with learners as an entry into story structure. During interactive storytelling, for example, connectives can be incorporated into the retelling of the text which emerges learners into this world of improving vocabulary. If this is then followed up with guided instruction of how to apply these words, what they look like when presented in written form can provide a way in to start to know the importance of these when creating their own written masterpieces.

Vocabulary/writing craft-word choice

Vocabulary is one of the strands in the reading rope and is represented in the writing rope as word choice in the writing craft strand. The significance of developing a strong bank of vocabulary is absolutely pivotal in enabling learners to navigate the worlds of reading and writing. When searching in 'EYFS Development Matters' (DfE 2023) the phrase 'vocabulary' points out the significance of planning for the type of words which will be shared with learners as well as the importance of developing an environment which allows for this direct instruction to continue in either independent learning and/or adult-initiated times. Immersion in a language-rich environment (implicit approach) is certainly a positive choice so learners appreciate the world of language, although in my opinion, this is insufficient in cultivating a knowledge of words and how they can be used to continue learning. The EEF in their 2021 guidance 'Preparing for Literacy' include accounts of recent research which currently advocate for a mixed approach to teaching vocabulary. They express too the significance of targeted intervention for those children who need more support to optimise their language skills. They state 'It can be helpful to think about targeted support through a tiered model of "waves" whereby high quality initial teaching is supplemented by small group support and subsequently individualised support as necessary' (page 22). Adopting this concept of a 'wave' could be useful for practitioners when contemplating how to pan for vocabulary teaching and learning in their own classrooms. Placing 'ambition for all' as the ultimate aim for all children, the wave approach guides planning to consider what is accessible for everyone, how my direct teaching transfers into the environment and what can be put in place to remove barriers for some children. This focus generates structure and a keen ongoing progress approach to becoming confident and competent readers and writers.

Word recognition/transcription

Within the reading rope, word recognition skills include knowledge of the alphabetic principle and spelling-sound correspondences (phonics) which are needed to fluently read and spell words. Advanced phonics include competence in knowing syllable types and morphology (prefixes, suffixes and roots as examples), and is important for decoding and spelling longer, multisyllabic words. Within the EYFS, certainly with reception and often nursery classes, a dedicated phonics programme is an expectation. Implementing one of the many validated DfE schemes has elevated the relevance of learning to read and has supported senior leaders in moving to improvement in their levels of confident readers in their schools/settings. The connection here between reading and writing cannot be overestimated. When children have the required knowledge and skills to recognise, make and process a series of word structures/patterns, a processing procedure is activated. Generating a blueprint of rules, exceptions to known rules, application in context, and so forth is an impressive achievement, especially for our youngest learners. Within this established processing system, which is supported by a sophisticated retrieval system, practitioners can maximise this by carefully and gradually showing the connection between what has been learnt when reading to mark making/writing following similar rules.This connection can help learners build confidence when learning to generate ideas in written form as they are being asked to use something which they have had experience of. A useful motivator, a helpful confidence boost.

In this first contribution, Rebecca Walsh, an Early Years practitioner, advocates for reading for pleasure to be given a place within the whole literacy curriculum and provision, asking for reflections on the role of this in the whole literacy provision.

Rebecca Walsh: the importance of reading for pleasure

Reading has been shown time and time again as being the biggest predictor for a child's future success, including their academic attainment (DfE, 2012). It has been shown to have more of an impact on a child's success than their family's socio-economic status (OECD, 2002, cited in DfE, 2012). It is crucial that those who work closely with young children support children to become readers from an early age, by engaging with reading material regularly and showing enthusiasm and enjoyment about reading.

Research conducted by the National Literacy Trust (2023) shows that children's reading enjoyment is rapidly declining; this is especially true of children from a disadvantaged background, for whom access to books and other reading materials can be the hardest, especially with library closures. Often the only way these young children access books is through nursery or school.

Research also shows that less than half of two-year-olds are being read to by their parents on a daily basis due to busy home lives or a lack of access to reading material (National Literacy Trust, 2020). A lot of settings share how important reading is with parents, but do they support them in setting good reading habits or support them in choosing appropriate reading material or provide reading materials? Some of my fondest memories from my childhood are of my dad reading daily to me from a young age, developing a strong bond between us and supporting me to become a life-long reader. If it wasn't for my dad introducing me to the power of literature, I don't know if I would be the avid reader that I am today.

Not only does reading improve a child's literacy skills, but it also improves their social skills when sharing stories with others, their understanding of the world as they gain an understanding of cultures and communities around them and their emotional skills as they learn how others deal with big emotions and explore these in a safe way. Reading helps to develop the whole child and can, of course, support a child hugely as they progress through the education system.

Practitioners need to share a range of high-quality literature with children and be engaged and enthusiastic when sharing stories, even when they've asked you for the tenth time to read the same story again. Share stories from a range of countries and a range of walks of life, including people who look like the children, people who don't look like the children, people with disabilities and people who experience life differently to them. Children should be exposed to a wide range of characters and life experiences to allow them to develop a better understanding of those that they share the world with, which will enable them to be more understanding of other and develop into well-rounded, kind and happy individuals.

In this second contribution, Holly May Andras, from the University of Cambridge, shares personal reflections on the impact of using Talk for Writing to support children who may need additional support with their literacy skills. The ideas shared in this contribution provide a very useful reminder of the significance of multi-sensory experiences in a child's learning experience.

Holly May Andras: reflections on using talk for writing to engage a reluctant learner

This reflection considers a pupil with a diagnosis of autism in an early years setting, who became particularly anxious whenever literacy activities were presented to him. This pupil lacked confidence and feared making mistakes, resulting in frequent dysregulation and emotional outbursts when given an adult-directed task (Deweerdt, 2020). This meant that practitioners could not accurately assess his levels of understanding, as his discomfort compromised his ability to demonstrate his full potential and caused concern amongst staff regarding his social and emotional wellbeing. It became clear that in order to engage him, a less risky and intrinsically motivating approach was required, which would simultaneously scaffold his learning. Talk for Writing was selected as a pedagogical storytelling technique (Corbett and Strong, 2017), which starts with a whole-class discussion approach and breaks the storytelling process into accessible stages, focusing on a high-quality story book to inspire interest and creativity (Bearne and Reedy, 2018; EEF, 2015). The text *Owl Babies* (Waddell, 2017) was selected as a motivational starting point, since this pupil took a particular interest in flight. The predictability of the repeated phrases in the text gave this pupil the confidence to take part in the initial Imitation phase of Talk for Writing, where he joined in with the actions and retelling of the story. Following this, I decided to create multi-sensory *Owl Babies* tuff-trays to allow the pupils to role play and manipulate the story during their self-directed busy learning time, using puppets and natural resources, with no obligation being placed on them to participate. This proved successful for the identified pupil, who was observed to gravitate towards these resources and act out the story using the repetitive phrases, due to the familiarity previously gained through this interleaved approach to learning, thus further embedding his confidence with the story. During the Invention Stage, where pupils adapt the text, this pupil was particularly motivated to engage, as he had the freedom to develop the story in an interest-led manner, allowing him to include his special interest of space travel, which he recorded on a visual story map. Talk for Writing encouraged whole-class collaboration of ideas, in line with Vygotsky's socio-cultural theory (1978) through allowing pupils to develop their own increasingly sophisticated language styles, sentence structure and ideas. Challenges with communication and language are key areas of the diagnostic criteria for autism (APA, 2013), making these opportunities particularly valuable for the focus pupil who was able to retell his story to the class. This is the first time I had observed him being intrigued and motivated by texts. The more dialogical approach to learning and assessment provided by Talk for Writing allowed practitioners to appreciate the pupil's creativity, a skill which had not previously been observed, further indicating the benefits of promoting comfort in learning through an interest-led approach.

Continuing the themes of the role of the adult in promoting high levels of literacy development, Crystal Cunningham, a literacy specialist and curriculum designer, presents a compelling account of a study which explored the impact on pupils' literacy skills when Early Years practitioners supported high school colleagues. The lessons learnt here serve as a useful reminder of the fundamentals of literacy skills.

Crystal Cunningham: the reading shift–from primary to beyond

Literacy. What image popped up in your head when you read that word? More than likely it was an image of a young child. Maybe the child was sitting with their teacher reading a book, pointing to each word as they read. Maybe the child was at home, cuddled up on the couch reading a great book with a parent or family member. But more than likely you thought of a YOUNG child.

Preschool and kindergarten are, for many reasons, the most critical and meaningful times of a young learners' educational journey. During this time, instruction and support for the five pillars of the science of reading is given consistently. Students learn the foundational principles of reading in their primary grades and then become strong, fluent, lifelong readers, right? Unfortunately, this is so often not the case. In many situations, students do not receive the necessary reading and early foundations in the primary grades. After second grade, we often see a 'reading shift' where students receive much less instruction and practice with basic phonemic awareness and phonics activities. When those struggling students move to the upper elementary grades, they begin to read for content, such as science and social studies. So now these students who were struggling in reading are now struggling in science and social studies as well. The beat goes on and the struggles continue, creating a domino effect of failure after failure. By the time these struggling learners get to middle and then high school, they are so behind, that many of them feel hopeless and make the decision to drop out of school. So what's to be done? That's a BIG question and one that many are trying to answer.

Back in 2012, I was fortunate enough to be part of a program that piloted putting early childhood educators into high schools to provide instruction and resources with foundational reading support. It was a brand-new program that the superintendent created. His thought process was that middle and high school students needed literacy instruction, but secondary teachers aren't typically trained with literacy foundations. If he put an early childhood teacher into the upper grades, it might just work! He received special permission from the state department and picked three early childhood teachers who had a track record of success with teaching students the bedrock of reading principles: phonemic awareness, phonics, fluency, vocabulary and comprehension. Myself and two others were chosen. We packed our belongings and each headed to a different high school in our district. Unfortunately, what we saw was a disheartening number of students who were reading below a third grade reading level. Those struggles expanded into every single one of their classes, creating a plethora of academic and behavioural concerns. Throughout the school year we focused on teaching through the use of research-based, systematic literacy programs and a LOT of hard work. Students met with me for one class period a day to consistently work on literacy skills. I also pushed into different classes (English, history, etc.) and would assist with the literacy side of the different content areas. Additionally, we worked with students who were ELL (English language learners) and would benefit from learning the foundations of the English language. Another big part of my position was to provide support and resources to the other teachers at the school. I even wrote a grant and bought a classroom library full of low-level, high-interest material. At the end of the year, we saw a huge impact! EVERY student had increased their literacy scores—in some cases 4 or 5 years of literacy development and growth in just one year.

It was during that first year that I realized just how important it is to provide instruction, support and intervention to not only our primary grades, but also to our secondary, older learners. While we hope that learners receive the necessary literacy skills in the primary grades, there should be safety nets and opportunities for 'refreshers' and 'spiraling back' along the way. Supporting our older learners in reading foundations is just as critical as primary grades.

The next contribution prompts reflections on the way that literacy learning can be planned and implemented. Tracy Hopkins, EYFS Associate Headteacher: Transform Trust, explains how experiences included in the aspect of 'understanding the world' provide a powerful context for children to engage with key literacy priorities.

Tracy Hopkins: bringing literacy to life through 'Understanding the World'

At Transform Trust our schools focus on creating engaging, meaningful experiences that inspire a love for reading and writing. By integrating literacy with the 'Understanding the

World' area of learning, we create vibrant, immersive learning experiences that bring literacy to life. This area of learning encourages children to explore and make sense of their physical environment and community. While this area is not part of the Good Level of Development (GLD) assessment in the profile, it plays a vital role in enriching literacy learning.

Example 1–Nature Journals

One exciting way we blend literacy with Understanding the World is through nature journals. This activity involves children exploring their natural surroundings–such as a garden, park or school–and documenting their observations.

Children collect leaves, flowers and small stones, and then use their journals to draw pictures and describe what they've found. We guide them in writing simple sentences or labels for their drawings, encouraging the use of descriptive language. This activity not only enhances writing skills but also builds vocabulary related to nature and science.

Example 2–Storytelling

Stories both represent children from our settings and around the world. Storytelling is another method to bring literacy to life. By exploring stories from different cultures, children can learn about the world while developing their reading and comprehension skills. Children are then encouraged to retell stories in their own words, either orally or by creating their own illustrated books. This activity promotes narrative skills, creativity and an appreciation for diversity, enriching both their literacy and understanding of the world.

Example 3–Virtual Field Trips

We know that trips and outings have been reduced due to budget and staffing constraints, but we still need to enhance children's cultural capital. By offering this virtually, children get an exciting opportunity to integrate literacy with real-world experiences. Through virtual tours of museums, zoos or historical sites, children can explore new environments and learn new concepts. They love to draw and label maps! We help the children construct sentences, guiding them in using new vocabulary and describing their virtual adventures. This activity links literacy with technology and global awareness, making learning both fun and educational.

> **Example 4–Market Day**
>
> 'Market Day' role-play is one of our most popular activities and is a fantastic way to integrate literacy with practical life skills. Children create signs and labels for different stalls, write shopping lists and even develop simple scripts for buying and selling goods.
>
> Through these activities, children practice reading and writing in a context that feels real and relevant to them. This hands-on approach helps solidify their understanding of literacy concepts while also teaching them about economics and social interactions.
>
> An integral aspect of these activities is their ability to enhance communication skills. We know that children need to be able to talk it before they can write it. Engaging in conversations, storytelling and role-playing activities helps children develop their spoken language, which is the foundation of writing. By discussing their observations in nature journals, narrating stories or interacting during role-play scenarios, children practice articulating their thoughts and ideas. This verbal practice builds their vocabulary, sentence structure and confidence in using language, all of which are crucial for effective writing. By blending literacy with 'Understanding the World,' technology and role-play, at Transform Trust we create a rich, dynamic learning environment that fosters a lifelong love of literacy. These approaches not only enhance literacy skills but also help children make meaningful connections to the world around them.

In this penultimate contribution in this chapter, Clare McKie, founder of DfE England and DoE W Australia Power Phonics reading and spelling program, explores the crucial aspect of phonics teaching and learning. Empowered teachers = empowered learners is celebrated.

Claire McKie: power phonics reading and spelling program

Phonics in the early years can be a controversial topic. There are many expert views and opinions to consider. Many believe teaching phonics in Reception is 'too early' and it is not developmentally appropriate. Others point out we must teach phonics in EYFS, not to do so would be to 'disadvantage' many children. As the founder of DfE validated Power Phonics, you might assume I belong only to the second 'group'. If only things were that simple! Social media often presents such debates as binary—you are in one camp or the other. Well, I can understand and appreciate evidence-based points raised on either side. I have seen many children make astounding progress in reading and writing through their love and application of phonics. I have also seen some children struggle against an inflexible, burdensome 'one size fits all' approach to phonics. Choosing an approach to phonics which is agile, which can flex according to teacher judgement, is essential in EYFS. Of course, as with most areas of learning, EYFS should be the blueprint for the rest of the school. Championing the importance of teacher judgement; the importance of using what you know your class need next... can and should be modelled by EYFS teachers to the rest of the school. Many children are depending on it.

What does that look like? Teachers know their children. They know what they need next, they know what would not be appropriate, they know what would be appropriate and how to support children through those next steps. They know all of this because they know their children. Phonics subject knowledge has to marry with teacher judgement, whilst not overpowering it. A phonics program FIT for EYFS will scaffold and support subject (phonics) knowledge. It will champion and empower teacher judgement whilst providing a simple, logical and incremental sequence underpinned by easy teacher tools. It will empower teachers to empower ALL learners. You cannot empower teachers by removing, circumventing, undermining teacher judgement. It's never a good idea—it can be catastrophic in EYFS.

Phonics in EYFS—the day-to-day experience of it, what it looks like, how it feels for children and staff is an important litmus test for any phonics program. The teacher tools and incremental sequence bound up in any phonics program must allow EYFS staff to respond to ALL learners appropriately, whilst maintaining consistency and fidelity to the program. This is only possible if the program itself is underpinned by teacher judgement and 'easy to use and flex' tools. Empowered teachers = empowered learners. ALL learners.

This chapter concludes with this fascinating contribution from Susanne Rice, Childminder and owner of Little Puddings, who shares how literacy skills are planned for, implemented and monitored within a childminder setting. This contribution acts as a reminder that literacy learning, if planned appropriately, has the opportunity to change children's lives.

Susanne Rice: supporting literacy in a childminding setting

Literacy forms a vital part of our day. In 2023, I was awarded the Communication Friendly Setting award based on how we promote and support children's communication and language and literacy development in my childminding setting. We have made literacy a part of our daily routine; the key is to make it a habit.

Books are an essential resource in my setting, probably one of the most used resources that we have available for the children to access freely during the day. Children will look at the books independently, sometimes together with their peers but often they will bring them to one of us adults to read. It is a wonderful sight when a nearly 3-year-old calls a younger child across for them to share a book together. Having a selection of books available allows for the children to be in control of when they want to access books and what book they want to read.

All our children are also read to as a group twice a day. Whilst the children have their morning snack I read our book of the week. The book will have been carefully chosen for the week, either to embed new knowledge (topic) or focus on something, like kindness, sharing, and so on. It may seem boring that the children get to hear the same story each day, however, repetition is good, and it is a good way for children to acquire new vocabulary. It also allows me to assess the children's comprehension and memory towards the end of the week. I will sometimes replace key words or names with something completely different for the children to correct me.

Before lunch the children will gather again as a group to sing nursery rhymes, they all get to have their turn to pick one, even our youngest children will join in, often starting with the actions before they can speak. This is also when we often first notice the youngest children 'speaking' when they join in singing. After they have all had a turn at choosing a song, they get their second story of the day as a group read by one of my assistants. These are also carefully selected based on our current theme, season or children's particular interests.

When you read it is important that you do not rush, allow the children to engage with the story, pause and ask questions, stop mid-sentence for the children to finish it off. If the children ask questions, then stop and answer them.

Most days we also do the 'squiggle whilst you wiggle' program from 'Spread the Happiness'. This is a set of movements/dances that we do to music using squares of fabric; these movements are then also drawn using both hands simultaneously. This program aids both children's cross and fine motor skills and is the precursor for letter formation and helps with mark making in general. The program consists of nine different movements, and we usually spend around three weeks on each one. This helps build muscle memory.

In conclusion

This chapter explores the dynamic relationship between reading and writing in early years literacy, accentuating how the two disciplines are mutually supportive rather than separate curricula. Drawing on research models such as Scarborough's Reading Rope and Sedita's Writing Rope, it illustrates how language comprehension serves as the foundation linking both aspects. The chapter also delves into pedagogical reflections–from integrating phonics effectively to fostering a love of reading through immersive storytelling and culturally diverse literature. It advocates for a holistic approach to literacy, ensuring that early years provision not only builds confidence in reading and writing but also empowers learners through enriched language experiences, cognitive flexibility, and structured support.

Summary of key points

- The development of literacy skills for the youngest learners is best planned using a secure subject knowledge of reading and writing developmental patterns with a focus on speech, language and communication skills.
- It is essential that links between reading and writing are explicitly taught, with further and frequent opportunities in place for children to revisit, rehearse and practise.
- The processes involved in storing and retrieving key literacy information need to be modelled and supported as part of the literacy curriculum.
- Recognising the interconnected nature of reading and writing allows practitioners to create literacy experiences that reinforce both skills simultaneously. Consider the experiences which will engage children in this duality.
- Teaching strategies that enhance working memory, cognitive flexibility, and self-regulation–such as structured storytelling, sentence building and guided reflection–can strengthen children's ability to process and apply literacy knowledge effectively.

References

American Psychiatric Association (2013). *Diagnostic and Statistical Manual of Mental Disorders: DSM-5™* (5th ed.). American Psychiatric Publishing.

Bearne, E., and Reedy, D. (2018). *Teaching Primary English: Subject Knowledge and Classroom Practice.* Routledge.

Corbett, P., and Strong, J. (2017). *Talk for Writing Across the Curriculum: How to Teach Non-Fiction Writing to 5-12 Year Olds* (2nd ed.). Maidenhead: Open University Press.

Deweerdt, S. (2020). Amygdala, the brain's threat detector, has broad roles in autism. Retrieved October18, 2023. https://www.spectrumnews.org/news/amygdala-the-brains-threat-detector-has-broad-roles-%20in%20autism/#:~:text=People%20who%20sustain%20damage%20to,diagnostic%20criteria%20for%20th%20e%20%20condition

DfE. (2023). Development Matters-Non-statutory curriculum guidance for the Early Years foundation stage. Available online: https://assets.publishing.service.gov.uk/media/64e6002a20ae890014f26cbc/DfE_Development_Matters_Report_Sep2023.pdf (Accessed 22 July 2025).

DfE. (2025). Early years foundation stage statutory framework for group and school-based providers. Setting the standards for learning, development and care for children from birth to five. Available at: https://assets.publishing.service.gov.uk/media/687105a381dd8f70f5de3ea9/EYFS_framework_for_group_and_school_based_providers_.pdf (Accessed 21 July 2025).

DfE (Department for Education). (2012). *Research Evidence on Reading for Pleasure*. London: Education Standards Research Team. Available at: https://assets.publishing.service.gov.uk/media/5a7c18d540f0b61a825d66e9/reading_for_pleasure.pdf (Accessed: 3 June 2024).

EEF (Education Endowment Foundation). (2015). Talk for writing. Retrieved October15, 2023. https://educationendowmentfoundation.org.uk/projects-and-evaluation/projects/talk-for-writing

EEF (Education Endowment Foundation). (2021). Preparing for Literacy. Accessed via https://educationendowmentfoundation.org.uk/education-evidence/guidance-reports/literacy-early-years

EEF (Education Endowment Foundation). (2023). Early Literacy. Accessed via https://educationendowmentfoundation.org.uk/early-years/evidence-store/early-literacy

OECD (Organisation for Economic Co-operation and Development). (2002). *Reading for Change: Performance and Engagement Across Countries – Results from PISA 2000*. Paris: OECD Publishing.

Scarborough, H. (2001). Connecting early language and literacy to later reading (dis)abilities: Evidence, theory, and practice. In S.B. Neuman and D.K. Dickinson (Eds.), *Handbook of Early Literacy Research* (pp. 97-110). New York: Guilford Press.

Sedita, J. (2024). Connecting the Ropes: Integrating Reading and Writing Instruction. Accessed via https://keystoliteracy.com/blog/connecting-the-ropes-integrating-reading-writing-instruction/

The National Literacy Trust. (2020). Reading to children is so powerful, so simple and yet so misunderstood. Available at: https://literacytrust.org.uk/blog/reading-children-so-powerful-so-simple-and-yet-so-misunderstood/ (Accessed 03 June 2024).

The National Literacy Trust. (2023). Our latest research reveals that children's reading enjoyment is at its lowest level in almost two decades. Available at: https://literacytrust.org.uk/news/childrens-reading-enjoyment-at-lowest-level-in-almost-two-decades/ (Accessed 03 June 2024).

Vygotsky, L. (1978). *Mind in Society: The Development of Higher Psychological Processes*. Cambridge, MA: Harvard University Press.

Waddell, M. (2017). *Owl Babies*. London: Walker Books.

9 Specific area
Mathematics

Jayne Carter

Introduction

We would like to build on the excellent contributions for this chapter by offering our explorations on the concept of maths anxiety. As included in the EYFS statutory framework (2025), the essential elements in becoming an early mathematician are clearly outlined (spatial awareness and number patterns for example). The following expectation, mentioned at the end of the mathematics section, says,

> It is important that children develop positive attitudes and interests in mathematics, look for patterns and relationships, spot connections, 'have a go', talk to adults and peers about what they notice and not be afraid to make mistakes.
>
> (DfE 2025: 10)

Our view is that if this vital aspect of being a competent and confident early mathematician was moved to the beginning of this overview, it would elevate its significance and secure its place for practitioners.

Pondering question: how can we connect explicit maths teaching to maths application and rehearsal?

The suggestion of elevating an understanding of maths anxiety is, of course, not intended to negate the overriding importance of developing a bank of mathematical knowledge and skills but, for us, the attitude of being a mathematician can be a real driving force towards becoming mathematically proficient. Perhaps this view is clouded by our own memories of maths.

Jayne, first author of this book, says: I can sum up my maths lessons in junior and secondary education with this quote ....'I just couldn't make any sense of it. It didn't seem relevant to me at all.' I needed to see the relevance in maths for me to buy into it, for me to be able to know how everything I was being taught fitted together. It all felt very separate; in distinctly individual compartments, with a clear focus on recall and barking out answers. The result of this view was extreme dread of each maths lesson which subsequently 'shut off' my mind to even the possibility of accessing the maths being taught. A self-fulfilling prophecy in play. I quickly became a student who wasn't any good at maths so purposefully found ways to avoid it or self-sabotage the thought of engaging in it. These historic feelings still remain with me to some extent, although I was able to channel them into something more positive by working with my local maths hubs in facilitating early years workgroups.

Maths anxiety: does it impact mathematical competence?

Exploring this concept of maths anxiety in more depth, the extensive and dynamic work of Jo Boaler leads the way in both providing a wealth of research on the subject, as well as providing a range of accessible and supportive pedagogical advice. In her groundbreaking work, *The Elephant in the Classroom–Helping Children Learn to love maths* (2017), Boaler found that a poor maths identity can develop as early as two years of age, with observations showing children moving away from activities where there is a 'right' or 'wrong' answer, instead preferring to take part in much more creative, open-ended activities which allow a sense of exploration, trail and error and creativity. From two! We all know how difficult it is to undo a learnt response and change emotions and narrative. Boaler used in their research commentary and examples from children, showing their views around maths.

> I don't like maths as I have to sit on the carpet for too long.
> I think it's hard as all the numbers get jumbled up in my head.
> Maths is too much answer time and not enough learning time.
> I think I would rather play with the cars or the dinosaurs.

Quite telling... children are very good at giving honest opinions. Already these children are developing habits of mind about maths. These findings have helped me consider how maths is 'sold' within early years. How do children at such an early age and stage of development make the differentiation between a required factual response to a non-factual response? These comments seem to be already negative and potentially could be a barrier to them moving forward in their learning, especially if this is an engrained long-lasting memory.

Influential in Boaler's work is the research of Carol Dweck, particularly about Dweck's views on fixed and growth mindsets. Dweck's pioneering research explores how a positive attitude to learning acts as a driver towards feeling that you CAN and whether this ultimately means that you WILL achieve. Barriers, worries are obviously still there, but the determination, resilience and grit to overcome them is presented as a fundamental indicator of progress and achievement.

Pedagogical reflections: tuning into your mathematicians

Think of the children who you support—what are the ones like who are successful at maths? What are the ones who find maths a struggle like? Do those who succeed at maths know how to apply their key maths skills in a range of experiences? Do they keep going, adapt and modify approaches when their first attempts didn't satisfy? Do they understand the power of mathematical language in helping them shape their emerging understanding of maths content? How does their positive attitude make a difference to their maths learning? Do the children who find maths more difficult have a narrower window of trial and error, relying on a limited number of strategies? Do they seek out a greater level of adult support to provide different strategies and ways of problem solving? Do they also have a sense of 'I know I already can't do it' when faced with a new problem? Consider what this means for us at our level—are we more inclined to be totally engaged in something if there is a glimmer of succeeding at it, especially anticipating wallowing in the positive feelings which generally happen as a result of that achievement? Or do we choose to override both the experience and the subsequent feelings, deciding instead to not even start the experience/feelings journey for fear of failure, dissatisfaction or anxiety?

The significance of Boaler and Dweck in considering maths provision

Boaler was able to use Dweck's theory and consider how to use this within mathematics teaching and learning. Building on the original Dweck mindset approach, Boaler wanted to explore how to move from the empowerment of a positive mind set to dissecting the qualities which would enable a learner to feel this way. In the article 'A mathematical mindset approach to student learning' (2024), Boaler states,

> A mathematical mindset approach starts from the premise that it is not enough to share mindset messages with students – messages that they can learn anything and that times of struggle are critical – if those messages are not supported by the teaching approaches they experience. In a mathematical mindset approach students are taught with rich mathematical tasks that give them opportunities to learn and grow, rather than short, closed questions. These tasks give students opportunities to struggle, and teachers support students with positive messages as they work.

The dynamic between what is being shared through positive personal and life skills messages can only be truly revolutionary if the corresponding approaches taught by teachers also support this specific empowerment approach. Any perceived dichotomy between them must be in sync to strengthen each other and maximise learning within both disciplines.

Boaler's website 'youcubed' https://www.youcubed.org/tasks/ stores a vast array of research, CPD webinars and classroom tools to aid this view. Central to this site is the absolute commitment to improving the opinion of maths as enticing, interesting, creative and adventurous. The intention of upskilling practitioners' own subject knowledge and confidence in extoling the virtues of maths has the aim of acting as a model to learners; feeding off the adults' enthusiasm and providing additional tools to the 'I can do it' bank. Boaler supported the teachers in their development of a positive maths mindset by asking them to consider the impact of task design and the planning of maths challenges and problems, including too the impact on the attitude to maths from their classes. The hundreds of classroom ideas help adults to move away from a seemingly default setting of asking for the memorising and recall of taught facts as the indicator of knowledge, to one which allows learners to represent this same knowledge in a much more creative method, drawing on their skills of reasoning, visualising and problem solving. For example, learners could work with peers to present a visual overview of the set problem or focus on an explanation of the method involved in the problem to share with others. This shift, argues Boaler, moves adults' whole belief model. 'The myth of the fixed brain is countered and a new way to approach mathematics is shared.'

Connecting key threads of maths teaching and learning

Where does this fit into Early Years? A reminder of the expectation stated in the EYFS statutory guidance,

> It is important that children develop positive attitudes and interests in mathematics, look for patterns and relationships, spot connections, 'have a go', talk to adults and peers about what they notice and not be afraid to make mistakes.
>
> (DfE 2025:10)

I can instantly see the connection between this statement and the aspects included in the EYFS characteristics framework. The latter, which is often thought of as the drivers or attitudes which contribute to being an effective learner could be the vital key to ensuring that maths, specifically, is embedded in a child's mind as something which they want to be part of; they make the choice to engage in maths problems and relish the opportunity to use their blossoming maths knowledge and skills. The Early Childhood Maths Group (ECMG) have developed an impressive framework which promotes the principles needed to support all children to be confident, competent and enthusiastic mathematicians. Engrained in this document is this powerful manifesto:

> 'Early years teaching is underpinned by practitioners' understanding of children's possible mathematical learning trajectories and a belief that all children are effective mathematical learners, although their previous experiences may differ.
>
> (The Early Childhood Maths Group, n.d.)

The efficacy of this framework lies in the blend of research-led views illustrated with accessible pedagogical ideas, with the target being that any classroom-based decisions are evidence led and individualised. It is hopefully clear to see too that the above statement makes more than a nod to those views from Boaler and Dweck: namely the power to change the view of maths as a priority is a responsibility placed on the adult.

One of the principles included in the ECMG framework is this:

> Adults are disposed towards behaviours and ways of thinking that promote positivity and success in mathematics.

Another confirmation expressing the role of the adult in teaching both maths content and skills as well as the key maths dispositions. The ECMG suggest that the nurturing of a whole class with a positive maths mindset can be best supported by all of the adults authentically demonstrating curiosity about children's mathematical reasoning skills and their choices to reveal their thinking in maths. They suggest that adults could include mathematical marking as an alternative to verbal communication. This suggestion offers another opportunity for children to access the maths concepts and for the adults, a window into their children's knowledge, application choices and possible misconceptions. I would add to this that by explicitly showing children what maths mark making means, the skills of using this approach, provides the model of how to create their own mathematical writing. When I have introduced this to practitioners and children, I have named them 'maths stories'. I hope by using this title, children are able to use their current understanding of what a story means, using this as their own blueprint and allowing me to add the mathematical aspect to this. I make sure I show them my maths story developing, so creating it in front of the class, using key mathematical language alongside my picture. Children, if so inclined to do so, can read their own story, with the adults scribing their own special maths adventure. This, as well as many other ideas included in the ECMG framework, ensure that all adults who support our early mathematicians this vision, expressed by Boaler (2017):

> Teachers need to offer mathematics as a learning subject not a performance subject.

Perhaps if we focus on the drives and attitudes involved in developing a love of maths as an aspect to explore and enjoy, rather than just providing them with more of the same content in the hope that it would 'stick', children may be able to appreciate and improve their own drive and motivation towards maths.

I wish I had had this clarity when sat in my year 5 mental maths test!

In this first contribution, Lesley Boyle, Senior Lecturer, Initial Teacher Training University of Hertfordshire, explores the key concept of subitising in more detail and how this can be used to provide a maths curriculum which is engaging, responsive to children's needs and informed by progress.

Lesley Boyle: subitising: how does this fit into early years maths?

In the teaching of early maths to children aged 2-5 years old, traditionally teachers and practitioners place an emphasis on teaching children skills associated with counting. However, humans have an innate capability to subitise (Trick and Pylyshyn, 1994; Choo and Franconeri, 2014) and this skill is something that has, until recently, been largely overlooked in an early years classroom. Subitising comes from the Latin word subito which means to 'arrive suddenly' (Clements and Sarama, 2021: 18) and is the ability to instantly recognise small quantities (usually up to 4 or 5) without needing to count. An example of this would be to notice a bowl of four apples and to instantly know there are four without needing to count.

In my research I have been examining the impact of early years maths in a classroom where subitising plays the dominant role in teaching children mathematical concepts such as cardinality, composition of number, unitising and place value. Through resources such as tens frame and rekenreks, teachers encourage children to notice and begin to form visual concept images which help them to develop fluency and see numbers in relation to one another, rather than as a linear process. As part of my research I interviewed a number of teachers who have adopted a subitising approach to teaching early years maths.

Their responses to subitising was overwhelmingly positive. These teachers felt that inclusivity was promoted because the subitising approach is so visual and is based on children's natural abilities. And for those children who are multi-language learners or nonverbal, they can show their learning in other ways rather than relying on speech. They also recounted how quickly children responded and began not only recognising quantities but also noticing differences. Some of the participants linked this to the principle of cardinality, enabling the children to understand that the quantity they could subitise relates to the 'how manyness' of a set, rather than learning that it is simply the last number you say. One participant explained it like this: '[the children] have a mental visual representation they can see either in front of them or in their head of what that quantity actually looks like'.

The participants gave examples of ways in which subitising supported children's composition of number: knowing that numbers are made up of other numbers. One teacher pointed out that they no longer had to encourage children to 'learn' their number bonds because the daily work they do on subitising, and partitioning numbers, meant that children over time, naturally began to see the number patterns. They also remarked on how children began to see groups of numbers within numbers, paving the way for multiplication and division.

Perhaps most importantly, all the interviewed teachers said that the children were also able to demonstrate their subitising abilities in their child-directed play and reported an increase in engagement and enthusiasm for maths that did not wane throughout the year.

In this next contribution, Erica McGinley, Maths Consultant, presents her personal findings on the power of counting collection. Using these collections as a vehicle for maths learning can contribute to how children engage in maths, with the significance of the role of the adult also being a determining factor to their success.

Erica McGinley: counting collections

I have a long fascination with collecting interesting objects and have always used them as starting points for inquisitive exploration or play in my classroom. Using counting collections has given many opportunities for children to explore the world, to make observations and be playful in their learning. I have found that children want to sort, arrange and classify. They select their favourite and set aside those of little interest. In this early play they are comparing and contrasting, spotting differences and similarities. Noticing the odd one out, the smallest, and the same is one of the first steps to making mathematical observations and connections. Children who are sorting and playing are reasoning and noticing. They are spotting patterns and making explicit links.

Children need to be supported to use their collections and draw out mathematical relationships and also show connections and how this relates to the number system. The role of the adult to pose questions such as 'I wonder', 'what did you notice' is a carefully timed and balanced intervention. Adults need to skilfully support children noticing and model connections, not to halt play and thinking. Careful noticing and talking through your own thinking whilst playing alongside can support children to talk about their own thinking.

Group and paired activities such as 'odd one out' or 'same/different' with the collections allows children to share their thinking and to practice maths talk. With guided talk, and very simple stem sentences such as 'it's the same because...'; 'I noticed......', children begin to make connections, using conjuncture and mathematical reasoning skills.

The type of object in a collection needs careful consideration. I prefer to use natural objects, but these are not always robust. Children need time to play and explore; the presentation and storage needs to be attractive and engaging. However, a beautiful maths table with interesting collections is not enough to develop children's maths skills or engage them in mathematical thinking. High-quality modelling with explicit language is essential to develop mathematical thinkers. Children need explicit teaching, time to explore and rehearse, to then apply independently.

The focus of the maths, how this will be modelled and with what objects must be considered carefully. The relationships and structure that I want to emphasise should be explicit in the choice of collection I model with. If I am spotlighting the composition of numbers within five, limiting the resources to two colours will show this relationship more clearly than a rainbow of objects.

One of my favourite resources is a fabric tens frame; it can be squashed into a pocket and carried anywhere. Alongside a counting collection it can be used to sort, count, see the relationships between numbers and the essential elements of early number, as well as comparing, counting, cardinality and composition of number.

Collections are exciting and engaging, they will become mixed up and go home in pockets, but they are essential for children to make connections and see the world mathematically.

Echoing a significant theme of this whole chapter, Kate Gingles, an independent Early Years Consultant, advocates for joyful maths to be included in practitioners' planning, implementation and evaluation of a maths curriculum. This contribution offers so many opportunities to personally ponder and consider how a positive maths attitude can be fostered in provision.

Kate Gingles: finding the joy in maths

I am lucky to have had a career path that has given me not only the time to research but also to put my research into practice. My fascination with early maths really arose around the time that Ofsted released its Bold Beginnings document. As a local authority advisor at the time I was working on a project with Reception teachers that aimed to exemplify how the challenging demands of this document could be met through developmentally appropriate EYFS practice rooted in a strong early years pedagogy. We found that phonics, unsurprisingly, was a huge focus in schools at the time and teachers could speak very clearly and coherently about how their programme of learning for phonics was structured but that maths was harder for them to pinpoint. There was wonderful practice happening and children were making great progress and achieving well in relation to the early learning goals at the time, but the subject knowledge of adults was less secure and the sequence of learning and pedagogy around this had been given less thought.

As a result of these reflections a range of training and CPD was developed for local teachers around maths and early number in particular, and, as somebody who definitely didn't consider myself an expert, I spent many, many hours delving into the rich range of materials that are out there to develop my own subject knowledge. Douglas Clements and NCETM became my go-to websites, as did work being done by colleagues in schools working with the local maths hubs. I also discovered the fabulous book *Making Numbers* around this time and this has shaped my practice and understanding ever since, as has my personal favourite *Playful Mathematics* by Helen Williams.

When I returned to a school-based role in 2021, I was determined to use what I had learned to positively impact on the maths provision in my new school. Out went the maths scheme and all its associated worksheets and in came a playful approach built around maths games and quality picture books (Publications from The Early Childhood Maths Group were an enormous help here!). My team and I worked together on developing our learning environment to reflect the curriculum we offered, with a strong focus on open-ended, authentic resources such as egg boxes, buttons, beads and pebbles and opportunities for children to revisit and embed taught concepts in continuous provision.

Stepping back into an advisory and consulting role my advice for EYFS practitioners is threefold:

- Know your stuff. Really explore and learn as much as you can about the concepts involved in early number sense.
- Hold true to your pedagogical beliefs. You know children learn through play and exploration and that it is their own interests and fascinations that best drive their learning, so make sure that your maths curriculum and the experiences you offer reflects this knowledge.
- Be fascinated and have fun! If you are curious to explore numbers and patterns your children will be too. Share the joy in this with them.

In this next contribution, Peter Foulds, a School Improvement Adviser, advocates for the role of 'always out maths', offering a personal perspective on the impact of ensuring purposeful maths provision is readily available for children to continue their explorations and discoveries.

Peter Foulds: always out maths!

Who would have thought that to predict the future mathematical proficiency of a child—all the way to adulthood—one would not look to number but spatial awareness and reasoning and patterning? Yet there is now a plethora of research coming to light that shows these strands of maths are indeed the key building blocks of future success (e.g. Rittle-Johnson et al., 2017).

How could this inform the way we use our provision? Simple—if it is that important, it should be what we now call 'always out maths.' By this we mean, if your maths units move on from these areas, the chance for children to experience patterning and spatial reasoning should not go away in the cupboard. It should stay out either as overt activities (e.g. a patterning station that is a consistent feature with the resources changing to match the curriculum—the patterning stays) or as incidental activities within other areas (e.g. picture prompts to copy in the construction area; patterns to copy with cereal hoops in the finger gym; obstacle course to navigate on the tricycle track).

Patterning, along with sorting, matching, ordering and comparing, make up what we know to be the key strands of very early maths and it is these ideas that underpin spatial awareness and reasoning at a young age. This knowledge then informs us about other types of activity that children should always be able to experience—always out maths! Do you always have chances for sorting, matching, ordering and comparing? Don't wait for that unit, see it as 'always out maths.'

However, the toys teachers once took for granted that children had experienced as toddlers—stacking rings, shape sorters, building blocks—that laid the foundation of patterning and spatial reasoning are rarely experienced by toddlers now due to the rush to electronic devices or poverty. So, what does this tell us? Don't assume children have had these hands-on building blocks and put these sorts of activities in your provision in an 'always out maths' way—not in cupboards.

What could 'always out maths' look like? Some simple ideas we find to be effective include:

- Story vote: children add their token to the pot matching the choice of book they want for story time. When it is story time, the teacher leads a discussion around comparing the pots and if it's too close to call we move to the count. Lots of maths that backs up democracy from PSHE.
- Silhouetting: key toys/equipment have a shadow under it so children have to match the shape to its home in the correct orientation.
- Tweezer match: in a fine motor area simply put coloured dot stickers in the bottom of an empty egg box and children match the pompom to the sticker and use the same colour tweezers. Then move it on so the dots form patterns. Patterning, spatial awareness, fine motor all rolled into one.

In this contribution, Jayne Carter, co-author and Early Years Consultant is able to draw on the recommendations included in previous contributions and consider how all adults can develop a maths mindset through high-quality maths environments and experiences. There is a reminder of how practitioners should 'question, challenge and ponder everyday'.

Jayne Carter: fostering adults to developing confident and competent mathematicians

- **Be a positive role model ourselves**: we all bring memories and experiences about our own subject knowledge and confidence. This may be positive which is great as your natural enthusiasm will shine through and enthuse your children about maths. But it may not be as positive—it may even be extremely negative. If this is an established emotion, there is even more importance, I would argue, to make sure that others never feel like this. That they instead develop and maintain a favourable view of maths. Enable children to see the magic in maths and by doing that you may also rediscover some of the magic for yourself.
- **Be conscious of making connections for children**: connectivity is vital as a motivator for children to not only learn the maths content you are sharing with them but also to help children feel propelled into applying their knowledge. Relevance plays a key role here. Like most things, children need to appreciate 'what's in it for them'. Will this enrich their lives, deepen their sense of exploration and bring them emotional satisfaction in what they are doing?
- **Acknowledge that for some children maths is a journey (with no sat nav!)**: the maths journey is full of roadside information, possible wrong turns and occasional pit stops whilst children are immersed in new information, then come to terms with it, apply and modify. For some children this journey will be quite direct where they soak up the new information and then are able to use this alongside a secure maths attitude to learn deeper and move forward. For many children there will be times that they need to stop and revisit, maybe even take a different route to ensure learning is deeply assimilated. Having this close collaboration between the *'what'* they are learning and *'how'* they are

learning ensures that all children reach their own destination, refreshed and ready for what meets them next.

- **Excite, enthuse and inspire: consider how you do this for your children**: consider the ethos that you nurture within your room and the role of the environment in this ethos. When planning ask yourself, 'Where's the maths in my environment?' Does it move pass the purely aesthetic also allowing for possibility thinking, creativity, exploration and challenge? Are you using your key mathematical manipulatives with an understanding of the mathematical potential within them? Perhaps scan your environment for a pattern of maths *enjoyment* as well as maths *content*.
- **Be brave to go with the children**: one of the most exciting parts of being in the early years is the way children can completely surprise you! Children can come up with a million more times more imaginative, amazing maths ideas then adults can think of. Consider all events within your daily routine as potential opportunities for maths content learning and maths skills learning. These could be incidental and spontaneous times but may also include routine times such as snack time, welcome and goodbye time. Edit your planning, scribble on it, celebrate the bits which worked well and equally those which took an unexpected direction. Planning which looks like it is used to inform how support can best meet the needs of the children is a priceless document, regardless of its less than pristine appearance.

As well as developing your own pedagogy, continue frequent professional discussions with your early years team to ensure that there is a level of consistency of beliefs and how these affect provision.

Question, challenge and ponder everyday

In this thought-provoking contribution, Hannah Foster, a Reception Teacher, presents what worked well when supporting a child excelling in maths. Negotiating this specific need enabled personal reflection, prompting both confirmation of current provision and extension to support learning.

Hannah Foster: supporting a maths genius in the early years

Being able to teach a Mensa-registered 4-year-old maths genius, I discovered that there is a real lack of support for exceptionally high-achieving pupils. There is not only a lack of support for the child and their family but also the teachers who teach them.

As practitioners, we get no extra time or additional support for these pupils, so unless they find themselves in devoted teachers' hands willing to go above and beyond, scouring the internet for ideas and taking the time to get to know them and their interests to tailor work accordingly, holding regular parent meeting to create continuity and a good support system, then these children run the risk of being left behind and even eventually falling behind. Their behaviour may deteriorate due to disinterest in the lack of challenge in their classroom environment and their abilities may be viewed as a hindrance rather than a wonderful gift. Devastating!

As a school we work exceptionally hard to go above and beyond to meet individual needs. I am aware that not every school or family can offer this, and it begs the question, how many child geniuses go undiscovered or unsupported? I reached out personally to the MENSA team and I gained some really useful insight but they too are facing the same hurdles with lack of research, funding and resources.

I have found this year to be incredibly exciting and rewarding but I fear for this particular pupil's future as they may not always fall into such willing teachers' hands and as they move higher up the school, the work will only become harder to tailor to meet their needs.

My belief is that everyone deserves their chance to shine and fly. I liken my job to that of a facilitator, laying the foundations to freedom and future by creating an enabling environment in the classroom that meets each individual's needs, so that my students can grow to be exactly who they are meant to be and fly.

There was a minimal amount of support for practitioners and to provide sufficient challenge for the pupil. Hours of work planning in the evening were spent trying to find extension tasks and problem solving/reasoning/maths mastery tasks for him to do in place of the lesson content.

The pupil had a keen interest in space so I tried to incorporate this and did a lot of 'on the spot' adaptations to lessons with whiteboard work, that is, everyone else is asked what $4 + 3$ equals and I would ask them what 40000 to the power of x would be. (They love big numbers!)

We found the approach of diving deep rather than stretching wide really useful.

Physical manipulatives were the way forward. The pupil's brain was fascinating; they could really 'see' number. It was a tangible approach that was hard to understand as my brain physically doesn't see numbers represented in the same way.

We implemented a kinaesthetic approach using open-ended resources such as number blocks which allowed the pupil to make visual representations of cubed numbers and more. Resources such as these allow numbers to be represented in a multitude of ways and allow visual and kinaesthetic learners to really understand concepts such as multiplication, division, subtracting.

Vygotsky's theory of scaffolding was put to the test lots last year. We saw some great benefits and interestingly, the whole class has an overall strong cohort above average in maths results. Is this because of this pupils' influence? Or the enabling maths environment that was created?

It was interesting to note that the pupils' fine motor skills and handwriting were not fully developed, so I had to work a lot on this to ensure their answers were legible (they could work out these incredible answers yet not write them clearly so that they could be read.)

It put the focus on the necessity of a well-rounded approach.

In this final contribution, Amy Stancer, Headteacher, expertly brings together the major threads from this chapter, offering an important reminder of the many aspects which contribute to a powerful maths curriculum. The role of the environment and the interactions adults initiate within these spaces contribute to an early years mathematician who has the knowledge, skills and positive attitude to fully engage in this aspect of learning.

Amy Stancer: developing number sense is a crucial part of any Early Years teaching

Paying attention to opportunities in play and adult interactions during routines allows young children to develop their counting, understanding of comparison and cardinality. Most mathematical play and conversations in early years will interweave spatial awareness, physical engagement and problem solving seamlessly.

Ensuring real opportunities for this indoors and outdoors encourages adults and children to talk about maths.

Organising relevant resources in your environment allows for mathematical play and problem solving to flow from the children. Resources do not need to be expensive but do need to be carefully chosen for their relevance to the play and opportunities for learning in all areas. Mathematical thinking can be explored as children play alone, together and with playful adults with continuous resources which are open-ended and aid imagination. A sand pit can be organised for enclosing, moulding, building, digging, mixing, sieving and pretending! It can be enhanced with crates, tubes, funnels, water, scaffolding and large balances over the year (Figure 9.1).

Figure 9.1 An outdoor sand provision area provided by the author for this submission.

120 *Early Years Essentials*

An outdoor sand provision area provided by the author for this submission

These skills can be supported with appropriate provision inside too. Damp and dry sand offer such different experiences related to number sense and special awareness.

Silhouettes and labelling are helpful when giving children independence and can grow in complexity as the children become able to match and arrange. This can include grids and/or five frames. Fabric, planks with lines drawn and cardboard fruit box layers are reusable and transportable ways of tailoring counting grids to the children's needs.

Including boxes in provision allows children to gain concepts of smaller amounts/objects being within larger objects. Adding in shapes which allow for matching and balancing offers opportunities for 1:1 correspondence.

A digging pit is rich in mathematics: a key gross physical skill, which allows amounts to be moved and collected; an early recognition of greater and smaller, more and less; and much talk about the stones, leaves and worms you uncover! Then the weather adds a different dimension–rain allows conversations about 'how deep' and 'I can't see your two boots or my two boots....'

Putting boots away and matching and selecting them, offers many visualisations of number. Children may recognise their own two boots, a group of boots and, with support and practice, may be able to recognise a row of ten as they move into Reception (Figure 9.2).

Figure 9.2 An outdoor wellies storage shelf provided by the author for this submission.

An outdoor wellies storage shelf provided by the author for this submission

Planting saplings. Here, this extension to planting seeds requires children to talk about number of saplings, whether there are a greater number planted in some containers, sizes, space, depth and the opportunity for purposeful mark making when recording the amounts in each container at the end to make a 'map' of the saplings. Over time the saplings are nurtured by the children; measures for water and non-standard measures for the growth extend their thinking yet further.

Making opportunities to revisit and apply your mathematical skills is crucial. Planting in lots of locations allows children to connect their knowledge of growing to the number sense and spatial awareness they are developing.

Opportunities to actively subitise both indoors and outdoors are key, adding numerals to label for purpose as the children have a concrete understanding of number order and amounts.

Understanding play schema can enable mathematical provision to be developed both indoors and outdoors.

With younger children this offers additional opportunity to play and explore as they develop their active engagement and problem solving for mathematics.

Babies and young infants thrive with closeness, physicality and interaction. A treasure mat which has multiple resources allows children to hold one in each hand or feel sensations on their hands, arms and legs. Choosing resources that inspire gentle touch on legs and hands allows them to make early recognition of non-visual amounts. This will grow into their dexterity and awareness of their bodies in contact with objects and allow them to control movements which will allow play for mathematics.

Noticing number is a key skill that adults and children can engage in positively.

In conclusion

This chapter explores the essential principles of early years mathematics, focusing on fostering mathematical confidence, competence and curiosity through effective pedagogy and engaging learning environments. It highlights the significance of developing positive mathematical identities in young learners, addressing factors such as maths anxiety, mindset theory and the role of open-ended exploration. Drawing on insights from influential researchers like Jo Boaler and Carol Dweck, the chapter examines how attitudes towards maths shape children's engagement and resilience in problem solving. Through expert reflections and practical strategies, the chapter reinforces the idea that mathematical proficiency is not solely about recalling facts but about cultivating a mindset where children feel empowered to explore, experiment and embrace challenges in their mathematical journeys.

Summary of key points

- Early maths involves the teaching of both key concepts and the skills/dispositions of being a mathematician.
- The role of the adult is crucial in promoting a positive view of maths.
- The role of the environment needs to be planned carefully so children can access a range of maths problems independently.

- The sequencing and connectivity in maths learning should be carefully planned to ensure it captures each of the developmental steps involved.
- The careful consideration of the type of manipulatives and resources children use to support their maths learning needs to be considered with a focus on their potential for maths learning.

References

Boaler, J. (2017). *The Elephant in the Classroom - Helping Children Learn to Love Maths*. Souvenir Press.

Boaler, J. (2024). A mathematical mindset approach to student learning. Accessed https://www.openaccessgovernment.org/article/a-mathematical-mindset-approach-to-student-learning/185160/#:~:text=In%20a%20mathematical%20mindset%20approach%20students%20are%20taught,support%20students%20with%20positive%20messages%20as%20they%20work

Choo, H. and Franconeri, S.L. (2014). Enumeration of small collections violates Weber's law. *Psychonomic Bulletin and Review*, 21, pp. 93-99.

Clements, D.H. and Sarama, J. (2021). *Learning and Teaching Early Math (Thirds)*. New York: Routledge.

DfE. (2025). Early years foundation stage statutory framework for group and school-based providers. Setting the standards for learning, development and care for children from birth to five. Available at: https://assets.publishing.service.gov.uk/media/687105a381dd8f70f5de3ea9/EYFS_framework_for_group_and_school_based_providers_.pdf (Accessed 21 July 2025).

Rittle-Johnson, B., Fyfe, E.R., Hofer, K.G. and Farran, D.C. (2017). Early math trajectories: Low-income children's mathematics knowledge from ages 4 to 11, *Child Development*, 88(5), pp. 1727-1742.

The Early Childhood Maths Group. (n.d.) https://earlymaths.org/

Trick, L.M. and Pylyshyn, Z.W. (1994). Why are small and large numbers enumerated differently? *A Limited-Capacity Preattentive Stage in Vision*, 101(1), 80-102.

10 Understanding the world

Poppy Gibson

Introduction

In early years education, 'Understanding the World' refers to a child's developing knowledge and curiosity about the world around them. Through play, exploration and hands-on activities, children develop their understanding of the world, which helps them become informed and responsible citizens. This tenth chapter explores the variety of early years research which highlights the teaching and learning in this area, as well as the statutory framework expectations. We have gathered a variety of contributions from all sectors of the EYFS, written by eight experienced professionals.

Pondering question: how can we make sure that children's key knowledge in this area of learning is in context and developmentally appropriate?

The EYFS curriculum has gone through many revisions since it was introduced, but the key themes remain widely the same along with the importance of children learning from their interactions with their environment, including people and places (Hirst, and Culshaw, 2024). In current early years education at the time of this book's publication, 'Understanding the World' refers to a child's developing knowledge and curiosity about the world around them. This includes **People and communities**: Learning about different cultures, families and communities, recognising diversity and understanding how people live and work; **The world**: Exploring the natural world, including plants, animals and the environment. Understanding basic scientific concepts and how things work; and **Technology**: Learning to use and understand simple technologies, such as computers and other digital devices. These themes are valuable in helping children develop identity and understanding in who they are and where they live (Louis, 2012).

Children as explorers of their world

Understanding the World, therefore, encompasses the humanities. Young children bring a wide variety of developing geographical experience with them when they enter primary school (Catling, 2006). Geography education and geographical learning is a great way for young people to begin developing a deeper understanding of their environment (Pratama, 2024). When looking to enhance children's understanding of the world, it is also vital that learning opportunities for STEM are integrated into daily play, developing curiosity in the world and scientific discover (Campbell and Howitt, 2024). Throughout this chapter, ideas for helping children understand their world are shared and discussed.

In this first contribution, Roisin Casey, Assistant Head of Early Years, explains how Bokashi Composting is being used to help early learners understand sustainability and the processes in our natural world.

Roisin Casey: little composters, big impact: how Bokashi Buckets empower early learners

An appreciation for, and understanding of the natural environment, as well as the development of civic responsibility, are essential tenets of the Early Years Foundation Stage (EYFS). One novel and easily accessible approach to accomplishing these aims in early childhood education settings is Bokashi Composting.

What is Bokashi composting?

Bokashi Composting is an anaerobic fermentation process that breaks down organic waste using beneficial microbes. Unlike traditional composting, the fermentation process creates a nutrient rich 'Bokashi tea' that can be diluted and used as a plant fertilizer, and the fermented solids can be added to traditional compost heaps or directly into soil for faster decomposition.

Benefits for sustainability

Bokashi composting empowers early years settings to:

- **Reduce Food Waste**: Instead of throwing away food scraps, children can actively participate in diverting them to a valuable resource. During the 2022-23 academic year our setting saved over 300kg of food waste from going to landfill and instead used the Bokashi Composting method to rejuvenate our soil and create a school garden for planting.

Understanding the World Through Bokashi

Bokashi provides a unique opportunity for children to engage with the natural world through hands-on experiences:

- **Observation and Exploration**: children can observe the changes in food scraps during the fermentation process, fostering curiosity and encouraging them to ask questions about decomposition.
- **Understanding Cycles**: Bokashi demonstrates the cyclical nature of life. Food scraps are transformed into valuable resources, nurturing new plant growth.

Vocabulary development

Bokashi introduces new vocabulary, enriching children's communication skills:

Composting, fermentation, anaerobic, microbes: these terms introduce children to scientific concepts in an age-appropriate way.

Decomposition, nutrient-rich, fertilizer: children learn about the natural process of breaking down organic matter and its role in plant growth.

Bokashi composting offers a valuable educational tool within the EYFS curriculum, promoting understanding of decomposition and sustainable practices.

Materials:

- Bokashi bin (We get buckets donated from a local fruit juice company)
- Bokashi bran (a fermented wheat bran mix)

Daily Additions:

1. **Food Scraps**: encourage children to add daily food scraps (fruit & vegetable peels, eggshells, coffee grounds) to the bin. Avoid meat, dairy and oily items.
2. **Layer & Sprinkle**: after adding scraps, use a scraper (if available) to gently press them down. Then, sprinkle a thin layer of Bokashi bran (1-2 tablespoons) on top.

Bokashi Tea & Solids:

1. The bin collects a nutrient-rich liquid called 'Bokashi tea.' Every few days, drain the tea using the spigot (adult supervision needed). Dilute it with water (1:10 ratio) and use it to fertilize houseplants.
2. Once the bin is full (4-6 weeks), the fermented food scraps become 'bokashi.' These can be buried in soil to break down further.

Learning Opportunities:

Throughout the process, discuss the importance of reducing food waste and the transformation happening within the bin.

Conclusion

When used in an EYFS context, Bokashi composting can be an effective means of promoting early learning and incorporating sustainable principles. Bokashi encourages children to value the environment, become responsible citizens, and create valuable resources by reusing food scraps. With its easy accessibility and small footprint, it is perfect for early childhood environments, where it can inspire a lifelong appreciation for nature and a commitment to sustainability.

In this second contribution, Nicola Wallis, Practitioner Research Associate, highlights the value of museums in helping children connect to the past and present of their local areas as well as wider afield.

Nicola Wallis: what do museums offer children in the Early Years?

The dictionary definition of a museum is 'a building where objects of historical, scientific, or artistic interest are kept' (Cambridge Dictionary, 2024). Perhaps this is also what you think of when you imagine a museum?

Having worked for many years in the Fitzwilliam Museum, which holds the art collection for the University of Cambridge, I can tell you that a museum is much more than the description above. It is a place for stories—some brand new, some very old; it is a bridge between communities who will never meet; it is a building that has the power to hush voices and to amplify them; and it is an opportunity for young children to experience feeling connected to the rest of the world.

So come with me up the big stone steps, through the grand entrance and let's explore what museums can offer young children.

A place for inspiration

The word *museum* comes from *mouseion* meaning 'seat of the Muses'—the goddesses who inspired music, science, literature and the arts in Ancient Greek mythology. Museums have incredible potential to inspire to this day. Their collections enable children to explore the world beyond anything available in an early years setting or a school (Shaffer, 2020). By connecting with museums, children can become fascinated with ideas and themes they would never have otherwise encountered, and who knows where those fascinations might lead?

A place to take time

Museums offer opportunities to play with time in exciting ways (Walklate, 2022): we can travel many centuries in a few steps in a historical display or capture a moment forever in an artwork. In our hectic lives, the benefits of slowing down, noticing and taking time to connect have benefits for well-being, for learning, and for relationship building (Chung, 2023; Clark, 2022; Honoré, 2004; Tishman, 2017). In my own research (Wallis and Noble, 2023), I have noticed that the context of the museum sets the mood for slow, careful looking with children and adults paying close attention and noticing more than they might do elsewhere.

A place for intergenerational learning

Another incredible benefit of museums is the potential they have for lifelong learning. These are places where both people of all ages can learn together (Eberbach and Crowley, 2017; Marinopoulos, 2019; Tazi et al., 2015). Making discoveries alongside those of different generations can challenge stereotypes and pre-conceptions about who knows best and can support relational learning through a shared experience.

A place for agency

Importantly, museums offer children a chance to exercise agency (Manyukhina et al., 2023). My research (Wallis and Noble, 2022) has demonstrated that both children and adults experience a sense of freedom in museum environments. Free from the structure of curriculum, planning framework, or everyday routines, children can make their own decisions and develop a sense of where their own interests lie (Falk et al., 2006). This is fascinating for curious and attentive adults, who often learn something new about their children too.

Let yourself be surprised by how the children you care for engage with museums!

In this next piece, Chloe Higgins, Teacher, reminds us how learning about the world develops curiosity in our children.

Chloe Higgins: is there a better way to understand the world than to go out and explore it?

I believe a great way to teach children about the world around them is by providing meaningful experiences that resonate with our children and build upon their current interests.

Often when observing or interacting with children, something sparks an interest or discussion, and we know we could do something to enhance that child's knowledge. For example, recently I asked, 'what hatches from an egg?' and almost all the children replied 'chocolate!' At that point, I knew we needed to teach more about lifecycles and arranged for the living eggs to come to Nursery so that the children could observe the changes that happen as a chick hatches from an egg. I wanted the experience to be the starting point for so much more learning about growth and change and something the children would remember!

Whilst this experience did cost money and was incredible for the children, there are so many experiences that we can offer children which are free and effective. We often take our children out into the local community, to the park, the library, the fire station, the postbox and more! We've also created experiences within nursery. For example, we asked the police to visit us. They arrived with a variety of equipment, uniforms and a car for the children to explore and learn about. This led to an enhanced level of role play and some interesting discussions surrounding other people who help us.

I believe it is important to show children 'real things' wherever possible rather than a photo or toy because of the value this adds to a learning experience. For example, seeing a photo of a duck versus visiting the duck pond. From the photo we can learn about the features of a duck but from a visit, we can observe them in their habitat, see their movements, hear the sounds they make. We can compare the similarities and differences from other birds, we can feed them and explore what they need to grow and live. With this, we can offer children multi-sensory and hands-on experiences and provide them with exciting and challenging new language. These experiences encourage children's natural curiosity and make them want to ask questions and learn more about the world around them. Whilst we might not always know the answers, we can teach children how to find them by researching, observing or asking an expert. A child asked a question as we passed a construction site, and I didn't know the answer. So, we asked a builder, and he was happy and able to share more knowledge and detail than I ever could!

Some ideas for experiences you could offer in your setting:

- Litter picking.
- Send letters at the post box.

- Visit the park, library and local sports team.
- Make a list and go to the shops.
- Visit your local care home.
- Create maps of your local area whilst walking.
- Invite people with different occupations to visit.
- Take part in community events.
- Take a bus trip.
- Go to a café.

In this next piece, Tara Paxton and Lisa Greener, from Childsplay Nursery, Newcastle, coauthor a valuable and sensitive explanation of how visits to a local care setting can help children—and older adults—form and enjoy respectful and enjoyable relationships.

Tara Paxton and Lisa Greener: our intergenerational project

Our intergenerational project began when we started visiting a local extra care setting. Taking 12 preschool children into a care environment was a daunting experience for staff who had little or no experience of older adults. Our priority was to allow the children and adults to develop reciprocal, respectful friendships in their own time and at their own pace.

As we all took our first tentative steps into the care village, the Nursery practitioners did not immediately believe that this special 'home from home' environment would be the start of a wonderful learning experience for everyone. On arrival, the children are respectful, taking off their coats and shoes just as they would do at nursery. They walk briskly, with huge beaming smiles to their grownup friends, embracing them and they immediately begin to chat about what they have been up to since their last visit. The children independently select their chosen resources for the day and off they go! Activities are not pre-planned by the staff and are instead chosen by the children or are provocations developed from child and adult observations. One child who had recently visited London wanted to share a book he had purchased with a resident who had worked as a London bus driver. In return, the resident explained he would bring his own London bus figurine on our next visit. Once back at nursery, the child wanted to look for more London memorabilia, so an email was sent out to the nursery families to support us, and we had an abundance of items donated. This was the beginning of a shared interest between the adult and child.

The children spend their time with their older friends and need little if any support from the practitioners. The high levels of engagement are an opportunity for practitioners to observe and record the quality interactions. The pace is slow. The room is filled with the sound of gentle, quiet voices of children chatting. They share everything from family life to what they are doing at the weekend and the residents listen intently. Their whole focus is on the child. The child is listened to, valued and respected. With more residents than children, time and interactions are precious. The children are heard and are responded to by caring, thoughtful and understanding adults.

These adults have a whole lifetime of experience and skills to share with us. They are the best storytellers, best listeners and best artists. They ask the children questions and are truly interested in the children's responses. In turn, the children ask the adults questions about their life. One of the residents worked on a farm for a period and this has been a huge topic of conversation. The children are fascinated by his stories of lambing season and sheep shearing antics. To observe the children and residents working in partnership is something to behold. They truly are 'best friends' and have shared a wealth of experiences in the time we have visited. They have made a connection with these very special people in their lives, and it is having such a huge impact on everyone involved.

Children's quotes

(names of residents and children have been changed)

I was holding the book for Emily because she couldn't. I readed the book for Emily. I told her what was happening using the pictures.

Helen

I loved drawing my pictures with Joyce and Barry. I drawed Brian, me and Bill. We were doing some binoculars and giving them to the residents. I miss the care home. I wish I could live there.

Robin

I feel happy because I love the care home people because they are the best people in the world.

Brian

In this next contribution, Erin Skelton, Senior Teacher at Worksop College|Chief Strategy Officer, Bright Field Consulting, shares some ways that we can have meaningful conversations with our youngest learners about faith and belief.

Erin Skelton: faith and belief in EYFS classrooms

As a Religious Studies, Philosophy and PSHE specialist, I fundamentally believe that some of the most incredible learning around faith, religion and belief can take place in EYFS. Curiosity, imagination and lateral thinking abound in EYFS settings, and when harnessed, the depth and richness of discussion, debate and understanding around culture, belief and identity far exceeds that of children in older years. In a universe of talking animals, fairytales and imaginary friends, there is no unlearning, suspending reality or grappling with rationality and scientific method that comes into play in later key stages.

When it comes to planning meaningful learning opportunities for EYFS around belief, faith and religion, scaffolding of learning episodes is vital, as are these key considerations.

There are no correct answers when learning about these topics and a key outcome for EYFS children is to understand the meaning of 'interpretation' and 'translation' to build knowledge of how people can infer and understand different experiences, texts and morals in different ways. A lovely way to undertake this is by planning an art activity but give the class little guidance about how to interpret the task—you could ask them to create a butterfly for example. The children might paint, colour, use 3-D materials. They will all produce a butterfly but no two will look the same.

Faith and belief are subjective, and we gain knowledge of the world around us in different ways and that affects what we believe and how we believe it. Teaching EYFS children the difference between 'subjective' and 'objective' understanding whilst also teaching about how we gain knowledge of the world is an important distinction. You may even want to delve into some basic philosophical ideas about how we gain religious knowledge, focusing on natural and revealed theological ideas.

Faith is complete trust or confidence in something without requiring any proof, or sometimes even going against logical reasoning. EYFS children have considerable faith in everyday phenomenon; they intuitively believe in the improbably and unprovable. Start with what they can relate to—talking animals, the tooth fairy, imaginary friends—and use this to form the basis of how to expand their understanding of belief. Good religious studies provision in EYFS can lend itself to supporting so many areas of the EYFS curriculum. A nice cross-curricular link is to also build in some science here too, for example that we can't 'see' forces, or you could relate faith to how we use a microscope—sometimes we don't always see what we know to be true.

EYFS children can handle the largest of the 'Big Questions'. For example—why do many people believe in a God that they cannot see? To a Year 11 student that question might be a real challenge as it requires a suspension of logic and a deep dive into a non-evidencable arguments.

Learning about faith, belief and belonging requires a prior understanding of Diversity, Equity, Inclusion and Belonging and civil discourse, so the building blocks of diversity, respect, equity, equality, lived experiences and inclusion should be interwoven into lessons around religion, belief and culture. It's also important to address words like 'tolerance' which they might hear in certain resources or settings, because in the 21st century, we need much more than tolerance in our approach.

In conclusion, teaching faith, belief and culture in EYFS opens a world of rich possibilities for young minds. By tapping into their natural curiosity and imagination, we can foster deep understanding and critical thinking about subjective experiences, diverse worldviews and how people make sense of the world. The flexibility and creativity of the EYFS curriculum provide the perfect framework to explore big questions in a way that resonates with children's innate sense of wonder. Through this early foundation, we not only build knowledge about religion and belief, but we also cultivate empathy, respect and a deeper appreciation of diversity, preparing children to navigate an increasingly complex and interconnected world.

In this next contribution, Danyah Miller, storyteller, writer, trainer, talks us through the innate value in storytelling. Reflections are invited around the impact of using this tool for cognitive growth.

Danyah Miller: shaping young minds: the power of oral storytelling

As far back as I can remember I've had a fascination for and love of nature; Mother Earth, Father Sky, Grandmother Moon, Brother Wind....

In recent times, I've been conscious that the four seasons I experienced growing up are changing, potentially merging into two. My gut instinct is largely backed up by scientific evidence, and I, like many millions of others, am horrified by our urgent climate crisis. The statistics, facts and figures often render me speechless and feeble.

In schools, libraries and at home, I listen to children voicing their fears about climate change and I'm struck that the message they often hear—*your generation will save the planet*—must weigh heavily on small shoulders, surely an impossible burden for them.

Therefore, for me as an oral storyteller, a key part of understanding the world, in EY education, revolves around fostering a deep connection to our planet through song, rhyme and story, using personification and metaphor as part of this. We know that stories engage children's emotions, imagination and intellect in a way that facts and figures cannot. I want to use my storytelling skills to help shape how children perceive the challenges we face, by focusing on a love of nature rather than on fear.

Children in early years learn through imitation. It's our actions not words that influence them most, with the notable exception of storytelling which, studies have confirmed, has a profound and lasting impact on young minds. Sharing simple seasonal stories, poems and rhymes during each season can have a lasting beneficial effect on young children.

By embedding a love of 'Mother Earth', I believe they're more likely to grow up wanting to protect and fight for the environment, at an age when they have agency to do so.

My recommendation is to make up simple, every day, tales about the current season, on a regular basis. By imbuing nature, animals, the weather with personality, children learn to view the world not as something distant or abstract but as something to which they are emotionally invested.

Each season has something unique to offer whether that be Prince Autumn, flying kites, kicking fallen leaves, filling pockets with shiny, smooth conkers, or meeting King Winter in our thick coats, gloves and hats, noses tingling from Jack Frost's icy fingers. You could welcome Lady Spring as she reveals the first tiny snowdrop shoots, the result of the unseen work of the Root Children beneath the soil. Hear the birds' chorus, smell the pink and white blossom, leaves unfurling.... And as Majestic Queen Summer arrives it's time to share stories of fluffy, light clouds morphing from one animal to another, sandcastles, beaches, picnics, blue skies, no shoes, open doors and windows.

Watch as their love for our planet blossoms and grows naturally and organically. Observe how, after sharing a simple story with them, they run out into the playground to experience these things for themselves.

Stories are incredible! They cleverly work their magic to transform children's play, strengthen language acquisition, inspire imaginations, impact their ability to empathise and increase their understanding of the world around them.

I've witnessed that when EY practitioners share oral stories, as well as those from books, it is an effective and profound educational tool, underpinning all literacy and learning.

I believe the foundations of environmental stewardship are laid in the earliest years, not through lectures or warnings, but through play, imagination and a sense of wonder for our beautiful, natural world.

In the final contribution of this chapter, Sandra Beale, Science Communicator to 0-6 and Founder of Toddler and Early Years STEM, shares with us an insight into her journey as a science communicator, and how science, technology, art and maths can be used to inspire our youngest learners.

Sandra Beale: toddler and early years STEM

The best learning environment I feel is one where a young child is unaware that they are learning, an environment where they can explore and discover and feel joy in their accomplishments and the 'I can do it' or 'I made that' moments, where they can seamlessly move from one activity to another without interruption.

I started my Toddler and Early Years STEM sessions almost 10 years ago to help very young children to discover and explore the science around them. Young children are naturally curious, and science and all aspects of STEM including art feed into that natural curiosity.

My sessions are very child led and children can spend as little or as long as they want doing a particular experiment. Very often when a new child starts coming to the session, they want to explore the house and the toys before they participate in the experiments.

I always encourage the parents/care givers to allow the child/children to dip and dive, until they are ready to sit around the table with the others and participate in an experiment.

The experiments are very messy as I often use lots of paint, water, water beads, flour, bicarb, vinegar, food colouring, ice, pom poms, feathers, leaves, sticks, pipe cleaners and many other materials including lots of balloons. Through my experiments children are learning new words, increasing their vocabulary, and developing the ability to look for and find solutions and begin to think creatively.

Unbeknown to them they are learning and absorbing through experimentation and exploration—what happens when colours mix, how to separate colour, the states of matter, how light bends in light refraction, why fruits sink and float, why does a flame burn, what happens when there is air in a bottle, what does carbon dioxide do in a fizzy drink and so much more.

They also come to understand the layers of the earth, the layers of the sea, the way our bodies work, the changing seasons and many other fun and exciting sciences that surround us all the time.

Here is a fun experiment that you could try in your early years setting or at home. It is one of my favourites and teaches children about gravity and elasticity. All you need is a plastic cup, a marble and a balloon.

Cut off the neck of the balloon, stretch the body of the balloon over the mouth of the cup making sure to smooth out any dimples or knobbly bits on the surface, then ask the child/children to drop the marble in the centre of the stretched balloon and watch as it bounces up and down for several seconds before falling off.

Explain to the child/children that the balloon is elastic and regains it shape when the marble bounces upwards. You could experiment with different textures such as a pompom instead of a marble or paper balls and ask the children what they think works best.

In conclusion

This chapter examines how early years education fosters children's understanding of the world through exploration, inquiry and meaningful experiences. Contributors share diverse perspectives, from Bokashi Composting as a tool for sustainability education to museums as spaces for intergenerational storytelling. Discussions explore ways to nurture curiosity, such as real-world experiences, outdoor learning, and engaging with local communities.

The chapter also underscores the role of oral storytelling in shaping children's perceptions of their environment from a young age. Through practical strategies and reflections, this chapter advocates for immersive, hands-on experiences that encourage children to engage with their surroundings, fostering a lifelong sense of curiosity, respect and agency.

Summary of key points

Encouraging curiosity in young people about their world offers numerous benefits:

- Fosters Lifelong Learning: curiosity fuels a desire to learn and explore. When children are curious, they are more likely to seek out new information and experiences, making them lifelong learners.
- Boosts Creativity: curiosity encourages children to think outside the box and come up with unique solutions to problems. It helps them develop their imagination and creativity.
- Enhances Problem-Solving Skills: curious children are more likely to ask questions, experiment and try different approaches to solve problems. This develops their critical thinking and problem-solving abilities.
- Builds Confidence: when children feel empowered to explore their interests and ask questions, they develop a sense of confidence in their abilities to learn and grow.
- Prepares Them for the Future: in our ever-changing world, curiosity is essential for success. It allows children to adapt to new situations, embrace challenges and thrive in a complex and ever-evolving environment.

References

Cambridge Dictionary. (2024). https://dictionary.cambridge.org

Campbell, C. and Howitt, C. (2024). *STEM in Early Childhood Education: Foundations for Scientific Thinking*. Melbourne: Australian Council for Educational Research.

Catling, S. (2006). What do five-year-olds know of the world?: Geographical understanding and play in young children's early learning. *Geography*, 91(1), pp. 55-74.

Chung, K.D. (Mitsy) (2023). Radical dialogue and slow pedagogy in early childhood art education. *Journal of Curriculum and Pedagogy*, pp. 1-18. https://doi.org/10.1080/15505170.2022.2154291

Clark, A. (2022). *Slow Knowledge and the Unhurried Child: Time for Slow Pedagogies in Early Childhood Education*. London: Routledge.

Eberbach, C. and Crowley, K. (2017). From seeing to observing: How parents and children learn to see science in a botanical garden. *Journal of the Learning Sciences*, 26(4), pp. 608-642. https://doi.org/10.1080/10508406.2017.1308867

Falk, J., Dierking, L., and Adams, M. (2006). Living in a learning society: Museums and free-choice learning. In S. Macdonald (Ed.), *A Companion to Museum Studies* (pp. 323-339). Oxford: Blackwell Publishing.

Hirst, N. and Culshaw, A. (2024). Understanding the World 21. In I. Palaiologou (ed.) *The Early Years Foundation Stage: Theory and Practice* (4th edn), London: SAGE Publications, p. 268.

Honoré, C. (2004). *In Praise of Slow: How a Worldwide Movement is Challenging the Cult of Speed*. London: Orion Books.

Louis, S. (2012). *Developing a Sense of Place: The Role of Outdoor Play in Early Childhood Education*. London: National Children's Bureau.

Manyukhina, Y., Haywood, N., Davies, K., and Wyse, D. (2023). Young children's agency in the science museum: Insights from the use of storytelling in object-rich galleries. *International Journal of Science Education, Part B*, pp. 1-17. https://doi.org/10.1080/21548455.2023.2244645

Marinopoulos, S. (2019). *Une stratégie nationale pour la Santé Culturelle-Promouvoir et pérenniser l'éveil culturel et artistique d l'enfant de la naissance à 3 ans dans le lien à son parent (A National Strategy for Cultural Health: Promoting and Sustaining the Child's Cultural and Artistic Awakening from Birth to the Age of Three, Within the Parent-Child Bond.*

Pratama, H., (2024). January. Introduction to geography education based on exploration of the surrounding environment for early children. In *Proceeding of International Conference on Education, Society and Humanity* (Vol. 2, No. 1, pp. 95-101).

Shaffer, S. (2020). *International Thinking on Children in Museums*. Routledge. https://doi.org/10.4324/9780429296697#

Tazi, Z., Vidal, H., and Stein, K. (2015). Arte juntos/art together: Promoting school readiness among latino children through parent engagement and social inclusion in a suburban museum. *Museum and Society, 13*(2), pp. 158-166.

Tishman, S. (2017). *Slow Looking: The Art and Practice of Learning Through Observation* (1st edn.). Abingdon: Routledge.

Walklate, J.A. (2022). *Time and the Museum*. Routledge. https://doi.org/10.4324/9781003248446

Wallis, N., and Noble, K. (2022). Leave only footprints: How children communicate a sense of ownership and belonging in an art gallery. *European Early Childhood Education Research Journal, 30*(3), pp. 344-359. https://doi.org/10.1080/1350293X.2022.2055100

Wallis, N., and Noble, K. (2023). The slow museum: The affordances of a university art museum as a nurturing and caring space for young children and their families. *Museum Management and Curatorship*, pp. 1-22. https://doi.org/10.1080/09647775.2023.2269145

11 Expressive arts and design

Poppy Gibson

Introduction

Expressive arts, like music, dance, drama and visual arts, ignite early learners' imaginations. Through these mediums, children explore emotions, develop creativity, and build confidence. Music fosters language skills, rhythm and coordination. Dance encourages physical expression and social interaction. Drama helps children understand different perspectives and develop communication skills. Visual arts nurture fine motor skills, problem solving, and self-expression. These experiences provide a foundation for lifelong learning, fostering curiosity, critical thinking, and a love for exploration. In this chapter, nine experienced practitioners and professionals share inspiration for how we can enjoy expressive arts and design in the Early Years.

Pondering question: how can we move teaching and learning in this aspect from being taught as discrete learning modules to be embedded into the curriculum?

Take a moment to think back to your own childhood; are there any songs, rhymes or dances that you can still remember?

Expressive arts, encompassing music, dance, drama and visual arts, play a crucial role in igniting the imaginations of children even as young as the early years (Crowe, 2006). These creative outlets provide a unique platform for children to explore, express and make sense of their world and allow spaces where young children can develop cognitive, social and emotional skills (Bloomfield and Childs, 2013). Looking at the range of children's toys and media available, it is clear that music, dance and learning through rhymes are ways that young children can be engaged and stimulated. Having experiences of the expressive arts can offer comfort and joy even from birth, through a parent or carer's singing of a lullaby or a toddler's activity with playdough (Lemon and Garvis, 2023). Learning through the arts for three- to five-year-olds also builds self-esteem, promotes development of important social and spatial skills, and contributes to wellbeing (Lemon and Garvis, 2023).

Why creativity is fundamental to development

The integration of expressive arts into early childhood education offers numerous benefits such as developing imagination, cognitive development and emotional development (Holochwost, Goldstein, and Wolf, 2021). Expressive arts also offer opportunity for physical development through movement in dance, drama and music. Music has been shown to stimulate a child's auditory senses and evokes a range of emotions. Singing songs, playing instruments and moving to music encourages imaginative thinking as children create stories, express feelings and explore different sounds (Liu, 2023). Research indicates that musical engagement enhances language development, memory and spatial reasoning, all of which are vital for imaginative thought (Ahern, 2023). Music literacy in the early years has also been shown to enhance good speech development (Arasomwan and Mashiy, 2021). Teacher confidence in teaching the expressive arts such as music is also important to consider, and this will be explored throughout this chapter as well (Chua, 2022).

We begin with an overview of expressive arts and design from Courtney McAllister, Post Graduate Researcher, who invites thoughts and analysis of how theory impacts decisions made to provision.

Courtney McAllister: expressive arts and design

Expressive arts and design (EAD) is a broad concept and should explore a wide range of what children see, hear and understand and how they then exhibit self-expression, vocabulary and their ability to communicate through the arts (DfE, 2025: 11). This area of learning is important to children's development where there is interpretation of the experiences they have participated in and observed, displaying cultural awareness and making connections to wider society. The Early Years Foundation Stage (EYFS) incorporates this area of learning into statutory guidance through early learning goals (ELGs) of 'Creating with Materials' and 'Being Imaginative and Expressive' where early years educators should make learning ambitious for all children (DfE 2025: 15–16). Ofsted (2024) emphasises the importance of children in early years education to enjoy learning and participating in this area of development, where there is a broad range of how this can evoke deep learning and connections to give them the best start in life.

There are links to early childhood education, dance education and movement having key relationships to children's cognitive development, brain development and intelligence (Faber, 2017). There is research of the existence of an 'Isadora Effect' which proposes the fundamental role that motor development has with brain development, where young children having an early understanding of movement and gesture can have symbolic meaning and impact on their individual development. There are additional benefits to shaping dance, music and movement with young children beyond enhancing physical health: focus, cognitive development and cultural and emotional benefits as a necessity for holistic development. Considering this, children can be given valuable opportunities to develop creativity and problem solving, and it is vital that early years educators know when children can be introduced to any techniques, tools or materials to apply this area of learning effectively.

There are complex views of EAD and how this can foster children's development through cultural and artistic awareness and how practitioners support learning through varied opportunities to experience different genres of expression, arts and design over time. Through the

ELGS in the EYFS (2025), children safely exploring and experimenting with tools, texture, form and function, through repetition and their experiences translating into their learning, can enhance their creativity and vocabulary to extend into role play and stories. This further supports children with their imagination and how they have quality experiences within this area of learning through regular opportunities of self-expression.

It is key that this area of learning should be well thought out and children are presented with a wide range of experiences and opportunities to understand this specific area of learning. With limited research relating to how EAD can be specifically planned or sequenced in children's learning, there is a broad range of learning and opportunities to be had for children to develop new skills, appreciation and become creative. The role of the adult is crucial, with their experiences and prior knowledge applied to offer children a responsive environment for their sensory experiences, and should focus on efforts children make and their skills.

By encouraging creativity, we nurture curious minds, prepare children for a future of innovation and lay the foundation for lifelong learning.

Building on an overview of EAD, in this next piece, Amy Marrison, Reception Class Teacher, Catton Grove Primary School, Norwich, reminds us how creativity is so important in child development.

Amy Marrison: nurturing creativity in the Early Years

Embedding expressive arts and design into the Early Years curriculum can be achieved through carefully considered provision, where children freely access the creative resources needed to develop their play and learning effectively. The following ideas are starting points for building opportunities for children to express themselves.

Stocking up resources

To encourage independent creativity, making resources easily accessible and appropriately challenging is key. When resourcing an art area, materials including paints, fabric and recycled plastics and cardboard all allow children to explore freely. Children choosing what is needed to complete a project develops the planning and organisational skills needed for the creative process. Providing paint tubes that are self-service, as well as pots and a range of brush sizes that can be freely chosen by the child, deepens the learning experience.

Provocations

Well thought out provocations can be added to the learning environment in order to further inspire expressive arts and design. These items should always be set up as a response to what has been observed in play (Haughley and Hill, 2017). Adults can then reciprocate by adding resources that are changeable in nature, in order to develop play further. For instance, an interest in drawing faces has been observed and cork mats, glass beads and mirrors have been planned into the environment to build upon that creative expression. Loose parts such as this can also be part of the continuous provision that is available every day. These are materials that have no specific directions, in turn supporting creativity and innovation. They allow children to manipulate, control and change the use of the objects provided (Daly and Beloglovsky, 2015) and possibilities are unlimited.

Imaginative play

Providing opportunities for children to take on new characters and explore scenarios through role play allows children to develop their creative ideas. Bryce-Clegg (2019) explains that role play is more effective when children have had the opportunity to experience the real situation prior to a scenario being set up in the setting. Arranging visits to local shops and libraries, as well as inviting members of the community into school who are experts in the field, will give the children a tangible starting point which they can base their play on. Providing open-ended resources such as colourful materials inspires children to make their own props for roleplay. This allows them to reach new levels of creativity, where they are involved in the process of planning and designing the roleplay, as well as the art of acting it out.

Finding a rhythm

Music, dance and performance are all forms of expression that are inherent within daily life in an early years classroom. Songs and rhymes can be used to establish routines and support children to remember facts quickly. Whether the children are learning the days of the week or recalling their number bonds, a song is a vehicle for productive thought processes. Musical activities allow children to show their identity and heritage and contribute towards their inner self-worth (Sarrazin, 2018). Props such as ribbons, colourful scarves and instruments enhance the environment, as does access to a diverse collection of music.

By integrating these elements, educators can create a rich, dynamic environment where children are encouraged to express themselves creatively and submerge themselves into a world of possibility.

In this next contribution, three coauthors, Sarah Eastaff, Sarah Clough and Alison Fleetwood, share their Tuneful Chatter arts workshops that have been running at a primary school in Doncaster. The workshops offer a useful platform for personal reflection and consideration of their role within am engaging EAD provision.

Sarah Eastaff, Alison Fleetwood, Sarah Clough: tuneful chatter: Embedding arts in early years practice

It's Thursday morning at a primary school in Doncaster, and the children in nursery are giggling, gasping and paying attention. They've started their weekly Tuneful Chatter arts session, and their hall has been transformed into a forest. Leaves, sticks and hues of green are everywhere. They can hear bird song, the wind blowing—today, they'll use their imaginations to meet insects, birds and hibernating animals around their forest. With the help of Emma, the artist leading the session, they will sing songs, warm their bodies up and continue developing key skills like taking turns, listening to each other, and learning new vocabulary. 'This is magic!' one student says.

Tuneful Chatter is a programme of artistic provision in Doncaster, delivered in partnership with the Local Authority, Cast theatre and Darts, the participatory arts charity. We work with nurseries, schools and family hubs to deliver arts workshops for children aged 0–5 and their adults.

This work is supported by a regular CPD programme, where artists and practitioners come together to learn from each other's expertise, plan together and build excellent practice. In a normal week in Doncaster in 2024, there are 14 arts workshops happening as part of Tuneful Chatter.

This work is funded by Arts Council England through their Place Partnership Scheme and by the City of Doncaster Council. In 2022, Doncaster Primary Schools told us that pupils aged 3-5 were struggling. They didn't know how to listen, focus, take turns or interact with adults, and these difficulties continue today. Tuneful Chatter was developed in response to a consultation with Doncaster Early Years practitioners in 2022, which highlighted that over 90% of specialists felt that the pandemic had a significantly negative impact on 0-5-year olds' development:

> I've worked in nursery 15-20 years. This year I could see a massive difference in terms of communication and language, PSED—they didn't know how to play with each other.
>
> We've noticed a downward trend in our children's vocabulary skills since the pandemic. This is particularly in our 0-3-year-olds.

By delivering regular, high-quality arts sessions in a range of settings, practitioners are seeing real changes in their children. 'Tuneful Chatter gives children the confidence to express themselves. Our children bring their confidence back into the room and practitioners have seen this through their purposeful interactions.' Early Years Practitioner. Baseline data captured at the start of the programme demonstrates that 74% of the children involved are not meeting their developmental milestones across CLL and PSED. Interestingly the baseline data suggests that there is a slightly higher level of delay in PSED than CLL with 75% being delayed in PSED in comparison to 73% in CLL.

We know there is incredible value in working directly with families and this is embedded across Tuneful Chatter. In our sessions with children and their parents/carers, we've seen relationships form between adults and between the children themselves.

> I always take my little boy to Tuneful Chatter, and he loves it so much. The artists are so great with him and I've seen a huge boost in his confidence because of the time and effort they put in.
>
> Parent

It is crucial that we meet each child where they are and follow their lead. One parent highlighted that

> For us, the biggest thing that has helped with that, for Flynn, is the fact that staff have been really understanding that he is developing a little differently to others, and they're giving him that space.... It has just been really welcoming and lovely.

This work is funded for three years, and we can build significant relationships with Early Years educators, artists, children and their grown-ups.

In this next contribution, Jayne Carter, coauthor and independent Early Years Consultant, invites considerations on possibility thinking, showcasing the importance all adults have in ensuring that this key aspect of EAD is understood and included in provision.

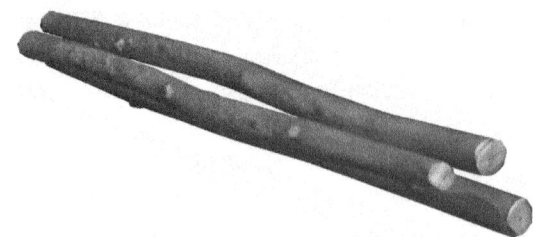

Figure 11.1 A collection of sticks or....

Jayne Carter: the role of possibility thinking in the Early Years

What is this?

Yes it's a stick.... but it could be a magical stirrer of a potion, a new and wonderful way of communicating with your friends, a guitar or whatever your creative Early Years child wants it to be (Figure 11.1).

A perfect example of possibility thinking.

What is possibility thinking? Literally, allowing yourself to think of possibilities; moving away from the given to a new place of 'it could be'.

When we allow ourselves to think of a 'possible' we adopt an air of trial and error, testing and let's see what happens-ness.

We are given the freedom to have a go and see if it fits in our own head; practising and using current ideas and thoughts to see if they gel with a new idea, challenge or scenario.

Possibility thinking offers the chance to wonder, to speculate and the permission to dare to dream.

What an opportunity! What potential to develop an inquisitive mind; thirsty to branch out and explore.

So why is the development of a possibility thinking attitude important for our children?

Possibility thinking can be seen implicitly in the EYFS framework; predominately in the characteristics of effective teaching and learning recommendations. There is evidence of the fostering of possibility thinking littered through each characteristic, which in my mind means that it should play an important part in the experiences which children are offered.

For example, in 'Playing & Exploring' there is the sub section of 'being willing to have a go'. This crucial characteristic suggests that the development and ongoing support of a positive mindset to take that chance and use possibility thinking to find out about the world could lead children to know about possibility thinking and its role in their ongoing adventures.

In 'Creative & Thinking Critically' the whole sub section called 'having their own ideas' encourages children to seek out alternatives, drawing on the usual and venturing into the potential to test and expand their emerging ideas and thoughts.

How can we support all our children to know the possibility of possibility thinking, be able to use it as an additional tool in their learning toolbox and meet their own personal challenges of exploration?

- Teach the skill of possibility thinking. This may come really naturally to some children (look out for the ones who have a secure grounding of the characteristics mentioned above) but to other children they may not have this already ignited within them. I would argue that it is there in everyone but like other things it just needs a bit of coaxing to flourish and embed.
- Look for opportunities to include this explicit teaching in everyday experiences and activities. (Do we always do this in literacy inputs for example? What would happen if more were included in scientific explorations I wonder?') Make **'WHAT IF'** a core driver. Helpful 'possibility questions' might include
    - What does that remind you of?
    - What do you think might happen next?
    - What do you/don't you like about this - why?
    - Is there another way?
    - How could we...?
    - What would you do if...?
- Be a possibility thinker yourself. Model the choices you make with explicit vocab, discussing your choices and the reasons for them. Sprinkled with a thick dose of excitement and enthusiasm it's sure to exude a positive vibe. It also gives children permission to have a go themselves. If you don't know that you can do this then chances are you won't even attempt it.
- Provide the resources to practise possibility thinking. Plan for resources which have the potential to be more than a single thing... resources which plant the idea of 'it could be anything' in your mind.
- Celebrate the extent of possibility thinking... strengthen the impact of ideas with additional representations, maybe in visual form, creative representations, dance, drama... anything to embed the ideas. The more connections children have between what they are learning, the deeper it remains as a working memory, ready to be recalled for future implementation.
- Foster a nurturing possibility thinking environment. These could includetaking risks—feeling comfortable with not knowing and embracing the opportunity for new learning that this provides: 'shall we see what happens if...?'
    - rising to new challenges—viewing 'being stuck' as a valuable learning opportunity and an opportunity for moving forward in our thinking.
    - being willing to share and make mistakes—demonstrating that this is an important part of the learning journey and not something to avoid: 'I've gone wrong here. How can I do it better?'
    - being imaginative—there is more than one way of solving a problem—playing with different perspectives and lines of enquiry: 'Can we do that another way?'

Empowering children to develop the skills of possibility thinking opens up the creative world for them. It provides them with the tools to be able to immerse themselves into the world of imagination, make believe and adventure.

In this following contribution, Natasha Nechat-Murphy, Teaching Assistant, London, United Kingdom shares her passion for art in the early years and the skills that high-quality art provision develops.

Natasha Nechat-Murphy: the value of art

Art is an invaluable and enriching experience that plays a crucial role in the early years of a child's development. Creativity, self-expression and exploration of the world are fostered, whilst also promoting mental, physical and social growth. As educators, it is important to expand our understanding of expressive art and design and recognise its contribution to children's holistic development.

Art is deeply embedded into various areas of the curriculum. For example, it enhances fine motor skills and control through mark making which serves as a foundation for reading and writing. This is crucial for physical development. Additionally, art provides opportunities for communication and language development, as children express themselves verbally or non-verbally, whilst boosting their confidence and fostering communication skills. Art also plays a significant role in personal, social and emotional development as children can share ideas, build relationships with peers and develop a sense of self. Moreover, art promotes mathematical skills by developing visual processing and spatial awareness. Children learn to remember and reproduce what they see through shapes, colours and fine details, while also considering proportions and size. Lastly, by using natural resources, planning outdoor art activities and exploring themes and topics, children develop a deeper understanding of the world.

Based on my own experiences, I have witnessed how much children value the opportunity to create their own drawings. It is important to allow independent selection of art resources, as this gives children a sense of choice and control. Freehand drawing nurtures problem-solving skills, critical thinking, adaptation, fine motor control, social skills, positive well-being and communication. Freehand drawing can be easily incorporated into any setting, whether indoors or outdoors, allowing children to further their learning across all developmental areas. This approach ensures that learning is not just short term but more memorable and long lasting. Themed activities, on the other hand, require more structure as the practitioner guides the process and outcome. It's important to incorporate children's previous experiences and artistic interests so these activities are engaging and stimulating. For example, during a Mother's Day activity, I decided that the children create their own heartfelt gifts with a hand-drawn picture of themselves and their mum or special person. By incorporating relevant early learning goals, I was able to focus on both their academic achievements and personal interests. Themed drawing may present challenges in deciding what to draw, but it also helps develop problem-solving, critical thinking, adaptation, communication and resilience skills in children. Striking a balance between choice and control in both freehand and themed activities allow children to develop holistically and thrive in challenges.

As a practitioner, I've learnt the importance of providing regular opportunities for children to engage in high-quality art experiences that explore and develop their artistic skills using a variety of materials and media. The quality, frequency, repetition and depth of these experiences are crucial for their overall development and progress, as they enhance their

Expressive arts and design 143

understanding, self-expression, vocabulary and communication skills. By fostering a love for art in the early years, we lay a solid foundation for their future learning, while also igniting their curiosity and imagination.

In this next contribution, experienced Primary Teacher Lucy Hennell shares an imaginative and fun activity, explaining both the 'what' and 'the 'why' involved.

Lucy Hennell: role play town

This activity aims to engage children in imaginative play while fostering understanding of the real world around them, the natural world, and various concepts related to science, social skills and creativity.

Materials Needed:

- Road tape (or masking tape with lines drawn on)
- Building materials (blocks, magnetic tiles)
- Free artificial grass sample (available online easily)
- Mini road signs and cones
- Mini fences
- Animal figures or character figures (including vehicles; tractors and cars)

Begin by planning the town and asking the children: What types of buildings do we see in our town? Where do these animals live? (linking to science) Who might live in your town?

Activity Steps

1. **Building the Town**:
    - Use the building blocks or magnetic tiles to create houses, schools and other buildings. Encourage children to work together and share ideas about what their town needs.
    - Discuss the purpose of each building and who might live or work there. For example: the doctors are where people go if they are unwell. The school is where children go to learn and make friends.
2. **Creating the Roadway**:
    - Lay down road tape to design roads in the town. Use mini road signs and cones to mark roadworks; have you seen these signs before?
    - Introduce concepts like traffic rules and traffic lights. Discuss how these signs help keep us safe, linking to road safety.
3. **Animal Habitats**:
    - Integrate animal figures into the play. Create areas where different animals live, like farms, forests or ponds.
    - Explore science concepts like habitats. Ask children questions about the animals: Where do they live? What do they eat?

4. **Imaginative Scenarios**:
    - Encourage open-ended play. Suggest fun scenarios, such as:
    - All the character figures going for a day out to a zoo.
    - A sudden storm causing houses to fall down, prompting a rebuilding project.

   This will support the children to narrate their own stories as they play, promoting creativity and storytelling.

5. **Fine Motor Skills Development opportunities**:
    - Use drawing materials to create maps or signs. Children can draw their own road signs or sketch out their town layout.

6. **Empathy and Community**:
    - Role-play different community members, such as doctors, farmers or construction workers. Discuss what these roles entail and the importance of empathy in these professions.
    - Create scenarios where children can help each other, like taking care of an injured animal.

This role play town activity not only encourages creativity and imagination but also helps children make connections to their own experiences and the world around them. By integrating science, storytelling and community awareness, children develop a holistic understanding of their environment, enhancing both social and cognitive skills. The possibilities for exploration and learning are endless, ensuring that every play session is unique and engaging.

Hannah Foster, Reception Teacher, offers additional ideas of how to implement EAD provision within Early Years, focusing on the significance of a thematic approach in helping children engage and connect.

Hannah Foster: expressive arts and design: where pupils really come to life!

One of my favourite quotes is: "If you judge a fish by its ability to climb a tree, it will spend its life thinking it is stupid." So many of our children have so much to offer the world but find the constraints of a classroom extremely challenging. Once we get to an older age, we pick the things we are good at and only focus on those things. Yet at school we expect so much from everyone despite their personal interests or talents.

I have found a 'thematic approach' to teaching extremely useful. Linking everything (all subjects) to interests or a story/theme that the children are familiar with helps to take away the sense of 'new' and any fear this may evoke. It can also provide them with a sense of achievement and familiarity before the lesson has even begun which can improve their confidence to tackle new concepts and as a result, improving their resilience and lesson participation too.

For example, we have been studying the 'Magic Box' poem by Kit Brown.

Our children scored below national average and we found their comprehension as a whole was poor, despite good reading ability. The children did not really understand what they were reading.

We took a different approach to comprehension and studied the poem first, acting out the words with actions and drawing, story boards and artwork. When they came to do the comprehension their answers and understanding had drastically deepened.

The use of expressive arts and design really helps provide the children with a vehicle for expression and allows them to communicate their thoughts, feelings and ideas to the world in their own magical and accessible way.

From my own research study 'What role do dance and drama play in supporting engagement in the Early Years?' I was able to explore the unique power of both these creative forms in enhancing learning in the early years. A key finding from the study included,

> Despite the obvious focus on core subjects in the curriculum, I believe better cross curricular links can continue to be made to incorporate dance and drama to benefit pupils. This is particularly evident from the research conducted which clearly demonstrated that schools should be adopting a more positive attitude and expansive approach to utilising dance and drama rather than merely restricting it to end of term plays.

Through the study, there was also significant evidence to show how this cross curricular approach is able to enhance not only knowledge, but the skills involved in being an early years learner, especially the skills, attitudes and dispositions included in the characteristics framework.

Whilst many of these cross curricular experiences occur naturally as supporting children in their play-based explorations, this study also reinforces the significance of planning for these. This planning could then be the 'hook' for children to use their creative skills further.

In conclusion

This chapter examines the role of expressive arts and design in early years education, exploring how music, dance, drama and visual arts support children's cognitive, emotional and social development. Contributors provide practical insights into fostering artistic exploration, including strategies for embedding expressive arts throughout the curriculum. Discussions cover the significance of open-ended resources, imaginative play and possibility thinking in inspiring curiosity, problem solving and collaboration. Case studies, such as the Tuneful Chatter programme, illustrate how engaging arts initiatives enhance children's confidence, language skills and interpersonal interactions. The overarching theme is that expressive arts should be integrated thoughtfully into early years provision, ensuring children have regular opportunities to engage, create and express themselves in ways that nurture their identity and holistic growth.

Summary of key points

- **Boosts Creativity and Imagination**: art, music and drama provide a safe space for children to explore their imaginations, experiment with different ideas and express themselves freely. Through these activities, they learn to think outside the box and develop unique perspectives.
- **Enhances Cognitive Development**: these activities stimulate various cognitive skills, including problem solving, critical thinking, memory and language development. For example, learning to play an instrument improves listening skills and pattern recognition, while acting helps children understand different emotions and perspectives.

- **Builds Confidence and Self-Esteem**: engaging in the arts provides children with opportunities to showcase their talents, receive positive feedback and build a sense of accomplishment. This can significantly boost their self-esteem and confidence, which are essential for their overall wellbeing.
- **Encourage possibility thinking to foster creativity**: by embracing possibility thinking, children learn to explore beyond conventional uses of materials, ideas and expressions. This approach nurtures curiosity and problem solving, allowing children to take risks, experiment with imaginative scenarios and develop a mindset of innovation that extends beyond the arts.
- **Embedding expressive arts and design throughout the curriculum**: rather than treating creative subjects as isolated experiences, integrating expressive arts across different areas of learning enhances engagement and deepens understanding.

References

Ahern, L. (2023). Exploring the development and integration of music in preschool settings in Ireland.

Arasomwan, D.A. and Mashiy, N.J. (2021). Early childhood care and education educators' understanding of the use of music-based pedagogies to teach communication skills. *South African Journal of Childhood Education*, 11(1), pp. 1-12.

Bloomfield, A. and Childs, J. (2013). *Teaching Integrated Arts in the Primary School: Dance, Drama, Music, and the Visual Arts*. David Fulton Publishers.

Bryce-Clegg, A. (2019). *The Family Interview, Alistair Bryce-Clegg*. Available at: https://www.famly.co/blog/alistair-bryce-clegg-interview. (Accessed 23 November 2024).

Chua, S.H.L. (2022). *Teaching music in Singapore early childhood settings: perspectives from early childhood educators, music educators and early childhood music educators* (Doctoral dissertation).

Crowe, S. (2006). *Dance, drama and music: a foundation for education: a study on implementing the performing arts in the Early Years of education* (Doctoral dissertation, RMIT University).

Daly, L. and Beloglovsky, M. (2015). *Loose Parts: Inspiring Play in Young Children* St. Paul, MN: Redleaf Press.

DfE (2025). Early years foundation stage statutory framework for group and school-based providers. Setting the standards for learning, development and care for children from birth to five. Available at: https://assets.publishing.service.gov.uk/media/687105a381dd8f70f5de3ea9/EYFS_framework_for_group_and_school_based_providers_.pdf (Accessed 21 July 2025).

Faber, R. (2017). The Isadora Effect: Movement, Gesture and Symbolic Meaning in Early Childhood, *Dance Education in Practice*, 3(2), pp. 12-19.

Haughley, S. and Hill, N. (2017). *Provocation: A Start Up Guide*. Available at: www.fairydustteaching.com (Accessed 23 November 2024).

Holochwost, S.J., Goldstein, T.R., and Wolf, D.P. (2021). Delineating the benefits of arts education for children's socioemotional development. *Frontiers in Psychology*, 12, p. 624712.

Lemon, N. and Garvis, S. (2023). The arts. In D. Pendergast and S. Garvis (eds.) *Teaching Early Years: Curriculum, Pedagogy and Assessment* (pp. 84-99). Abingdon: Routledge.

Liu, Y. (2023). The influence of music activities on children's creative thinking development. In L. Zhang (ed.) *SHS Web of Conferences* (Vol. 180, p. 04001). Les Ulis: EDP Sciences.

Ofsted. (2024). *Early Years Education: Best Start in Life*. London: Ofsted.

Sarrazin, N. (2018). *Music and the Child*. Geneseo NY: Open SUNY Textbooks.

12 Observation-assessment and planning cycle

Jayne Carter

Introduction

In the revision of the EYFS (DfE, 2021), Early Years practitioners and leaders welcomed a change to the assessment process. Reassuringly, this change remained in subsequent versions of the statutory framework (DfE, 2023a, 2025). More flexibility was given to practitioners to plan and implement a bespoke curriculum, with an emphasis on increasing time spent with children, rather than spending this precious time completing paperwork. The wealth of contributions included in this chapter provide a comprehensive, insightful and beneficial account of how practitioners have embraced this shift in their own practice. They have all illuminated their personal journey, acknowledging the plans, the adaptations and steps they have taken towards developing a secure observation, assessment and planning cycle.

Pondering question: what are the fundamental aspects which contribute to an OAP cycle which supports all children's learning?

One somewhat expected response to the 'no more endless tick sheets' feeling was that some practitioners took this to mean that no paperwork at all was necessary, especially as the EYFS and Ofsted advocated 'professional judgement' as the overriding evidence to support judgments. Whilst not denying that professional judgment is indeed vital (after all practitioners in the early years are really good at developing strong relationships with their children and families), with no means of recording, however basic this may be, the OAP cycle may not even be looked at or not followed in its entirety. In my opinion, this would potentially mean that the curriculum would move to a simple set of activities, with no relevance to whether they were supporting the child at all.

A vision for assessment

Julian Grenier, in his book *Working with the Revised Early Years Foundation Stage: Principles into Practice* (2021), provides such a useful model of what this new world of assessment could look like.

Page 28 of Grenier's book shows a cycle of planning, observation and assessment, intending to illuminate the importance of each stage in the ongoing professional reflection of provision. With practitioner subject knowledge and expertise at the heart, this diagram includes

148 *Early Years Essentials*

further questions to shape practice. I have found it so helpful in either beginning the development of what a school/setting OAP cycle should like for their own community or to act as an audit to reinvigorate the process once again.

Being given the opportunity to reflect on the impact of this cycle for my own early years support, I am reminded of the value of Alison Clark's body of work on the mosaic approach (Clark & Moss, 2011). This approach provides a valuable insight into the child's world and upskills practitioners in not only understanding the importance of this world but also direct ways to maximise their own children's voices within their own settings/schools. Is it possible to integrate both of these expert approaches into a model which both supports practitioners and celebrates children's active involvement in a true inclusive manner? By including children's voices, through the choices they make and the representations they choose, does an OAP cycle provide the golden thread for professional decisions? I am considering how a child's voice could be added to this (or any other model of OAP) so it becomes manageable yet useful. Clark stipulates in the mosaic approach a myriad of strategies which capture the process a child goes through as well as the outcome of all their deliberations when learning. It blends traditional assessment procedures (observation, specific task-based activities) with more participatory activities to emphasise true involvement. The latter include children's photographs of what they deem important or special and interesting, making maps to present their own adventures in their classrooms and consultation into any redevelopments to their inside or outside learning spaces.

The OAP cycle in practice: shared conversations, shared purpose

The way I have found beneficial when supporting an early year's team is to start with an honest conversation about their own views and opinions on their existing OAP cycle. Allowing them to articulate this offers a useful insight for me in knowing what is important to them, as well as, hopefully, providing opportunities for practitioners to evaluate and reflect themselves. These shared conversations ensure that there is a collaborative agreement on what each part means for them as the adults in the room, with next steps generally moving from the '*what*' to the '*how*' and systematically moving towards the '*why*'. When introducing the 'voice of the child' aspect to these conversations I am mindful of not simply paying lip service to the phrase. I want this particular discussion to be fruitful in changing opinions, dynamic in being authentic to the children. Starting again from what they already do well is an effective place to start, evoking a sense of established and shared success. I find that there are so many ideas which many early years teams put into practice; some not consistently, some integrated to what normally happens. Capturing these and adding to the OAP model connects their '*what*' to their '*why*' within a bigger pedagogical framework. For example; planning for children to take photographs is without doubt a useful, engaging, fun activity to do; it provides children with the opportunity to be grown up, take on a role, even adding to a child's ongoing narrative and story. As illustrated in the OAP model, a reasonable question should be 'what's the point/purpose? Does it provide additional opportunities for me as the practitioner to know more about what the child thinks, feels, communicates?' Without this solid foundation of purpose it is practically impossible to move to the analysis or the next step's reflections the OAP dictates. This is where a seemingly participatory activity, such as taking photographs, paradoxically ceases to be truly participatory. Its potential for supporting and sustaining learning stops if or when the child is involved in it. What can move it towards an active engagement model; one in which full engagement comes from everyone engaged in it? Agreeing on the purpose of taking photographs is a reasonable place to commence but 'purpose' for whom? Is it to enhance learning by offering another media tool for the child to use, is it to act as a summative assessment tool to capture a bank of newly learning knowledge and skills or is it for the child to provide their thoughts through a different communication model? Any or all of these deepens the photographs use. I would like to suggest here that a practitioner's purpose can be added to discussions of the OAP cycle as a way to cement this deeper reflection. If I am using photographs into my provision and expect children to take the photographs and talk about them, what will I, as the practitioner, contribute to this improvement plan? The precious photographs are worth more than simply being stored on a shared drive or printed out and stuck in a book never to be visited again! On page 71 of Grenier's book, the significance of practitioner feedback is emphasised, presenting not only the notion of this in practice, but also granting the 'permission', or reassurance to interact with children through play. Perhaps this is an example of one of those trickier aspects to navigate when there is a period of change. I distinctly remember, both as a practitioner and as an Early Years curriculum adviser, the 'tiara age' where assessments were very clearly a passive experience whereby practitioners adapted a mute model of interaction, merely observing the slightest movement or utterance from the child which was quickly noted on a post-it or included in a novel-length observation. What a relief that we can actually be involved in play with our children! The example included in Grenier's book shows very practically how this can take place.

> Whilst some observations are written down, analysed, and acted on in planning, there is a second, more powerful and more immediate cycle. That's when practitioners notice something about what a child is doing, or saying, and they give the child helpful feedback there and then. They might point something out: 'I think that block there is a bit wonky, perhaps that's why your tower is shaking?' Or they might encourage a child to notice something whilst they draw: 'can you see that the petals aren't quite that colour? You've done a really good job, but maybe it's worth another try at mixing the paints?
>
> (Grenier, J. 2021)

The above advice propels the practitioner and child towards a more secure partnership. The child knows that their adult has noticed something that they are doing and wants to talk about it. A powerful motivator definitely for the child but also hopefully for the practitioner. Another example of truly including children's voices. I would add here my personal favourite, 'If I wanted to do that just like you, what should I do first?' Who doesn't want to be acknowledged, valued and given the status of the expert? Returning to the OAP model, empowering the child to take the teacher/practitioner role provides such a valuable insight into the child's world, which can certainly be added to the journal of a child's achievements, as well as directing their next steps to either enhance current joy or introduce new adventures to them.

Involving a wider audience into the OAP cycle

As well as supporting brilliant early years teams, I am often asked to support leaders who would like to understand more about Early Years. Such a privilege to be able to do this! In similar conversations regarding the OAP cycle with early years teams, when asking for similar conversations with leaders, often conversations about the cycle start with the assessment category, more specifically the data generated. Phrases like value added, narrowing the gap, accelerated progress and outcomes direct these discussions. It is understandable that these conversations are like this, especially in a system where quality is often measured by looking at endless spreadsheets or number crunching analysis. Not to diminish their importance in a whole school approach to teaching and learning, but gently guiding back to the entire OAP cycle places the data and excels in perspective and context. Supporting a respectful and informed dynamic between practitioner and leaders, managing the expectations important to both groups is essential. Without this, an imbalance could happen which could result in additional workload being added to the already crowded to-do list, evoke miscommunications and stir feelings of inequality in expectations. In these conversations, I have engaged leaders in considering their role within each part of the OAP cycle, in order to create appreciation and cohesion. What do they want to happen at each stage? What's the intention at a leadership level of, say, the observation stage? What are the practical decisions which could be made and put in place to ensure it's a shared process between practitioners and leaders. For example: deadlines, correct resources, time. Are practitioners involved in the data discussions or do they (as in one of my past schools) receive a data report, including a printed summary of what their numbers mean?!

The current Ofsted School Inspection Handbook (2024) includes the following descriptor when inspecting, emphasising further the power of these interactions in ultimately improving progress and outcomes for the children.

'449. Inspectors will take account of all the judgements made across the evaluation schedule. In particular, they should consider:

- the extent to which leaders and other staff plan, design and implement the Early Years curriculum'

Whilst any occurrence of change can be tricky, it's important to make sure that any challenges are discussed and people feel that a shared agreement is reached, particularly when maintaining quality in teaching and learning. Where the transition from the previous to the current EYFS was smooth, key changes were fully understood by all, with the unique opportunity to re-evaluate provision welcomed.

> My final point is this: let's remember why we all went into working in the Early Years. We're here because we want to give every child a great first experience of playing and learning outside their home. We want to play our part in giving them the best possible start to their learning. Should we be putting so much effort into creating masses of unhelpful tracking data about children? I'm arguing that it's time to stop that. Instead, let's put our efforts into improving learning for all children.
>
> Grenier, J (2021)

In this first contribution, Tricia Mohamed, Early Years Consultant: Play Practitioners, builds on the importance of an effective OAP cycle by sharing a personal example of how this is used within their own early years setting.

Tricia Mohamed: harnessing the unique potential of every child

The following is based on my experience as a class teacher, EYFS leader and consultant in London-based and International schools.

Why is observing children necessary?

Recognising that a child possesses their thoughts, ideas, feelings and motivations is an affirmation of their autonomy. Observing children is crucial because it provides valuable insights into each child's unique capabilities and helps us understand their individuality. Taking the time to observe play allows us to uncover a child's authentic voice and gain a deeper understanding of their needs, providing better support and guidance for their learning experiences (Sahlberg and Doyle, 2019).

Challenging adult biases when assessing

It's crucial to address bias in early years observations to ensure fair and accurate assessments of children's development. Our observations are often influenced by our biases, whether we realise it or not. How we interpret and respond to a 5-year-old's perspective depends on the educator's experience, knowledge and self-awareness.

I've observed a colleague engaging with a child who called out during story time because 'he's just a boy' and ignoring another child who did the same thing because 'she didn't follow the class rules.' Stereotypes based on race, gender or ability can lead to biased observations.

Educators should actively question their assumptions and avoid generalising children's behaviours based on stereotypes. Focusing on each child's unique traits helps reduce bias. Adults' willingness to honestly reflect with colleagues and the child's family leads to better observational outcomes.

When making final assessments or using tracking systems, it's important to be mindful. While a tick may neatly fit into a specific age band and seem convenient for tracking, it can lead to deficit models of assessment. Making judgments about a student's ability, such as 'they can't speak English' may overlook the child's linguistic and other unique skills. Developmental ideas, as Cannella (1997) has argued, have developed from a global north perspective. We should be mindful of what we consider to be 'normal'. In my experience the pressures of showing 'improving outcomes' means there is a dance to be had between tracking and acknowledging the unique child. I will always advocate for the unique child.

Planning a response

Following careful observations and assessments, it becomes essential to strategically plan a deliberate and purposeful response. This planning may unfold in real time or over an extended period. Meaningful and high-quality interactions with children throughout the day are conducive to ongoing assessments and the strategic planning of appropriate responses (Fisher, 2008).

For instance, when a child encounters difficulty while attempting to zip up their coat, the adult can quickly assess that the child is in need of learning how to independently accomplish this task. Subsequently, in that moment, the adult formulates a plan to support the child, drawing upon their comprehensive knowledge of the child. The adult may opt to assist with the initial part of the zip to ensure the child can subsequently pull it up independently, or they might choose to hold one side of the coat and encourage the child to connect the bottom of the zip before independently pulling it up. Another approach could involve verbally guiding the child through the entire process and providing support and encouragement throughout. Importantly, these planning and response processes should be characterised by collaborative engagement with the child through sustained shared thinking (Sammons et al., 2002).

Following the implementation of a response, the observation cycle recommences. At times, the cycle may involve observing, assessing, observing and assessing before a response is enacted. The appropriate response may take time and as Clarke (2023) argues, it's important to take time to understand what we are observing. This process of ongoing observation, assessment and thoughtful reflection is continuous and acknowledges the autonomy, distinctive voice and individuality of each child.

By creating a well-planned environment, conducting mindful observations, eliminating adult biases and embracing the present moment, educators can establish a space where children's voices are not just heard, but also respected and valued. This journey involves understanding, empathy and ongoing learning, benefiting the children, educators and society.

Danielle Kelly, an Early Years Lecturer from The Trafford Stockport College Group, also offers a personal reflection on how each part of the cycle can be effectively included in everyday practice.

Danielle Kelly: the observation, assessment, planning cycle in practice

The observation, assessment and planning (OAP) cycle is central to early years practice. This cycle enables you to capture a holistic view of children, support their current interests and build on their learning and development. Before beginning the OAP cycle, there are key factors to secure in place to enable the OAP cycle to be successful. These are for children to have a key person, practitioners to have a strong knowledge and understanding of the areas of learning and development and to provide children with an enabling environment. An enabling environment should be warm and positive, which offers a range of resources and experiences for children to learn and flourish. These experiences, both indoors and outdoors, should reflect the areas of learning and development so children can begin to explore, play and interact whilst being supported by their key person. By having these factors in place, children can begin to foster a love of learning and practitioners can then begin the OAP cycle.

Observations are your starting point. As children explore, play, interact and join in with the daily routines, this gives practitioners the opportunity to look at the levels of children's engagement, identify how children learn and what their interests are. Practitioners may find children enjoy and engage with one activity more than another. They may find children interacting with each other in a certain area of the room more than others. Additionally, they may find children consistently playing with the same resources and some resources may not be touched. As practitioners carry out observations, they begin to make their own assessments.

Practitioners assess the skills the child can do. For example, they may assess children confidently using simple words such as 'car' in play. From this, your next step as a practitioner is to 'plan'. Through observing and assessing what children know and can do, your role as a practitioner is to identify a next step to build on these existing skills. This would be a specific skill you intend for children to learn next. Therefore, practitioners may identify a next step for children to build two words into play. Practitioners would plan an opportunity for children to be able to build two words into their play. For example, you may set up painting with cars, with different colours so you can implement two key words such as 'blue car' or 'red car'. Additionally, you may set up a building activity so you can encourage 'big brick' or 'small brick'. As children enter and join in with your planned activity, your OAP cycle will begin again, and you may notice children learning more new skills and not just your 'intended next step'. However, a key point to remember is that children will not secure their next step in one learning activity. This will need to be repeated several times for children to consistently explore this skill. The key is to consistently sequence children's learning, build and extend children's learning and development.

By following the OAP cycle, it is important to understand that practitioners and children begin to shape their curriculum together. A curriculum can be defined as what you 'intend' for children to learn throughout the areas of development. However, this can be flexible; not all parts of the curriculum need to be 'planned'. As Early Years Coalition (2021) explains, children are all unique and they are 'constantly learning'.

In this next contribution, Louise Smith, EYFS Lead at Coldfair Green Primary School, shows how using an online system not only streamlined the whole OAP cycle but enabled for each part to be implemented effectively.

Louise Smith: using online learning journals to support the OAP cycle

My pedagogy which is deep rooted in an enabled and play-based environment, ensures that the observation, assessment and planning cycle is completed in the moment, repeatedly, several times a day with each child. In my classroom, children complete tasks linked to a skills progression-based curriculum, written by me lifted from Development Matters (DfE, 2023b) and Birth to 5 Matters (DCSF, 2009).

Each day, tasks are set for the children to complete as well as levelled continuous provision. These tasks are designed to enable children to independently practice skills and embed previous learning across the day. Children can complete their tasks whenever they want throughout the day, as long as they complete them all and to a high standard.

The children usually have four tasks or jobs a day which increase in complexity over the year. Each task is modelled by me at the start of the session meaning that there is a reduction in the cognitive load for the children as they are watching a task completed live. Photographs and an explanation of each task are also sent home via an online learning platform before the children arrive at school so that parents can almost pre-teach before the day has even begun.

I quickly realised that recording and evidencing this was a huge workload for me to manage so I devised a way for the children to independently record their own work. From the second week that the children start school, each child has their own QR code, they log onto their own online learning platform using iPads and take photos of their work and upload it to their journal. The work is then sent to me to release it to their journal. This means that I can live mark their work and correct any misconceptions immediately and then send the work directly to parents. This also means that the OAP cycle is completed in the moment. Any misconceptions or new interests that arise from the live marking, feed into the planning for the next day or within that moment. It also allows staff to be free from an assigned task; they are able to look for 'teachable moments1' to complete the OAP cycle there and then.

The uploaded work is checked at points in the day where we naturally come together as a class, such as before a transition. This means that gentle reminders can be given to children yet to complete tasks and we can share, talk and peer assess our work with each other. Each task can also be added to a subject folder, enabling subject leaders to quickly see what their subject looks like in the EYFS. Using an online learning journal has allowed the children in my class to become autonomous, keen learners completing the OAP cycle instantaneously.

Next is a contribution by Karl Eaveson, Nursery manager, who reminds us of the value of nurturing a good partnership with parents within the OAP cycle.

Karl Eaveson: observation assessment and planning cycle

At our Nursery setting based in York, I am a believer that children's individual interests should be the start point to any learning opportunity. We have recently adapted the Early Years Foundation Stage to create our own in-house curriculum.

As a setting, we recognise that following an effective observation, planning and assessment cycle tailored to our ethos and pedagogy enables us to get the most out of each interest. From here, we create outcome-based next steps to enable children to progress at their own pace.

We regularly use formative assessment to measure our children's learning and development. This method enables us to start with the child, match their unique interests and actions to an area/areas of development and then match to the correct links. It is imperative that children's observations are objective at their very core, writing only what we see and hear happening throughout to ensure our framework links are accurate.

As much as observation and assessment is child centered, it also goes hand in hand with partnership working with parents and carers. We build knowledge-informed professional relationships which create a healthy foundation in which to really understand children's learning. This creates a situation where with honest, accurate handovers, we can all leave singing from the same hymn sheet.

The next step when looking at our curriculum is 'responsive practice'. My aim as a manager each day is to create and observe a challenging, supportive and enabling play environment for the children where they can freely demonstrate their understanding and learning within a wide range of contexts.

Responsive practitioners are those who tune in to children's play and interactions to really immerse themselves in what is happening before deciding from here how best to proceed through next steps to keep learning moving forward.

Within this process, interests are priority. To get the most out of our interactions, we are listening, guiding and modelling processes and behavior together with asking open-ended questions which support both learning and reflection. Done correctly, our children are then equipped to apply newly learned skills and techniques taken onboard throughout. These will stick with them in a variety of different scenarios during both activities and independent play.

Once per term, we then look at the process of summative assessment which is simply us gaining an overview of all of the interactions, observations and reflections we have on each key-child that term. This information is tracked for us using a learning and development app but it is important that we cast an eye over this to ensure accuracy and to tweak and adjust before deciding how best to support moving forward the next term.

Within our staff team, practitioners are at different levels in their professional journey but generally will hold in their mind key details around each key child's learning and development. We offer lots of support in this area and also take the time to read and approve all observations and assessments before they are published to offer accuracy.

In this penultimate contribution in this chapter, Kate White, EYFS Teacher from North Cockerington CE Primary School, emphasises the significance of using checkpoints as a framework of quality observations, assessments and planning.

Katie White: planned observation and assessment opportunities to ensure an effective observation, assessment and planning cycle

Observation, assessment and planning were always key principles within my early years practice, however developing an approach whereby these are clearly linked to form a robust cycle has ensured each child's learning, needs and next steps are at the forefront.

Long-term planning specifies the termly learning progression and checkpoints for children to be on track to achieve the Early Learning Goal in each area. These checkpoints steer the medium-term planning so activities and provision are skill driven, focusing on what children need to know or be able to do. Cross referencing these from the long-term plan to the medium-term plan allows me to ensure the quality continuous provision, and structured enhancements I am providing give opportunities for children to learn and rehearse the specific skills needed. The medium-term plan then feeds directly into the weekly planning which includes more targeted challenges or activities for specific children, along with planned assessment for learning observations throughout the week.

Several checkpoints are selected each week as planned assessments opportunities, with observations of the linked activities then carried out. My observations, notes and knowledge of the children directly then inform the next week's short-term planning, enabling me to plan learning bespoke to the needs of each child. Assessment opportunities are neither missed nor left until the end of the term but are ongoing throughout child led and adult led learning each week. Precise, planned observations and interactions allow me to identify what children are doing, both across a range of learning areas and within the specific assessment checkpoints, then diagnose potential difficulties and plan next steps as a response. The 'Notice, Diagnose, Response' document is an integral part of the weekly plan as this assessment for learning process ensures I reflect on what I am observing in the classroom and use it to inform the next steps of individuals and groups. Identifying the focus checkpoints also steers more meaningful and targeted interactions with the children to the intended learning skills and outcomes, further driving progress.

This assessment for learning process is built on week by week with aspects crossed off once planned for or achieved and likewise added to where needed. This ensures the narrative of each child's needs and next steps is kept as a record and built upon. I am, therefore, able to continually reflect on what I am seeing and plan a response to this within the next week. These observations are then used to inform my summative assessments at the key data points.

In order for the observation, assessment and planning cycle to truly impact on each child's development I have ensured that each stage of my planning clearly flows, observations are carefully planned to support robust assessments, which then inform what is planned next. Without the precisely planned observations and assessment opportunities my planning was not driven by the needs of the children and became activity led. All three elements of the observation, assessment and planning cycle woven together has heightened my knowledge of the children, their needs and what I need to plan for next in order to support keeping children on track of the intended learning progression. Having these explicitly identified on my planning ensures opportunities to drive the progress of all children are utilised to the full.

The final contribution by Diana Wilson, Educational Leader and former Head of EYFS, provides a comprehensive collection of checklists which provide a structure to build the OAP cycle upon. They are intended to offer practitioners the opportunity to reflect and evaluate current systems for capturing children's achievements and how plans continue to guide and challenge.

Diana Wilson: instrumental case study

The purpose of this chapter is to support the implementation of observations in the early years of education. Planning and assessment of teaching and learning through observations is crucial which this chapter expands on to provide insight into the importance of rigorous practice of observations in early years settings. Data drawn from observations is productive to recognise various needs for accommodations. The key factors that indicate the need for observations in early years for support and collaboration with parents for effective development of children are accumulated below in the form of observation checklists across areas of speech and communication, listening and motor skills.

Observations are conducted through playful activities. Next on the list below are indicators for play in early years. Teachers or childminders would need to organise a learning environment to include some of the key measures as mentioned below to allow for observations.

- Set up a play situation using a child's interests such as pretend play or imaginative play and build conversation with the child in order to record observations for later use.
- Gather additional information from parents.
- Observe peer interaction.
- Provide the data as collected to the other committees on the team for planning and assessment.
- Consider the impact of background noise and other distractions.
- Use the knowledge of all staff members working with the child to inform your assessment.
- Build up learner profile over several observations of play/interactions.

Below is an example of a checklist to assess children's listening skills (Table 12.1).

Table 12.1 Example of an assessment checklist for children's listening skills in the Early Years Developed & supplied by & with the permission of the author for this submission. Diana Wilson

Observation Checklist for EYFS

Assessment of Listening Skills

Teacher:	Group of Learners		
	FS 1	FS2	Year 1

Response to Listening	Indicate as observed Yes/No	Name of students	Observation notes
1. Listen with interest to noises adults make when they read.			
2. Recognise and respond to many familiar sounds such as of animals, vehicles, weather sounds, turning to a knock on the door etc.	Yes	Rishi and Rami	Rami is also seen imitating sounds and sings along. Rishi has speech difficulty, and does lisp and urges to listen to songs more than once.
3. Can focus on what is said directly to them.			
4. Stay in a group activity if supported by an adult.			
5. Listen to stories with increasing interest and recall.			
6. Can follow directions.			
7. Join in with repeated refrains and anticipates key events and phrases in rhymes and stories.			
8. Takes a long time processing spoken language.			
9. Has difficulties following game rules or class routine.			
10. Unable to understand or follow gestures.			
11. Tendency to watch your lips when you speak.			
12. Need high volume of speech directed at him/her.			
13. Can understand a question or instruction that has two parts, such as 'Get your paper and wait at the teacher's table.'			
14. Can understand 'why' questions, like: 'Why do you think we need to eat fruits?'			

Observation checklist supplied with permission by the author of this submission

Additional checklists which assess children's skills in communication and motor skills can be found here: https://padlet.com/dianawilson321/observation-checklists-5azz0u4odcwlu0li

Developed and supplied by and with the permission of the author for this submission Diana Wilson

Padlet developed with permission of the author Jayne Carter

Additional checklists which assess children's skills in communication and motor skills can be found here.

In conclusion

This chapter examines the observation-assessment-planning (OAP) cycle within early years education, emphasising the shift towards a more flexible and child-centred approach. It explores how practitioners have adapted to reduced paperwork while maintaining structured assessments that support children's learning journeys. The chapter discusses practical applications, including shared reflections among practitioners, responsive feedback and collaborative planning with families. Key themes include balancing professional judgment with recorded evidence, ensuring assessments remain purposeful and fostering inclusive participation from both educators and children. Through case studies and expert insights, the chapter underscores the importance of a well-designed OAP cycle in creating meaningful, responsive learning experiences.

Summary of key points

- All aspects of the OAP cycle need similar dedication, commitment, knowledge and skills if they are to create a collaborative proactive framework.
- A key mantra to evaluate the impact of the OAP cycle could be 'what's the purpose for me (practitioner), the children and their family'. If it's difficult to answer these questions, then a readjustment needs to take place.
- Practitioner interaction offers a credible connection which binds each aspect of the OAP cycle together. How can we maximise our own language to provide information for our children?
- Children have the right and are capable of being involved in this cycle. We need to find the right model for them to show and tell us their thoughts, feelings and opinions.
- Balancing professional judgement with recorded evidence ensures a structured approach to monitoring development. Thoughtfully combining intuition with tangible records supports informed decision-making and strengthens the quality of provision.

References

Cannella, G.S. (1997). *Deconstructing Early Childhood Education: Social Justice and Revolution*. New York: Peter Lang Publishing.

Clark, A. (2023). *In Slow Knowledge and the Unhurried Child: Time for Slow Pedagogies in Early Childhood Education*. Abingdon: Routledge.

Clark, A. and Moss, Peter. (2011). *Listening To Young Children: The Mosaic Approach* (2nd ed.). London: National Children's Bureau.

DCSF. (2009). Learning, Playing and Interacting, National Strategies guidance document. Available at: Resources – Birth To 5 Matters.

DfE (2025). Early years foundation stage statutory framework for group and school-based providers. Setting the standards for learning, development and care for children from birth to five. Available at: https://assets.publishing.service.gov.uk/media/687105a381dd8f70f5de3ea9/EYFS_framework_for_group_and_school_based_providers_.pdf (Accessed 21 July 2025)

DfE (Department for Education) (2021). *Statutory Framework for the Early Years Foundation Stage: Setting the Standards for Learning, Development and Care for Children from Birth to Five*. London: Department for Education.

DfE (Department for Education) (2023a). *Early Years Foundation Stage Statutory Framework for Group and School-Based Providers*. London: Department for Education. Available at: https://assets.publishing.service.gov.uk/media/65aa5e42ed27ca001327b2c7/EYFS_ (Accessed: 13 September 2025)

DfE (Department for Education). (2023b). *Development Matters: Non-Statutory Curriculum Guidance for the Early Years Foundation Stage*. London: Department for Education. Available at: https://www.gov.uk/government/publications/development-matters--2 (Accessed: 13 September 2025)

Fisher, J. (2008). *Starting from the Child: Teaching and Learning in the Foundation Stage* (2nd edn). Maidenhead: Open University Press.

Grenier, J. (2021). *Working with the Revised Early Years Foundation Stage: Principles into Practice Sheringham Nursery School and Children's Centre*. London: Sheringham Nursery School and Children's Centre.

Ofsted (updated 2024). School inspection handbook. Available at: https://www.gov.uk/government/publications/school-inspection-handbook-eif/school-inspection-handbook-for-september-2023#evaluating-early-years-and-sixth-form-provision-on-graded-inspections

Sahlberg, P. and Doyle, W. (2019). *Let the Children Play: How Play Will Save Our Schools and Help Children Thrive*. New York, NY: Oxford University Press.

Sammons, P., Sylva, K., Melhuish, E., Siraj-Blatchford, I. and Taggart, B. (2002). *The Effective Provision of Pre-School Education (EPPE) Project: Technical Paper 8a – Measuring the Impact of Pre-School on Children's Cognitive Progress over the Preschool Period*. London: Institute of Education, University of London/ Department for Education and Skills.

The Early Years Coalition. (2021). Birth to 5 Matters: Guidance by the sector, for the sector. *Early Education*. Available at: Birth To 5 Matters – Guidance by the sector, for the sector.

13 Quality adult-child interaction

Jayne Carter

Introduction

Interacting with young children is more than simply being present. It is being truly available to commit to using the skilful power of precise engagement to create an irresistible synergy. Summarising the conditions for this collaboration to be both productive and mutually successful is often complex, as it can be dependent on adult knowledge, temperament and vision. The essence of these pivotal characteristics is captured clearly in this chapter through a variety of research into practice examples and models. This chapter aims to support practitioners in considering the impact of their own interactions, identifying strengths and potential professional next steps.

Pondering question: do we consider the range and impact of approaches and strategies we use in our interactions?

Consider a typical interaction with a child in a setting or school. The child may have initiated this; seeking out a responsive and unconditionally available adult for listening, for participation or for simply being a play partner. Likewise, the adult may have started this collaboration; wanting to generate curiosity, planting ideas for further exploration or offering much needed companionship. Throughout any interaction there is a recognisable ebb and flow to the adult and child conversations which occur, with verbal and nonverbal messages seamlessly conjoining. Akin to a shared dance, the adult and child meander and adopt a variety of roles throughout this interaction. These roles include labels such as 'the observer', 'the challenger', 'the cheerleader' or 'the connector'. Each of these may naturally blend and redesign throughout the interaction, presenting the very highest example of adult and child collaboration. Moving towards this more precise reflection of roles drives thinking beyond the notion of merely creating a quality adult-child interaction; it hopefully nudges deliberation further, offering the adult personal and professional evaluation choices. I am also interested in exploring the interplay that these interaction characteristics may also create for the child. What is the impact for the child on being part of an interaction which moves beyond simply being 'effective'? The range of submissions included in this chapter contribute to this line of enquiry, with each author carefully crafting their own opinion piece and pedagogical conclusions.

In this first contribution, Agnes Kosek, Lecturer at The University of Greenwich, prompts reflection and thought by exploring the question of how children learn.

Agnes Kosek: deconstructing the myth of progressive education in early years settings: how do children learn?

The publication of Jean-Jacques Rousseau's novel *Emile or Treatise on Education* (1762) and those of other progressive thinkers (Froebel, 1887; Montessori, 1912) had a profound impact on educational philosophy and on teaching practices in many early years settings, and significantly impacted the understanding of how learning happens in early years classrooms. Their ideas were largely reflected in the 19th-century Plowden report (1967), which challenged traditional education classroom practices, and argued that schools must meet 'needs and interest' of children, that learning needs to be fun and that the learning 'environment needs to stimulate [children's] growth along natural lines' (SED, 1965: 4). In other words, the report reflected the progressive ideas that continued to develop from the time of French Revolution and stressed that children develop at different ages and stages, that they should not be made to learn and should instead develop their own interests, in their own time, and that learning unfolds naturally unhindered by adult interruptions. Although *some* of these ideas are important and valid, they were somehow poorly translated into many UK early years classrooms.

What is particularly problematic with this line of thinking is that it developed into a kind of ideology (Standish, 2006), diminished the epistemic authority of the teacher and overly emphasised child-led learning 'along natural lines' (SED, 1965: 4). That is, it neglected the importance of reasoning and co-construction of knowledge at the critical periods of children's cognitive development and contributed to the deterioration of early years education (Darling and Nordenbo, 2003).

This is largely because many radical progressives developed a *different concept of learning and freedom* compared to that advocated by many liberal educators (Oakeshott, 1962: Hirst, 1965). They prioritised children's *exploratory freedom* and learning through the senses, emphasising 'playing and exploring' and 'hands-on experiences', and significantly neglected the importance of the development of children's intellectual freedom, epistemic agency, and the role of teachers in scaffolding their understanding. That is, many progressivist practitioners overlooked the fact that the development of *intellectual freedom* and higher-order thinking capacities takes place when practitioners *disrupt* children's current ways of thinking, *introduce* a source of novelty into their conceptual scheme and take them *beyond* their existing capacities (Oakeshott, 1962; Hirst, 1965) and the impressions they acquire through exploration of their environment using their senses. Radically progressive classroom practices therefore carry a great risk of leaving many children intellectually where they are instead of enabling them to access complex and abstract concepts which they are unlikely to access on their own through playing and exploring in the enabling classroom environment.

There is no doubt that child-centred ideas have had an important impact on the way practitioners view the child, as a person with their own autonomy and their own rights. But we need to bring back to Early Years classrooms the ideas promoted by many liberal educators and many Ancient Greek thinkers such as Plato and Aristotle. Learning and the true pursuit of knowledge happens when practitioners take children on an 'unrehearsed intellectual adventure' (Oakeshott, 1962: 198) and familiarise them with new ways of thinking and looking at the world. Exploratory *and* intellectual freedom are both important, and practitioners should introduce children to new forms of knowledge and understanding as they are newcomers to this world.

Next, Nick Robinson, from Nick Robinson Sports Coaching, extends the enquiry of how children learn, adding a sports teaching and perspective.

Nick Robinson: quality adult-child interactions

The most important consideration if we are to develop our early years children into becoming well-rounded and balanced adults are the relationships between adults and children. A child's community can have a lasting impact on our children. The journey for our children becoming adults can be a long and winding road, developing relationships with many adults. Parents and family would be the first adults that early year's children develop relationships with, then friends, nursery teachers, teachers, head teachers, sports coaches amongst others.

Children's positive development is reliant upon balanced supportive adults who meet the needs of the children. Our duty as adults and caregivers is to provide a safe environment physically and emotionally to support our children. Early years children are at the beginning of their own journey and adults' behaviour can be mirrored by our children. The adult-child interaction at early stages can be crucial for development as children's brains develop at the fastest rate between the ages of 0-5 years old.

As every child is unique and will have different needs, every caregiver and adult have their own journey too; our unconscious bias from our own journey could influence our interactions with the children. An adult's tone, mannerisms and body language all play a part in a positive or negative relationship.

Understanding how the brain's structure and growth impacts on the adult and child relationship is vitally important. Teaching children to understand feelings and how to manage those feelings is crucial for long-term development. Allowing children to fail without pressure and sometimes struggle can be positive in the long term if supported in the correct environment. This can help to gain resilience and will help our children's growth through different and challenging stages through their lives.

Co-regulation is vitally important in the development of a quality adult-child interaction. Supporting children as they experience different emotions, making sure they have time to express and communicate their emotions, can contribute to a strong adult-child bond and quality relationships. Developing children's emotions, self-esteem, and positive attitudes can support them to become independent children, helping them to make positive choices and building resilience.

Personally, I am very privileged to coach, support and interact with many early years children and start their journey in physical development. My role within early years sport is to develop a love for sport, improve resilience and self-esteem, nurture independent confident children who will become valued members of their own community.

The impact of a positive, supportive, knowledgeable, enthusiastic and patient adult can have an incredible influence and impact on an early years child and will set the foundations for the children for the rest of their lives.

In this next contribution, Yria Polydoropoulou, considers the importance of enriching adult-child interaction through a growth mindset lens. The significance of children independently using this to learn is a key point for consideration.

Yria Polydoropoulou: the effect of a growth mindset on children's interactions

Promoting interactions and encouraging conversations between children and adults in the Early Years is one of the quintessential characteristics of effective learning. However, the quality of interactions has a decisive role in the development of self in children and the formation of beliefs around their being.

A growth mindset, as Carol Dweck states, is about 'people's belief that their most basic abilities can be developed through dedication and hard work. Brains and talent are just the starting point. This view creates a love of learning and a resilience that is essential for great accomplishment' (2015). Hence when adults (teachers, parents, caregivers) integrate a growth mindset in their interactions with children they are providing a crucial aid for fostering children's cognitive, social and emotional development.

When one is wondering the ways to embrace a growth mindset in the classroom in order to enhance learning and meaningful interactions, one has to refer to Carol Dweck's (2021) approach 'The Power of Yet'. This approach encourages children to embrace challenges and persist in the face of difficulties. For example, instead of commenting on a child's incorrect answer as simply wrong, a teacher might say, 'You're not there yet, but with more practice, you'll get it.'

Additionally, when teachers focus more on the *process* of learning instead of the *result*, they create an environment where children feel safe to explore, make mistakes and try again. In order to create this environment adults could integrate a positive language that emphasises effort over innate ability. Phrases like 'You worked so hard on this!' or 'You didn't give up, and look what you achieved!' reinforce the idea that effort leads to improvement.

On top of that, open-ended questions and resources help children to reflect on the process and on different ways to approach their task. As Matt Bawler states, 'It is great to challenge children but when they root their sense of self-worth in whether they win or not that's the problem', and there follows the argument of the quality of interactions and the story we say to our students about their skills and abilities (Dweck, 1986).

Introducing growth mindset concepts to children through stories, games and activities is an effective way to update our approach to learning. Furthermore, practices like creating a 'Yet' Wall where children reflect by drawing or writing their weekly challenges, successes and areas they want to improve on, including the ways to achieve that.

As the interactions we have with our students play an important role in their development, a growth mindset will help us to provide better practices to our students.

In this next thought-provoking contribution, Alexander Walsh, a Speech and Language Therapist, offers a perspective on how to implement quality adult-child interactions, highlighting the value of practitioner reflection when planning for shared conversations with children.

Alexander Walsh: fostering early communication: some guiding principles

When you're a little kid, interacting with adults can be tricky.

As adults, we can use some strategies when communicating to make things easier. More enriching and enjoyable for both parties, hopefully too. Here are some guiding principles which can help support quality adult-child interaction.

1. Get down to their level

   Yes I know... it's a long way down but to a little kid, you're *enormous!* Think of it like this: if they can sit on the floor, you probably can do the same. Coming down to a child's level makes communication so much easier for them. They can share what interests them with you, they're more able to hear what you're saying and read your facial expressions. You're reducing the distance between the two of you, both literally and psychologically. Close proximity makes their interactions predictable... and predictability is a big deal for all children.

2. Praise! Give lots of praise

   If a child in your care is pumped as they have built the biggest Duplo tower in their short life, celebrate with them! Use an astonished tone. Tell the child exactly what you think is great (so it's clear) and pair it with an awed expression. Give a high five. They'll love the fact you share their joys and will return to share more in future.

3. Ask less questions

   Do you like being asked questions when you're having a great time? Children don't either! If a child is getting into the flow of painting something and really enjoying it and someone asks 'What are you painting?' they've been put on the spot to find an answer. Some children may be able to come up with one, others may not. Play it safe just in case!

4. Meltdowns aren't always messing around

   Looking after children is rewarding but can be really challenging too. I remember an explosive meltdown my stepson once had, aged four, when he lost his favourite Lightning McQueen toy. It was as theatrical as it was sudden. In cases like this, take a breath. Your child may be howling with despair when he's lost a toy because for him it *is* the end of the world. Regulating emotions is not something children excel at so validate their emotions:

   'You look really sad. Did you lose your favourite toy? I'd be really sad if I lost mine, too.'

   Drawing attention to emotions is a first step for children to be able to recognise their own. This helps them control them as they get older.

5. Use gesture or expression if needed... lots of it

   Think of pairing gesture and expression with spoken words as putting training wheels on your bike. With the added support you go so much further. This can be natural gesture:

   'Look at the bird in the tree. It's very pretty'. [pointing]

   Or you might want to pick up a few Makaton signs to reinforce messages to children who need it (the signs for 'more' and 'help' are particularly useful). Use these consistently with matching words or phrases and children will make the links.

6. Follow their lead in play
   Play is a vital driver in a child's communication growth. Interactions are more enriching for them if play is on their terms, not yours. If they don't like your ideas when you're playing together, that's fine. After all, they benefit more from leading and creating the play than you do.

In this contribution, Declan Dowkes, provides a fascinating account of the importance of including children's voices within a shared participation interaction.

Declan Dowkes: challenges to the 'gradual, authentic, reciprocal' relationships that underpin feelings of 'Professional Love' during an era of increased accountability within early childhood spaces

Appreciating and actively advocating for young children's autonomy both within and beyond the confines of the early childhood classroom is, for many, characteristic of supporting their continued holistic learning and development, as well as their identity establishment within the world (Harris and Manatakis, 2013). Seeking young children's experiences, perspectives and opinions (through their unique and individual lenses) is something which is enshrined within the United Nations Convention on the Rights of the Child (UNCRC, 1989) and subsequently born out in much of today's contemporary early childhood research, policy and practice (Hayes, 2024: 831). Aspects of my own research profile now as an Early Years academic is akin to this tradition. Consequently, actively recognising the important contribution that the child themselves can make to decisions and events concerning them (Hayes, 2024; Wall and Robinson, 2022).

However, Hart's (1992) ladder of participation (a model which helps to identify participation levels) warns those seeking to facilitate children's voices for the purposes of 'manipulation, decoration and tokenism' as this is a classic form of non-participation. As Grimmer (2021) rightly points out, rather than encouraging a pedagogy based on love, the absence of fully committing to enabling the child's authentic voice to thrive within how practitioners' approach their practice, is a barrier to feelings of love. In an era of ever-increasing standardization and accountability measures influencing early years work (Roberts-Holmes and Moss, 2021), building and maintaining a level of trust as a practitioner through completely implementing the child's wishes in the classroom may be challenging. Rogers (2010) alluded to this when remarking that a notable disparity exists between how much child-led learning early years educators want to facilitate, and what they are able to facilitate due to the external pressures of their roles. With these external pressures, coupled with recent developments such as the introduction of 'teacherless' classrooms such as those introduced at David Game College (Carroll, 2024), it would be easy to downplay how important children's interactions with their significant adults can be (Macdonald et al., 2021). Bronfenbrenner (1989) infamously alluded to this importance when characterising those closest to the child as being most influential to shaping and empowering them. During my time as an Early Years practitioner, I found this to be particularly observable in two-year-olds where despite striving for increased independence away from their key adults, the developing two-year-old typically returned to the safety net of nurture, reassurance and love that myself and their other significant adults in the setting afforded them. Far from child development happening in solitude therefore, the value of quality practitioner-child interactions provides a high level of unwavering benefit (Romeo et al., 2018).

In short, whilst the context within which the modern practitioner now practises may face a myriad of pressures that could pose a legitimate threat to sustaining interactions characterised as 'Professional Love', opportunities for practitioners to forge such bonds with the children in their care ultimately remain. It is therefore incumbent on practitioners to seek to pave a way (via providing platforms for authentic participation in decision making in the classroom) for a loving pedagogy to thrive and survive.

Carys Jennings, Curriculum Tutor at The Open University, shares a delightful example of adult-child interaction at its most effective. The spiders web experience provides a wealth of practitioner reflection and personal next steps planning.

Carys Jennings: making opportunities available- the spiders webs

Developing quality adult child interactions are key to ensuring effective learning provisions, as was found in the Effective Provision of Pre-school Education Project (EPPE) (Sylva et al., 2004) and continues to be the case in more recent inspectorate reports across the four UK nations.

A class of 28 Reception children in a rural school in Wales were enthusiastically in the throngs of their 'Wonderful wild world' project and had arrived at their legs and wings discovery week. In their planning session the children (most of them) were keen to explore spiders further and reluctantly those who were not so keen agreed. The starter activity on the Monday was recalling their mind map planning and discussing the questions they had set to answer by the end of the week such as 'Do all spiders have eight legs?' 'Are spiders friendly?' 'Do we need spiders?' 'How many different spiders are there?' were among the key questions. Given that some were unconvinced of the theme at first, they too soon began to enjoy all things 'octo'. I, as the class teacher, introduced a poem to encourage the children to care for spiders.

They learnt the poem and role played placing spiders outside carefully. It was the knowing adults' preparation of the environment that had ensured engagement from the children. Creating spaces with resources that would evoke interest and excitement such as glue and glitter to create spider drawings on black paper, thinking of ways to fix spiders legs that had been injured or broken by using various craft materials or placing boxes of books and magazines about spiders in the quiet area as well as next to the painting and computer areas to stimulate interest.

The most memorable of activities was placing interest baskets outdoors; one filled with twigs and blu tack and Sellotape, the other filled with different lengths and types of string, wool, pieces of material, lengths of crepe paper. Mid-morning on the third day of the theme, two of the boys came running in, eager to get the teacher to come out to see what they had created. After almost 40 minutes of collaboration with another three boys and two girls, the pair had created a garden full of webs and spiders, from the items they found in the baskets. This led to an afternoon of conversation about the spiders, their homes, spider eating habits and creating a fact file about their spiders.

It is no surprise that staff who understand child development and early years pedagogy and who have a greater understanding of holistic early childhood development foster effective relationships with young children. These relationships are based on trust, respect, and reciprocal interactions where the adults are knowing and in tune with the children's varied interests, needs and developmental milestones. The baskets were a product of those knowing adults understanding and enthusiastically adopted by the learners in their care.

In this next contribution, coauthors Hannah Robinson and Kelly Thompson, EYFS practitioners, consider how a focus on developing a consistent approach to how adults engage with children has shown positive results for their diverse school context.

Hannah Robinson and Kelly Thompson: fostering language development in a diverse school context

Within education, language development stands as a cornerstone for academic success and social integration. However, in a diverse school such as Park Academy, which has significantly high levels of need, such development can pose significant challenges. With a particular focus on interactions, this case study explores how educators navigate the convergence of various factors.

Park Academy welcomes pupils from diverse linguistic and cultural backgrounds. Upon entry, a significant proportion of students face substantial hurdles, including language barriers compounded by limited exposure to English prior to enrolment. Currently, 80% of the Reception cohort are EAL learners. Moreover, a growing number of students present with speech and language difficulties, necessitating specialised support to foster effective communication skills. Compounding these factors is the high mobility rate among students, leading to disruptions in continuity and consistency within the learning environment. A considerable proportion of students lack preschool experience, further exacerbating the developmental gap in language acquisition.

The school has implemented a comprehensive approach to promote language development, focusing on fostering high-quality interactions within the learning environment. The school recognises that by prioritising the development of communication and language **all** children will benefit (Higgins et al. (2017).

Ensuring staff have a deep understanding of the multifaceted nature of language development within our school has been paramount. Professional development has centred around ensuring the team are equipped with the necessary skills to facilitate language-rich interactions. Timetables have been adjusted to afford educators dedicated time for meaningful engagement with students and the school recognises that staff who wonder and listen during interactions and talk just at the right moment are vital to enhance children's learning (Fisher and Frey, 2013). Both the indoor and outdoor environments have been carefully considered to ensure they are 'inspirational environments that change and include quirky objects and things that lie outside the ordinary' (Bottrill, 2018).

Daily routines incorporate opportunities for language-rich activities such as songs, rhymes and 'snack and chat' sessions. Additionally, the school provides frequent, daily opportunities for shared reading and ensures a diverse range of meaningful, interest-led activities that promote active and real-life experiences.

The school places a strong emphasis on building positive relationships between staff and pupils. Home-school links are actively nurtured through parent workshops, online learning journals and stay-and-play sessions.

The implemented strategies have had a profound impact on student's language development for all, not just those with a significant language gap. Children have made significant strides in language proficiency and have developed essential communication and social skills necessary for thriving within and beyond the classroom.

Next, in this contribution, Maxwell Davies, Lecturer at Arden University, advocates for adults to take the lead in using a gender creative approach when interacting with children.

Maxwell Davies: the future is gender creative

Bronfenbrenner's ecological systems theory (1979) conceptualises a child's world view is influenced by external environments which impact their developmental growth through a process of socialisation. These influences can determine and reinforce aspects such as one's gender through the divisions of different roles, status and power reproduced through the treatment of children based on how they are expected to act and behave determined by their sex assigned at birth (Mischel, 1966). This is important because: 'Gender differences have long captured the public's interest and have been used to justify myriad laws, policies, and practices in the public and private spheres' (Zosula et al., 2011).

Children are socialised within a combination of interconnective web of experiences within their social systems, where they learn to accept and continue their expected roles, status and positionality of power. Gender stereotyping can happen through actions and words. The language we use and how we engage with children will be forming their ideas of the world around them (Salsabila et al., 2024). Therefore, it is important to consider our role within a child's social system and how we contribute to their development of gender and how we reproduce ideas that create inequality in society. Combating gender stereotypes would need to start early; it is within the first three years that we can influence children to see differently about gender. After that, stereotypes become so ingrained that they can become difficult to shift (Brown, 2014; Mischel, 1966).

Zook (2017) proposes that for the benefit of children, we must confront the segregation of people within society which leads to their marginalisation and oppression by challenging the injustice and inequalities that happen based on one's gender. Every environmental influence within a child's ecological system could create and hold space for freedom of expression, limiting segregation based on sex, using inclusive language, and lastly, reducing gender stereotypes, the ethos of Gender Creative (Open) Parenting (Davies, 2020; Morris, 2018; Myers, 2020).

These considerations have already entered into parenting practices and also in schools, such as Eglia in Sweden, who take a 'gender neutral' approach to teaching and learning (Erodal, 2018). Interactions with children as well as toys, language and material are all neutralised of gender.

Both Eglia and Gender Creative (Open) Parenting offer an alternative to building connections with children and supporting their development while simultaneously creating an environment for them to establish their own positionality removed from pressures based on one's gender or sex assigned at birth.

This is not advocating for the neutralisation of gender in children for a society of people without gender identity. What the proposal here is that children have the space to explore and build their idea of gender, making connections based on their own leadership towards finding out who they are and what identity means to them, without being forced or persuaded by others.

In this very interesting contribution, Dr Lucy Parker, Deputy Headteacher at Ludwick Nursery School, uses cooking as an example of how adults can involve children in meaningful conversations and experiences.

Dr Lucy Parker: developing quality adult-child interactions through cookery

Cookery is an engaging, first-hand activity for young children to experience and provides many opportunities for quality interactions between adult and child.

In our large, maintained nursery school, we have established cookery as a core part of our curriculum. Through a recent action research project, funded by The Froebel Trust, we focused on developing our community connections through cookery. This helped us to develop our curriculum in many different ways, but particularly around developing cookery for inclusion and thinking about how we include parents and carers.

Cooking in small groups, with each child having their own bowl and utensils, ensures cookery is an active and meaningful experience for all. Using a simple recipe card, as well as visuals and key Makaton signs, ensures all children can follow the cookery steps and engage with the process. Thinking about how to include children with additional needs in cookery is important, and some of the process can be adapted or changed to suit the needs of the child. This might be cooking in smaller groups, or on a one-to-one basis. For children who have high sensory needs, focusing on one aspect of cooking might be beneficial. For example, when making biscuits, just focusing on rolling and cutting the dough might be enough. Having the end product ready so children can see what they are making is also helpful. Being able to have a little taste of what you are cooking can be very motivating!

Cookery is a first-hand experience, and an active process so it provides a wealth of opportunity to develop quality interactions and have meaningful conversations. For example, the excitement of learning how to crack an egg, and learning about what is inside the egg and how the egg changes the consistency of the cake ingredients provides many opportunities for questions and conversations. Involving children in the whole process of cooking, from preparing, to tidying away and also growing and composting enable them to have many rich learning opportunities. Some of the cookery processes that the children experience during their time in nursery range from cracking an egg, grating cheese, kneading pizza dough, chopping vegetables, harvesting vegetables, rolling and cutting pastry, cooking over a bonfire –to name a few.

Cooking and sharing food is a universal, shared experience and brings us together as a community. Having a focus on sharing what has been cooked is important. As well as sending cookery home, so children can share what they've cooked with their families, we also make a point of sharing food in the nursery. This might be sharing an apple crumble that's been made as a small group or cooking some crackers or bread and adding them to the snack table so all of the children can enjoy them during the session. Eating food together provides many opportunities to talk and share, providing another opportunity for quality interactions.

Finally, in this contribution, Stephen J Morgan, Nursery Teacher at Summer Lane Primary and Early Years coach and mentor, beautifully illustrates the power of shared conversations and interactions.

Stephen J Morgan: creating memories

In 1974, I was not to know that my enthusiasm for role playing, by taking the register with my toys, would be something that would be the starting off point of a fabulous career working in the early years.

Interactions are something we all work hard on and for some people it's harder to adjust to a very young audience, but with practice and dedication it's something that becomes so characteristic that you would be able to do it in your sleep. My analogy tends to be the breakfast TV method that when you see men and women working well together a school community benefits. The dads that relate to the male teacher and then feel comfortable to engage in the classroom makes the classroom more inclusive to all. Or the child whose dad is no longer about or the child who sadly has seen the worst of men gets a refreshing insight that when the appropriate male is about who is keen to see a child thrive has a lot to offer. I once announced my promotion from the nursery school to a maintained nursery to the community I was leaving. A single mum with her young child was tearful. I asked why she was upset.

She said, 'It's not fair her dad is leaving.'

'That's sad,' I said 'but I didn't realise you had a partner?'

She replied, 'You are the dad that she never had. It's been amazing for her over the last 18 months that every weekday she had a positive male who has interacted with her.'

You couldn't rate this feedback!

I have seen the child hiding behind the couch when arriving on a home visit to adjust during the visit and become a different person by the time you leave. They might then tell you when in year 6 that they still remember with a smile that you dedicated enough time to visit their family when starting in nursery.

Can you end a career that you started at 5 years of age? Probably not, as it's in your heart.

Good relationships and essential interactions make any nursery special.

In conclusion

This chapter explores the significance of quality adult-child interactions in early years education, prioritising the nuanced and dynamic nature of engagement beyond simple presence. It introduces a framework for understanding interaction roles—such as observer, challenger, cheerleader and connector—illustrating how adults can enrich children's learning through intentional dialogue and responsive participation. The chapter shares practical strategies for fostering meaningful connections, highlighting co-regulation, growth mindset applications and the importance of practitioner reflection in shaping high-quality interactions. Through case studies and diverse expert insights, this discussion underscores how effective interactions contribute to children's cognitive, emotional and social development.

Summary of key points

- There is a powerful dynamic between the adult and the child. Creating, nurturing and maintaining this dynamic takes time, effort and dedication.
- The adult's role in the anticipated effective partnership is to both have a vision for themselves but to understand and align this with the aspirations for the child.
- Knowing what interactions mean and how they can serve the art of learning is a specific skill which needs both explicit teaching and frequent provided opportunities for rehearsal.
- Clarifying the different roles of the adult could provide a useful framework for evaluation: what am I?
- High-quality interactions require practitioners to continuously evaluate their engagement strategies, questioning how their approaches–whether as connectors, challengers or observers–shape children's learning experiences. Regular reflection on interaction styles ensures that adult responses remain intentional, adaptive and impactful.

References

Bottrill, G. (2018). *Can I Go and Play Now? Rethinking the Early Years*. London: SAGE Publications.
Bronfenbrenner, U. (1979). *The Ecology of Human Development: Experiments by Nature and Design*. Cambridge: Harvard University Press.
Bronfenbrenner, U. (1989). Ecological systems theory. In R. Vasta (Ed.), *Annals of Child Development*, Vol. 6, Greenwich, CT: JAI Press.
Brown, S.C. (2014). *Parenting Beyond Pink and Blue*. United States: Ten Speed Press.
Carroll, M. (2024). UK's first 'teacherless' AI classroom set to open in London. *Sky News*. https://news.sky.com/story/uks-first-teacherless-ai-classroom-set-to-open-in-london-13200637
Convention on the Rights of the Child (1989) Treaty no. 27531. *United Nations Treaty Series*, 1577, pp. 3–178. Available at: https://www.ohchr.org/en/ohchr_homepage (Accessed: 7th October 2025).
Darling, J. and Nordenbo, S.E. (2003). *Progressivism: The Blackwell Guide to Philosophy of Education*. Oxford: Blackwell.
Davies, M. (2020). Raising theybies; navigating within a gendered world. Unpublished.
Dweck, C. (2015). Carol Dweck Revisits the 'Growth Mindset'. *Education Week*. Retrieved from: http://www.edweek.org/ew/articles/2015/09/23/carol-dweck-revisits-the-growth-mindset.html?cmp=cpc-googew-growth+mindsetandccid=growth+mindsetandccag=growth+mindsetandcckw=%2Bgrowth%20%2Bmindsetandcccv=content+adandgclid=CjOKEQiAnvfDBRCXrabLl6-6t-OBEiQAW4SRUM7nekFnoTxc675qBMSJycFgwERohguZWVmNDcSUg5gaAk3I8P8HAQ
Dweck, C. (2021). Growth Mindset - The Power of Yet - Ted Talk from: [video] Available at: https://www.youtube.com/watch?v=dxa2r8kpWcg [Accessed 14 Sep. 2025].
Dweck, C.S. (1986). Motivational processes affecting learning. *American Psychologist*, 41(10), 1040–1048.
Erodal, E. (2018). Practicing gender pedagogy: The case of egalia. *Journal of Qualitative Research in Education (JOQRE)*, 7(4), pp. 1367–1390.
Fisher, D. and Frey, N. (2013). *Better learning through structured teaching: A framework for the gradual release of responsibility*. 2nd edn. Alexandria, VA: ASCD.
Froebel, F. (1887). *The Education of Man*. Paris: Applewood Books.
Grimmer, T. (2021). *Developing a Loving Pedagogy in the Early Years: How Love Fits with Professional Practice*. Routledge. https://doi.org/10.4324/9781003023456
Harris, P. and Manatakis, H. (2013). *Children as citizens: Engaging with the child's voice in educational settings*. Adelaide: University of South Australia.
Hart, R.A. (1992). *Children's Participation: From Tokenism to Citizenship*. Florence, Italy: Unicef International Child Development Centre.
Hayes, N. (2024). 'It's not fair': Hearing the voices of young children. *Education 3-13*, 52(6), pp. 830–842.
Higgins, S. et al. (2017). *Sutton Trust - Education Endowment Foundation Early Sutton Trust - Education Endowment Foundation Early Years Toolkit | Communication and language approaches*, London: EEF. https://educationendowmentfoundation.org.uk/evidencesummaries/early-years-toolkit/communication-andlanguage-approaches/

Hirst, P.H. (1965). *Liberal Education and the Nature of Knowledge*. London: RKP.

Macdonald, N., Gealy, A.-M., and Tinney, G. (2021). Exploring the effect of an attachment intervention in areas of multiple deprivation on adult-child interaction and the implications for children's social, emotional and behavioural development. *Early Child Development and Care*, 191(5), pp. 670-684.

Mischel, W. (1966). 'A social learning view of sex differences in behavior',. In Maccoby, E. (Ed.) *The Development of Sex Differences*. Stanford: Stanford University Press, pp. 57-81.

Montessori, M. (1912). *The Montessori Method: Scientific Pedagogy as Applied to Child Education in "The Children's Houses"*. New York: Dover Publications.

Morris, A. (2018). It's a Theyby. *New York Magazine*, 2 April, pp. 40-43.

Myers, K. (2020). *Raising Them: Our Adventures In Gender Creative Parenting*. New York: Topple Books.

Oakeshott, M., (1962). *Rationalism in Politics and Other Essays*, London: Methuen.

Roberts-Holmes, G. and Moss, P. (2021). *Neoliberalism and Early Childhood Education: Markets, Imaginaries and Governance* (1st; ed.). Routledge.

Rogers, S. (2010). Chapter 1: Play and pedagogy: A conflict of interests?. In S. Rogers (Ed.), *Rethinking Play and Pedagogy in Early Childhood Education: Concepts, Contexts and Cultures* (pp. 5-18). Routledge.

Romeo, R.R., Segaran, J., Leonard, J.A., Robinson, S.T., West, M.R., Mackey, A.P., Yendiki, A., Rowe, M.L., and Gabrieli, J.D.E. (2018). Language exposure relates to structural neural connectivity in childhood. *Journal of Neuroscience*, 38(36), pp. 7870-7877. https://doi.org/10.1523/JNEUROSCI.0484-18.2018

Rousseau, J.J. (1762). *Emile or Treatise on Education*. New York: Appleton and Company.

Salsabila, I.N., Umam, A.F., Nurjanah, A., and Wahyuningsih, O. (2024). The role of gender in language and communication: A linguistic perspective. *Journal of Universal Studies*, 4(1), pp. 260-269.

SED (1965). *The Primary Memorandum*. Edinburgh: Scottish Education Department.

Standish, P., (2006). *Moral Education and the Limits of a Liberal Education*, London: Springer.

Sylva, K., Melhuish, E., Sammons, P., Siraj-Blatchford, I., and Taggart, B. (2004). The Effective Provision of Pre-school Education (EPPE) Project: Findings from Pre-school to end of Key Stage 1. Available at: https://dera.ioe.ac.uk/id/eprint/18189/2/SSU-SF-2004-01.pdf

Wall, K. and Robinson, C. (2022). Look who's talking: Eliciting the voice of children from birth to seven. *European Early Childhood Education Research Journal*, 30(1), pp. 1-7.

Zook, T. A. (2017). *Justice... Not Just Us: How One District-Level Social Justice-Oriented Transformative Leadership Team Addresses Marginalization and Oppression*. Wayne State University.

Zosuls, K.M., Miller, C.F., Ruble, D.N., Martin, C.L., and Fabes, R.A. (2011). Gender development research in sex roles: Historical trends and future directions. *Sex Roles*, 64(11-12), pp. 826-842.

14 The characteristics of effective learning

Poppy Gibson

Introduction

What does effective learning look like? This chapter presents the characteristics framework as included in the statutory framework for the EYFS, making direct reference to its importance within a holistic curriculum. Six experienced practitioners, who have embedded the teaching of the characteristics included in the framework into their own curriculum, share thoughtful reflections on the ways effective learning has taken place in their settings.

Pondering question: how can we ensure that the way children learn is given a similar consideration as what children learn?

An overview of the characteristics framework

In EYFS, effective learning is characterised by three key elements: playing and exploring, active learning and creating and thinking critically. These characteristics are foundational for developing confident and capable learners (Lowe and Kilgour, 2024). Step into any playgroup, childminder's home, nursery or Reception class and it is likely you will hear the practitioner asking children what they are doing; questions such as 'what are you making? What are you creating?' encourage communication and connection (England, 2025). With regards to playing and exploring, early years settings are the perfect space for 'playing and exploring' to take place. Children engage in play to learn, experiencing the world through various activities and investigations. This includes 'playing with what they know' and 'finding out and exploring', fostering curiosity and a willingness to try new things (Kay and Buxton, 2024). Active learning in EYFS may present as children taking an active role in their learning, demonstrating motivation, concentration and persistence (Thouless and Veale, 2024). Children should be absorbed in what they are doing and show a sense of purpose (Kay and Buxton, 2024). Children should show fascination and engagement, and have resilience in tasks that they may find tricky, but often keeping on trying when facing challenges (Bryce-Clegg, 2025). To create and think critically, there will be evidence of children developing their own ideas, making connections between concepts, and learning to think creatively in their early years space. They should use problem-solving skills, paying attention to details and developing strategies. These characteristics are not just about what children learn, but also about how they learn, fostering a lifelong love of learning and developing key skills and behaviours.

DOI: 10.4324/9781003505266-14

In this first contribution of this chapter, Glenn Denny, Nursery Manager, York, helps provide an overview of the Characteristics of Effective Learning (COEL) and provides practical explanation of what these look like in an early years setting.

Glenn Denny: Characteristics of Effective Learning (COEL)

In my setting, the Characteristics of Effective Learning (COEL) are woven into everything we do when it comes to setting up the environment. These characteristics: Playing and Exploring, Active Learning, and Creating and Thinking Critically, are embedded in our daily routines to support and enhance children's development.

When we design our learning spaces, we ensure there is a variety of open-ended resources to encourage children to engage and explore. An important aspect of this is natural materials such as sand, water and pebbles, alongside traditional toys, as we believe this invites curiosity and enables children to investigate and experiment freely. It's also important that we rotate these materials regularly, but also sensitively, to maintain interest and excitement, ensuring that the environment remains dynamic and engaging.

An example of this is our 'nature table' which was set up, for a child's interest, to include magnifying glasses, leaves, twigs and small plastic insects. Children were encouraged to touch, examine, immerse themselves and ask questions, fostering their natural inclination to explore and discover. This activity also fostered a link between our indoor and outdoor environments, as we took the exploration outside, moving the learning away from the plastic insects to looking for real minibeasts in the garden.

Our approach prioritises child-led activities that promote persistence, resilience and the enjoyment of achievements. The team observe children's interests and provides opportunities to extend their learning through invitations and provocations to learn and scaffolded support and encouragement through that process. Celebrating small milestones fosters a sense of pride and accomplishment in the children, reinforcing their motivation to learn.

During a morning session, a child struggled to build a tall structure with the wooden blocks. With gentle guidance and encouragement from their key person, the child persisted and eventually constructed a stable tower. This experience not only developed fine motor skills but also built resilience and determination, essential components of active learning.

As a team, we like to nurture critical thinking in our children, presenting them with challenges that require problem solving and independent thinking. As far as possible, the team will use open-ended questions and encourage children to come up with their solutions; we help them develop their ability to make connections and think logically.

One of the team had devised a 'mystery box' activity, in which children had to guess the contents of a box using clues and sensory exploration. This activity sparked discussions, predictions and collaborative problem solving, enhancing their cognitive skills and encouraging them to think critically about the information they gathered.

As a setting, we feel it is essential to embed COEL throughout the daily routine, from arrival to departure:

- **Morning Greetings**: each child is welcomed into the setting individually, promoting a sense of belonging and encouraging them to express their feelings.

- **Gather Time:** a space where children can share their thoughts and experiences, developing their communication and social skills. This is never a 'forced' activity; children are free to come and go as they please.
- **Free Play:** allowing ample time for self-directed play is crucial; this takes up the majority of our day and is vital for supporting their autonomy and decision-making abilities.
- **Outdoor Play:** the outdoor environment is essential for providing opportunities for physical activity and exploration of the natural environment, promoting both physical development and a sense of wonder about the world.

By embedding the Characteristics of Effective Learning throughout our nursery environment, we feel we are creating a rich, supportive and dynamic setting for children to thrive. Our commitment to Playing and Exploring, Active Learning and Creating and Thinking Critically ensures that each child can develop holistically, preparing them for future learning experiences. This approach not only supports their current development but lays the foundation for lifelong learning and curiosity.

In the next contribution, Dr Diane Boyd, Honorary Research Fellow School of Education University of Hull, offers a valuable consideration of how we can support young people to develop the key characteristic of agency, highlighting the importance of nurturing personal opinions and how to communicate with confidence.

Dr Diane Boyd: authentic agency through early childhood education for sustainability

The influential Brundtland Report highlighted the urgency of climate action and demonstrated the interconnected nature of Education for Sustainability (WCED, 1987: 47). There are three pillars of Sustainability (economic, environmental and socio-cultural) which are holistic, interconnecting and must not be viewed in isolation. The foundations of Education for Sustainability are laid in early childhood (Boyd, 2018) with pioneering giants such as Montessori and Malaguzzi positioning the child as a protagonist of their own learning, giving them authentic agency, resonating with the Tickell report (2011: 87) which first introduced the *Characteristics of Effective Learning*. In viewing the child as an agent of their own learning, the adult is positioning them as actively constructing their thinking, by seeking out questions and being authentic and confident decision makers. In 2021, the government introduced the Sustainability and Climate Change Strategy (DfE) which also highlights the challenge of climate action and that children must be given 'knowledge-rich education' through active hands-on learning. The three Characteristics of Effective Learning clearly resonate with children exploring their natural world, being active reflective participants in challenging issues and problems through critical and creative divergent thinking.

Environmental sustainability is the most understood and practised in early childhood, with wonderful projects that support children's awareness of their ecological and deep connections to their planet. Examples of this pillar would include children 'finding out' about their natural world over the four seasons, growing their own vegetables, gardening, encouraging bees through wildflower areas and developing empathy for the other non-human world. But children need to understand the rights of the environment too and become the 'voice' of the non-human world. When deciding where to position a bug hotel at a nursery in Liverpool, the children were conscious of the worms already living in a possible site. Through discussions they decided they wanted the worms to carry on living safely and securely in their homes and the bug hotel was moved elsewhere.

This empathy and care resonate with the socio-cultural pillar which is identified through terms such as participation, self-determination and activism. The DfE strategy on Sustainability and Climate Action (2021) asks children to have the capacity to translate 'knowledge into positive action and solutions'. Key components for Education for Sustainability were defined by UNESCO (2017) and there are clear alignments with 'critical thinking, self-awareness, and integrated problem-solving' and the Characteristics of Effective learning (DfE, 2025: 17). Before building their newly positioned bug hotel, the children had initially researched what indigenous bugs were local to Liverpool and what sort of environments each bug needed to thrive, as well ensuring sunshine and shade. This was a clear example of agentic children being involved in the planning, trying different solutions and concentrating and finding new ways (DfE, 2025: 17).

The economic pillar of Sustainability is considered the least understood in pedagogical practice (Siraj-Blatchford et al., 2010) but again clearly aligns with early childhood. The foundations of early childhood are built upon practical hands-on skills using real tools and terms of trade. Reflecting on Froebelian practice, the children in the gardens sold their vegetables to the local community and had opportunities to handle not just tools of the trade, but the terminology and practice of trading. In Liverpool when the children needed to purchase the materials for their bug hotel, the teacher, Kate, took them to the local hardware store—the 'fix it shop' as the children called it. Each child was given a five-pound note and a shopping list. They communicated with the trade personnel and identified their building supplies, added them to their shopping trolley and purchased them at the till, being given change and a receipt. This whole experience resonates with the three prime areas as well as the characteristics of effective learning (DfE, 2025: 8, 17) demonstrating the holistic nature of early childhood. Once back at the nursery the children were scaffolded by Tom the caretaker who provided the knowledge to build the bug hotel. This case study example, which includes the designing, planning, purchasing of materials and building the bug hotel, demonstrates how all three pillars of sustainability are interconnected and holistic. By 2025, the DfE is expecting all settings to have both a Sustainability lead and a Climate Action Plan in place, and this case study demonstrates how early childhood easily aligns with this requirement.

In this next section, Deborah Haddon reminds us of the value in upskilling practitioners so they are best placed to understand and provide effective learning.

Deborah Haddon: investing in practitioners

A few years ago, we were asked to create a unit for two-year-olds alongside our foundation unit (nursery and reception). Our current provision was part of an inner-city primary school serving a complex community: one-parent families, social deprivation and generations of patterns of neglect and trauma. The starting point, as conscientious practitioners, was to research schemas, visit other provisions and talk to colleagues who had been on this journey. They also revisited the characteristics of effective learning and checked that within the planning cycle there was opportunity for finding out, exploring, application, making links and so on.

In addition to this, resources were ordered, the space was created, and we were ready to welcome our first group of two-year-olds.

The first two or three weeks were chaos! Lots of screaming and crying, very few of the young people settled and there appeared to be little learning and/or development happening. Constant discussions and a review of resources and opportunities for 'effective learning' were considered; we seemed to spend hours observing staff interactions and the behaviours of the children. Staff were doing everything to encourage play and exploration by providing an environment based on individual interests but the children were not making progress. The two-year-old unit was becoming a battle ground and potentially unhealthy for both the young people who attended and the practitioners.

One of the nursery colleagues was a particularly skilled and effective practitioner and they were invited to observe, reflect and provide feedback to support the practitioners in the two-year-old unit. Their particular strength was building healthy attachments and relationships with young people, fostering a culture of safety, trust, connection and belonging. It soon became noticeably clear that, whilst the staff had been trained in the EYFS, what hadn't been communicated was the importance of those four key elements: safety, trust, connection and belonging. This was the missing part of the jigsaw. It seemed so obvious to those of us who had been practitioners for a number of years and, let's face it, had perfected the art of developing these relationships naturally.

Subsequently we embarked on a fast-track journey to upskill our existing practitioners. They observed exemplary practice in these four areas through observation of modelling, peer/team facilitating and discussing videos of ways to develop and nurture connections.

The outcome was that the safety of the young people and the relationship/healthy attachment encouraged and developed was paramount to them leaving the attachment with their carer initially, becoming more confident to explore, play, to 'find out.' What we realised is that whilst the characteristics of effective learning are absolutely fundamental in any provision, the foundation to this is a sense of safety, belonging and the relationships firstly with staff members and widening to developing relationships with peers.

In some ways it seems obvious: a child will explore more freely given a safe and nurturing environment, and it does state in the Statutory Framework 'Children need to build an attachment with their key person for their confidence and well-being' (p. 17).

However, does this really communicate to practitioners the importance of this? It did provoke questions and considerations of the EYFS. Does it actually explain the importance of this for a child to make progress? Is there an assumption that practitioners will already know and implement it?

Next, Marianne Hixon, Early Years Teacher, advocates for a secure connection between the characteristics framework and the observation, assessment and planning cycle in order to strengthen progress and outcomes.

Marianne Hixon: embrace every child's learning style through the characteristics of effective learning

In my experience children can be motivated and exposed to more richly resourced play activities when linking in the use of the Characteristic of Effective Learning framework within the teacher's planning, implementation and observations continually.

They fully support the seven areas within the Development Matters document, including the process of learning and development, a unique child, positive relationships and enabling environments which will provide opportunities for children to learn and develop at their own pace.

On reflection, I can see that the three areas enhance the child's natural curiosity and the skills they are building on, by instilling a love of learning, through the thrill of discovery. Playing and Exploring builds on the ability to get engaged, whilst Active Learning builds on their resilience and Creating and Thinking Critically fosters a sense of excitement and reflection for their learning. I believe the best way to get the children motivated in their learning is to use the play-based ideas that interest them but use the characteristics to gently nudge them into other activities, ensuring that they have learning experiences in all seven areas of the curriculum. We have all had a child who just loves the bike and will happily spend their time whizzing around the playground and does not engage in other activities. So, by using the characteristics that the children get to know well, they can start to bring in other elements of learning. For example, the child who demonstrates playing and exploring on only the bike can be encouraged to actively learn through set challenges such as the will to succeed at the new assault course we set up, then onto creating and thinking for themselves as they are given resources to build a different course. By scaffolding their learning we can then introduce the idea of mark making, writing simple instructions for the bike riders, alongside maths such as arrows pointing to which way to ride and assigning numbers to bikes. They can then be offered resources that motivate and encourage further active learning and creative thinking such as making a garage from large boxes, finding out different surfaces of roads and even exploring what it would be like for the rider to travel through water on the bike. Using the framework, the list is endless and a very powerful tool for ensuring all areas of the curriculum are promoted, implemented and engaging.

In my opinion, observations and next steps that are supported by the characteristics provide the teaching staff with insights not only into what children are learning but also into how they are learning. This knowledge is invaluable for end-of-year reports and formative and summative assessments, as well as for sharing information with the next teacher as the child progresses into their next year. Most importantly, it allows for effective planning to ensure that any learning gaps are addressed for all children, including those with SEND and EAL.

I find that the best way to record each child's progress and utilise all three characteristics is by using a Venn diagram. In this diagram, we plot their names to reflect their transition from one area to another and ultimately encompass all three. If a child stays in the Playing and Exploring and never goes into the Creating and Thinking Critically, we can then identify what is needed in the environment, ensuring they are given the opportunities to make more sense of their experiences by linking ideas and choosing how they do things. This enables them to succeed and develop their ability to reach their own goals using the strategies that work for them, placing them in all three areas.

I truly believe that the implementation of the characteristics must always be in place throughout the provision and can be achieved in many different ways. I personally like the use of the dinosaurs, Shareadocus, Tryatops and an Askaraptor where the children will take on responsibility for recognising which dinosaur their learning achievements was, by moving their name or photo on to that character on an interactive display board and getting a sticker of that character. They also love to share their success during reflection time by talking about and showing the class any photos that they took themselves of their learning.

This gives them the ability to develop listening and speaking skills, build on vocabulary and grow the skill for articulation and confidence. The children are also supporting each other, learning to praise others, developing ideas for challenging themselves to succeed in each dinosaur, and building their self-esteem.

The Characteristics of Effective Learning can ensure that children are inspired, motivated and stimulated through play that develops imagination and creativity whilst enriching their experiences and giving them the reassurance that the adults value their ideas and achievements.

In this contribution, Catherine Mather, Early Years personal tutor, champions the characteristic of active learning, providing a wealth of practical ideas for implementation.

Catherine Mather: active learning

Active learning is a continual process; it is engagement and collaboration with others and ultimately children constructing learning for themselves. The adult's responsibility is to provide children with rich learning environments where they can explore, investigate, experiment and manipulate. Children's learning is fluid and knowledge of their individual needs, likes, dislikes and preferences ensures a potentiating environment that provides positive outcomes for children. The context in which learning takes place and the relationships with the children can have profound effects for future learning and personal, social and emotional development. It is therefore essential that significant relationships are qualitative. It is during play that children develop their critical thinking and by asking open-ended questions. Children are active learners. They seek to explore and make sense of their surroundings. The learning environment should be carefully planned, to provide children with optimum opportunities to make choices, decisions and solve problems (Montessori, 1967).

Playing with a variety of loose parts assists the approaches mentioned above. The concept has been around for many years, as children have always played with whatever they discovered in nature. 'In any environment, the degree of inventiveness and creativity, and the possibility of discovery, are directly proportional to the number and kind of variables in it' (Nicholson, 1972: 22). In other words, loose parts help to provide a rich play environment for children of any age. Loose parts are materials that can be carried, moved, combined, taken apart and put back together in a variety of ways. They can be natural or manufactured and can be used in infinite ways. Natural objects, such as pinecones, twigs, flowers, sand and stones can provide rich opportunities for creativity and can be used in transient art activities. The indoor environment also provides a multitude of resources, such as bottle caps, buttons, beads, cardboard tubes and fabrics. These enable children to develop their skills in symbolic play (Goldsworthy, 1997). Children are creative and crucial learning experiences come from being involved in the creating process. Providing children with the opportunity to play with a wide variety of loose parts empowers them to create and use their imagination (Nicholson, 1972). Loose parts have no defined purpose; they can be anything and can be used in any way.

Loose parts provide child-initiated, age-appropriate skills including mathematical development through ordinal numbers and one-to-one correspondence. Emotional intelligence, social and emotional skills, negotiating and communicating are all supported by opportunities for this approach to play. Loose parts play enables creativity and imagination. When observing young children playing with loose parts and everyday objects, they explore more effectively in contexts. Pretend play and make-believe play are facilitators for creative and flexible thinking. When considering creative thinking in children, loose parts and recycled objects can be used to enable creativity. Using recycled items can improve a child's flexible thinking skills because recycled items may be used to produce a diverse range of products. Children can practise their problem-solving skills as they manipulate objects in different ways. The use of such unstructured materials helps to support children's divergent thinking and helps them to think of innovative ways to use objects (Rule, Zhbanova, Hileman, Evans, and Schneider, 2011). The development of perseverance is supported by construction and problem-solving play (Sylva, Bruner and Genova, 1976).

In this final contribution, Michael Charles Fransen Cresswell, Tutor in Education at Coventry University, urges reflection on the wealth of research exploring the characteristics framework and its role in both teaching and learning.

Michael Charles Fransen Cresswell: integrating diverse educational philosophies in the early years

As Early Years educators, embracing a multifaceted approach to learning is paramount. An exploration of the symbiotic relationship between classical and postmodern theoretical perspectives provides a lens through which practitioners can enhance their pedagogical strategies.

Classical theories aim to objectively determine development in a universal state (Ryan and Grieshaber, 2005). This theoretical perspective incorporates concepts like psychosocial development, behaviourism and maturational perspectives and provides a foundational understanding of child development (Aubrey and Riley, 2022; Bates, 2023; MacBlain, 2022). These approaches, underscored by the works of Piaget, Erikson and Skinner (to name a few), are echoed across early years contexts, emphasising apparently predictable stages of growth and the transformative role of educators in driving or shaping the learning journey. Such theories advocate for a structured approach, where play and interaction serve as cornerstones of child development.

In contrast, postmodern theoretical perspectives, such as humanism and social constructivism, challenge these linear narratives, positing that learning is a complex, socially constructed process—found in some of the ideas from Vygotsky, Rogers, Dewey, Bandura and Bruner et al. (Aubrey and Riley, 2022; Bates, 2023; MacBlain, 2022). This paradigm shift questions the ability to define these universal developmental laws, suggesting instead that our understanding of learning is coloured by the values and power dynamics of its proponents (Ryan and Grieshaber, 2005). This critique invites Early Years educators to consider the broader implications of their teaching methodologies, recognising the diverse contexts and 'unique child' (DfE, 2025: 7) from which children emerge.

The task at hand is not to choose between these paradigms but to weave them into a cohesive 'educational woven mat' of pedagogy and curriculum. By integrating the structured guidance of classical theories with the adaptive, inclusive ethos of postmodernism, educators then embody the curriculum in their knowledge and skills as 21st-century practices. This is important for Early Years practitioners because they can then create environments that not only support developmental milestones but also respect the unique identities of each child.

This blended approach has profound implications for the continuity of educational experiences as children transition beyond the early years. It underscores the need for subsequent educational curriculum or frameworks to embody the same ethos of inclusivity and adaptability, ensuring a seamless progression for children and families alike. It is possible to see examples of this already in place, such as the values and principles in the Norwegian primary and secondary curriculum (Ministry of Education and Research, 2019), while in other places in the world, reform may have not yet evolved.

In crafting this narrative, the aim is to inspire Early Years practitioners to reflect on their practice, embracing the complexity and richness of educational theories, and push the boundaries of possibility in curriculum and practice. Such reflective practice, grounded in a deep understanding of both classical and postmodern perspectives, empowers educators to foster learning environments where every child can thrive, laying the groundwork for a lifetime of curious, adaptable and critical thinking.

Championing a practice informed by diverse educational philosophies enables us to have the characteristics of effective learning, paving the way for a more inclusive, dynamic future for early childhood education and reform in further stages of childhood education.

In conclusion

This chapter explores the Characteristics of Effective Learning (COEL) in Early Years education, sharpening the importance of fostering curiosity, resilience and independent thinking. It examines the three key characteristics outlined in the EYFS framework: Playing and Exploring, Active Learning and Creating and Thinking Critically, showcasing how practitioners embed these elements within their settings to create rich learning environments. Contributions from experienced educators illustrate practical strategies, such as integrating open-ended resources, scaffolding children's problem solving and cultivating agency through sustainability projects. The chapter also highlights the role of secure attachments, practitioner reflection and continuous professional development in ensuring that children's learning experiences are meaningful and engaging.

Summary of key points

- **The importance of safe and secure relationships**: a foundation of safety, trust, connection and belonging is essential for young children before they can begin to explore and learn effectively. This reinforces the importance of building strong relationships between children and caregivers.
- **Characteristics of Effective Learning (COEL) as a framework**: several educators in this chapter emphasise the value of COEL (Playing and Exploring, Active Learning, and Creating and Thinking Critically) in designing learning environments and activities. This framework promotes exploration, curiosity, problem solving, and critical thinking in children.
- **Play based learning for holistic development**: there is a strong consensus among the contributors in this chapter that play is crucial for children's development. Active, child-led play fosters not just cognitive skills but also social, emotional and physical development.

- **Importance of diverse learning materials and environments**: creating a rich and stimulating environment with a variety of open-ended materials is essential. This allows children to explore their interests, experiment and be creative. Natural materials and loose parts are particularly valuable in this regard.
- **The teacher's role as a facilitator and observer**: the teacher's role is key in providing stimulating environments, scaffolding learning and observing children's interests and progress.

References

Aubrey, K., and Riley, A. (2022). *Understanding and Using Educational Theories* (3rd ed.) Sage Publications.

Bates, B. (2023). *Learning Theories Simplified* (3rd ed.) Sage Publications.

Boyd, D. (2018). Early Childhood Education for Sustainability and the historical legacies of two pioneering giants. *International Journal of Early Years, 38*(2), pp. 227-239.

Bryce-Clegg, A. (2025). *Effective Transition into Year One: A Practical Guide to Creating a Successful Play-based Learning Environment*. Bloomsbury Publishing.

Department for Education (2021). Sustainability and climate change strategy. [online]. Available at: https://www.gov.uk/government/publications/sustainability-and-climate-change-strategy/sustainability-and-climate-change-a-strategy-for-the-education-and-childrens-services-systems

Dfe (2025). Early years foundation stage statutory framework for group and school-based providers. Setting the standards for learning, development and care for children from birth to five. Available at: https://assets.publishing.service.gov.uk/media/687105a381dd8f70f5de3ea9/EYFS_framework_for_group_and_school_based_providers_.pdf (Accessed 21 July 2025).

England, L. (2025). *Schemas: A Practical Handbook: Explains What Schemas are and How to Identify Them with Ideas on How to Expand on That Knowledge*. Bloomsbury Publishing.

Goldsworthy, A. (1997). *Andy Goldsworthy: A Collaboration with Nature*. London: Thames & Hudson.

Kay, L., and Buxton, A. (2024). Makerspaces and the characteristics of effective learning in the Early Years. *Journal of Early Childhood Research, 22*(3), pp. 343-358.

Lowe, A., and Kilgour, S. (2024). *The Inclusive Early Years Educator: A Reflective Toolkit*. Taylor & Francis Group.

MacBlain, S. (2022). *Learning Theories for Early Years Practice* (2nd ed.). Sage Publications.

Ministry of Education and Research (2019). Core Curriculum – values and principles for primary and secondary education, Government.no, Norway. Available at: https://www.regjeringen.no/en/dokumenter/verdier-og-prinsipper-for-grunnopplaringen---overordnet-del-av-lareplanverket/id2570003/

Montessori, M. (1967). *The Discovery of the Child*. (ed. 1972). New York: Ballantine.

Nicholson, S. (1972). The theory of loose parts: An important principle for design methodology. *Studies in Design Education, Craft and Technology 4*(2), 5-14.

Rule, A.C., Zhbanova, K., Hileman, A., Evans, J., and Schneider, J.S. (2011). Exploring Torrance's Creative Strengths by Making an Object from a Set of Given Materials. *Cutting beyond the edge: New realities in gifted education: Iowa Talented and Gifted Association Annual Conference*, October 17-18, Des Moines, Iowa: Airport Holiday Inn.

Ryan, S., and Grieshaber, S. (2005). Shifting from developmental to postmodern practices in early childhood teacher education. *Journal of Teacher Education, 56*(1), pp. 34-45, American Association of Colleges for Teacher Education.

Siraj-Blatchford, J., Smith, K.C., and Samuelsson, I.P. (2010). *Education for Sustainable Development in the Early Years*. World Organization for Early Childhood Education.

Sylva, K., Bruner, J.S., and Genova, P. (1976). The role of play in the problem-solving of children 3-5 years old. In J.S. Bruner, A. Jolly, and K. Sylva (Eds.), *Play: Its Role in Development and Evolution* (pp. 55-67). Harmondsworth: Penguin.

Thouless, H., and Veale, V. (2024). From 4 to 104: The characteristics of effective learning. Available at Thouless and Veale Special Edition 2024.

Tickell, D.C. (2011). The Early Years: Foundations for life, health and learning, An Independent Report on the Early Years Foundation Stage to Her Majesty's Government.

UNESCO (2017). *Education for Sustainable Development Goals: Learning Objectives*. Paris, France: UNESCO.

WCED (1987). *Our Common Future: The World Commission on Environment and Development*. UK: Oxford University Press.

15 The importance of implementing EYFS principles as a whole school

Jayne Carter

Introduction

For most EYFs professionals, being given the opportunity to talk about EYFS could be classed as a default professional setting! Any avenue to share how effective teaching approaches and strategies support children in the early years ignites the personal and professional fire of a passionate practitioner. As more and more schools and settings are exploring the potential of either replicating an EYFS model totally or adapting some of the key principles to implement throughout the whole provision, we can learn from others pioneering this. The contributors included in this chapter have shown how they have worked towards developing their own whole school or setting approach, secure in their own vision of collaboration. Their reflections of what has worked well for them, as well as the acknowledgment that ideas need to be continuously adapted, offer so many fruitful points for others to learn from.

Pondering question: what are the key EYFS ideas you would like to implement through your own school? Why?

Ofsted, in their research and analysis document, 'Strong foundations in the first years of school' (2024) present their findings from exploring effective practice in schools who have adapted their provision to ensure that their children in EYFS and KS1 have secure foundational aspects of learning. Their key recommendations from this research state:

Schools should:

- make sure that the curriculum clearly identifies the foundational knowledge and skills, as outlined in the EYFS and national curriculum, that children will need for later learning
- give children sufficient high-quality opportunities to practise using foundational knowledge and skills so that they become fluent
- choose teaching methods that are suited to what is being taught and what children already know
- make sure that assessment picks up children's misunderstandings quickly and gives teachers early opportunities to help children who need extra teaching and practice
- make sure that end of key stage 1 assessments do not disproportionately influence decisions about curriculum and teaching methods

All recommendations included in this report advocate for a strong collaborative culture, where there is a commitment to understanding and planning a curriculum for their children which demonstrates aspiration for all.

EYFS led conversations: continuing a developmentally rich discussion

In my work as an Early Years consultant I am always delighted, a little surprised and sometimes bemused when I share key aspects of the EYFS with others. My absolute favourite is when I share the characteristics framework, particularly with key stage 2 or secondary colleagues. It is mostly met with cries of 'where has this framework been' or 'is it ok for me to use this?' I always respond with a 'yes, we want you to know about it!' I am also sure that most schools and settings include in their policies a dedication to developing both knowledge acquisition and skills to be able to apply this learnt knowledge; a commitment towards a holistic approach to teaching and learning. Often an aspect already used in EYFS can offer a solution to a school's and setting's ongoing intention for improvement and may provide both the academic and pedagogical process for the school team. Any change is frequently a process to be navigated, often with the need to include both a leadership guiding model and a collaborative model simultaneously in order to drive a change in beliefs and practices. Whilst adopting a new approach or a new 'way of doing things' is a crucial start of the journey, it should be acknowledged that it is it firmly the beginning, with more parts to be added. Contributions in this chapter stress the absolute importance of using this start to cement a whole school approach, emphasising the importance of moving away from a simple list of new approaches and moving towards communicating the reasons behind these choices. Being involved in a shift of teaching methods involves a shift in how the adults feel, understand and skilfully use the proposed new approach. Without this being an integral part of any change model, adults could feel that they are part of a 'done to' model rather than a united 'done with' model. Ensuring everyone's 'buy in' is a significant motivator in achieving success and desired change resulting in improvement.

Decisions and choices

Why do some schools and settings initially decide to make a change using EYFS principles? These changes could happen as a result of recognising the existing outstanding provision in Early Years and/or the commitment and visionary approach to support all children's holistic development. When exploring analysis around reasons and desired change, the theme of improving mental health and wellbeing is pivotal to many of the schools and settings pioneering alternative approaches. In fact, this intention is at the top of most leaders' agenda, with the thought that improving this aspect of the whole school community would act as a catalyst for further adaptations/modifications to teaching, learning and outcomes. The development of nurturing spaces, a redesigning of learning environments to facilitate collaboration between children and an increased inclusion of further independent opportunities for co-regulation throughout all classes have been both popular and effective. The impact has been enlightening for those adults who have more experience in KS1 and KS2. They have noticed increased levels of engagement and much more collaborative talk between children as well as a reduction in reminders of accepted behaviour. Another key EYFS adoption in schools has been the planning, observation and assessment process. In early years, practitioners use a child-led approach which is underpinned with secure practitioner knowledge of child development and individual strengths/needs. As a result of this ongoing record of achievement, children's successes can be enhanced and potential misconceptions or gaps supported early to ensure that learning continues.

Learning from others

In the Department for Education's video (Chapter 2) showcasing schools who have adopted an EYFS approach as a whole school, one school shared how they completely changed their existing assessment policy to reflect the sound processes in place in their EYFS unit. Fundamentally, as a school leadership team, they removed the historic expectation to report data each half term, choosing instead to have more regular professional supervision meetings on the most vulnerable children. Obviously, just removing this data-led expectation was initially met with immense agreement, which the leaders swiftly captured and trained all staff in what the new observation, planning and assessment cycle would look like. They gave this responsibility to their EYFS team as the experts in this area, through a peer-to-peer model. Time was also given to the understanding and implementation of this new model, with frequent meetings to reflect on its use, practitioner confidence and space for troubleshooting. As a result, staff felt that they had far more autonomy in their own classrooms as the necessity of generating results had been replaced by deeper conversations and support with their children. Leaders had much more useful evaluations which could be firmly focused on demonstrating their school vision of personalised achievement.

In this first contribution, Lucy Fox, Early Years Leader, invites reflections on how continuous provision can be used effectively within KS1, sharing their own journey of implementing this beyond Early Years.

Lucy Fox: using continuous provision in KS1

It is mid-June. It is sweltering in the tiny classroom I am sat in. Surrounding me are groups of haggard-looking teachers, sat amongst piles of folders, scrapbooks and laptops. We are mid-way through our annual network moderation for early years and I am neck deep in a discussion with a fellow Early Years Lead about a child of mine who, bless his heart, just doesn't like to sit for very long. As our discussion becomes more animated and together, we cannot reach a mutual decision, a small crowd begins to gather around us. Taking the opportunity amongst the silence, I hear somebody say above the noise:

> At the end of the day, you need to ask yourself this: Is this child ready to sit for an hour every day at a table and write? That is what GLD (Good Level of Development) is about.

This was a turning point for me. I don't think I will ever forget that conversation. It was at that moment that I decided with my whole heart that the little boy in question was going to be given ticks for all his goals. Rather than second guess my own judgement, I turned to the lady who had spoke and said back:

> We don't expect our children to sit still and write for an hour here.

At my school, we implement a continuous provision approach across the whole of Key Stage 1. For us, it is a no brainer. As you reach the end of the early years, it is very easy to scale down the level of play offered to the children in a bid to get them 'school ready'. But what does it mean to be 'school ready'? Should it be measured by a child's ability to sit still? To listen for long periods of time? By the amount of writing in a blue book? Or instead, should we be measuring the term 'school ready' by taking a deeper look at the EYFS Characteristics of Effective Learning?

What is clear from current and relevant research is that a child can make significantly more progress throughout their primary school career when they have been given the chance to lay a strong foundation and by this, I mean the development of solid behaviours for learning.

Continuous provision allows children to develop several schemas which are important when we talk about the creation of life-long learners:

- A willingness to take risks. Play allows children to take risks in a variety of settings set up and created by them. Taking ownership of risk allows the children to experience failure in a measured way which they are in control of.
- A curiosity to ask questions. Asking questions about play allows children to develop further thinking, leading to deeper knowledge building and an ability to self-evaluate.
- The ability to show learning in a variety of ways. As adults, none of us think the same way. We all organise our knowledge and thinking using different approaches and the same chance should be given to children.

We are new to the building of continuous provision beyond early years, but so far, we have only positive outcomes and stories. Our children have never been more passionate or articulate about their learning and the difference in them as learners is huge. Developing a strong progressive policy on 'Play as Learning' is now our main priority across the early years and KS1. We adapt to meet the demands of the National Curriculum by making the environments in Year 1 and 2 as open ended as possible, whilst introducing a set of tasks/learning that the children must show or document during their school day. We call these 'must dos' and the children love them. The beauty of asking a set of children to demonstrate their understanding of the continents using their environment and then watching the *'play residue'* that comes from that is immeasurable.

Should the time arrive where we feel that there is a place for continuous provision beyond Year 2, I feel confident in the knowledge that it will fit right in and that our children will thrive. For now, though, our children across the EYFS and KS1 are excited about their learning and are some of the most articulate learners I have come across. That is all that matters.

In this next contribution, Dr Rachel Briggs, a Reflective Supervision in Education practitioner: illuminates the vital practice of supervision which, if implemented effectively, should provide a framework of professional support for the whole setting/school.

Dr. Rachel Briggs: mandatory supervision in EYFS

The Tickell Review (2011) recommended that supervision should be available to EYFS practitioners as a tool for supporting the management of practice and for giving practitioners a route for raising concerns and accessing support (e.g., related to clarity of roles and responsibilities, safeguarding, professional development, children's care and challenging situations). In 2012, supervision became a statutory requirement and remains so for all EYFS staff who have contact with children and families (DfE, 2025: 29).

Despite its mandatory status, I regularly talk to EYFS staff who are not receiving supervision and to leaders (particularly in primary schools), who, due to a lack of clarity and guidance, are unaware of the process of supervision as it is meant in this context. Here, supervision is not about being watched, controlled and judged as might be expected if applying its 'common' usage. Instead, what is meant is supervision akin to that offered in other 'helping professions' such as health and social care.

So, what is supervision?

Even within sectors where there is a strong tradition of supervision, there are lots of differences in terminology, for instance, related to supervision type (professional, reflective, clinical, safeguarding) and its functions. Despite the different terminology, lack of universally agreed definition and multiple models, there is agreement that supervision does not imply that the practitioner is 'in deficit' or can't be trusted; rather, supervision involves developing what Professor Peter Hawkins (Hawkins and McMahon, 2020) calls a 'super form of vision'.

The functions, common across all models, can be summarised as:

- Educative–focusing on developing the supervisee's skills, understanding and capacities
- Supportive–focusing on the emotional and psychological impact of the supervisee's work
- Qualitative–focusing on best practice and upholding professional standards.

These are achieved through a non-judgemental, reflective and collaborative conversation. This could be 1:1s, pairs or groups and provided by a colleague or supervisor external to the school. Conversations should facilitate a deeper look at work experiences (and if relevant, factors beyond work), with practitioners being supported to reflect on their values, practice (e.g., leadership, teaching, safeguarding), relationships, the emotional demands of their work, the wider education system and the impact (both positive and negative) that these have on their work, themselves and others.

Although empirical research and anecdotal evidence in supervision in education are limited, available evidence suggests that supervision can contribute to best practice, effective relationships, enhanced wellbeing, professional and personal development, and reduced sickness absence and turnover.

Supervision is confidential (unless content indicates a serious mental health concern, risk to self or others, professional misconduct or illegal activity) so governors should not be informed of content discussed in supervision sessions. Although currently there is no guidance from the DfE on delivering effective supervision in education, governors should ensure that there is an appropriate supervision policy in place (see further reading suggestions for support) and check that supervision is occurring in line with it and any future DfE guidelines. To support a culture of supervision, governors should promote a healthy balance between challenge, accountability and support. They could also check that staff have appropriate professional development and wellbeing support opportunities.

In this next contribution, the pivotal role of leadership, especially through governance, is discussed and presented as a model for whole setting/school improvement.

Nicola Carvell: reflections on Governors and Leadership

Effective Governance is critical for a school and specifically, EYFS Governance is an area of leadership which cannot be overlooked. In schools, Governors are often appointed to year groups or subjects, but the EYFS is a specialist area of provision and needs to be understood, at a deep level, to ensure that the minimum, legal requirements are met. As OFSTED makes a separate judgement on the early years, having the support of a well-versed, rehearsed and passionate Governing Body is critical for a positive outcome.

As a school we have a Governor-led Nursery (which stands alone to the school and the school's budget) in addition to two Reception classes. We are fortunate that we have a Governing Body who understands the value and importance of early childhood and children's learning and development. This does not happen by chance. Appointing people to the Governing Body who have the right skills, interests and passion is critical to the success of the school's wider leadership. The role of a Governor is to listen, reflect and challenge the school's leadership and to understand and support the actions needed to secure best practise. In order to do this, the Governors need to be well informed of this unique phase of a child's education and development.

As a school, we have invested time in building our relationships with our Governors. We have offered training in the Statutory Welfare Requirements and regularly invite the Governors into our settings. There are no sessions put on for 'show.' To support us and our needs and our drive for continuous improvement, we want our Governors to see us as we are. An example of this would be that last year, the EYFS Governor observed us administer a Reception Baseline Assessment. This enabled our Governor to understand what was involved and the time taken away from our new children to deliver the assessment. Our Governor was asked about the assessment by Ofsted and they were able to competently talk from experience.

At full Governor meetings, the EYFS is a standing agenda item. As EYFS lead, I support the EYFS Governor in writing a report to help them communicate our key priorities and the challenges and the barriers we face to achieving them. Importantly, we also ensure that our achievements and moments of great pride are also shared and celebrated.

Through visiting our settings and meeting and talking to staff, parents and children, our Governors fully understand the complexities of the EYFS. Governors attend our new intake meetings to meet our new families, and we also invite Governors to special events. Termly, together we review our EYFS action plan and monitor the progress we are making. As EYFS lead, I share links to the latest research from the EEF and other bodies with our Governors.

We are fortunate to have a highly effective relationship with our EYFS Governor, but this does not happen by chance. Appointing the right person to the role and having a positive partnership, whereby you collaborate effectively and receive and welcome challenge as an opportunity to reflect and grow, is the key to good governance. Having Governors who understand the complexities of the EYFS is a critical factor in ensuring that you, your team and the children can all thrive, develop and celebrate great opportunities and outcomes.

Next, Laura Douglas, ITT leader, L.E.A.D. Teaching School Hub, Lincolnshire, presents a collection of top tips for both trainees and mentors which are essential in the early years and beyond. They offer a framework to ensure that high-quality teaching and learning is paramount.

Laura Douglas: Top tips for trainee EYFS teachers and mentors

Five top tips for trainees in the Early Years:

1) Build positive relationships
   Relationships are key—this is true when working with the children, your mentor, colleagues in school and with parents. There are lots of people to get to know as an EYFS teacher—teaching is very much a 'people profession' and the importance of valuing such relationships cannot be underestimated.
2) Spend time getting to know the children and their interests.
   As young learners, they will be keen to get to know you and will no doubt ask you many questions! Answer these with a smile and ask the children questions to find out more about their interests and what they like to do in the setting.
3) Get down to the children's level.
   This is key to building positive relationships with the children. As another 'grown up' in class, you will tower above the children in height and will be unfamiliar to them at the beginning of placement. Therefore from day one, sit on the carpet with the children, sit at the tables and be involved in what the children are doing.
4) Be positive
   The saying 'the teacher sets the weather in the classroom' is very true. It is understandable to be nervous, particularly at the beginning of a placement. However, if you look nervous and worried, this will be noticed by the children and can affect the climate for learning. Therefore, smile and be positive!
5) Ask questions
   No question is ever a silly question! Asking questions is how we learn, no matter what the age of the learner. There will be lots of new words and phrases and many acronyms which can feel quite overwhelming when training. Work with your mentor to develop your understanding of this as you move through your placement.

Five top tips for mentors:

1) Reflect
   Thank you for taking on this very important role. The role of a mentor is a privilege—you are shaping a teacher of the future, who will impact the education of countless lives. Think back to when you were training… how did you feel? Were you nervous? Excited? Both? What kind of mentor did you have? What kind of mentor do you want to be?
2) Support the trainee in building positive relationships
   From the beginning of a placement, ensure the trainee feels welcome as part of the 'setting's family'. There will be lots of new faces, both adults and children, for the trainee to meet and get to know and the more welcome and settled the trainee can feel from

the beginning, the more effective the transition will be from an extra adult in school to trainee EYFS teacher.

In the classroom, both indoor and outdoor, model to the trainee how to work with the children. Each trainee will be very different in their approach—some will be keen to be involved from day one and will confidently ask the children about what they are learning. Others will be quieter and will require you to model how to get down to the children's level.

Building relationships with parents is important. Encourage the trainee to shadow you when you welcome the children into class, introducing the trainee to parents as a trainee teacher.

3) Be positive

Just as a teacher 'sets the weather' in their classroom, a mentor is highly influential in the mindset of the developing teacher. Therefore, the importance of being a positive role model cannot be understated. Modelling how to be solution-focused, for example how you prioritise, will build good teacher habits and will stand the trainee in good stead as an early career teacher.

4) Have clear, manageable practice points

As an expert-colleague, you will do so much without even realising; the art of teaching young learners has become second nature to you, and there will be so many things that you do automatically. Consider the analogy of learning to drive – to begin with, you consciously think about mirror-signal-manoeuvre, and over time, this becomes second nature.

In this next contribution, Tracy Hopkins, EYFS Associate Headteacher: Transform Trust, shares a useful description of how EYFS provision is strategically planned for within Transform Trust.

Tracy Hopkins: developing early years pedagogy across a multi-academy trust

At Transform Trust, our schools are 'United but uniquely different' so when I was tasked with developing an early years vision, I had to ensure that this could be individualised and embedded throughout all of our schools. So, we decided to explore 'What does excellence look like in the EYFS?' First of all, I explored our dedication to early years pedagogy.

We acknowledge the remarkable diversity within the communities of our Trust schools. Consequently, our approach to early years pedagogy is richly informed by this diversity. We recognise that every child is unique in their experiences, languages and cultural backgrounds. We promote research-informed practice together with a thorough knowledge and understanding of the context-specific needs of the children and families.

A robust Early Years Foundation Stage (EYFS) curriculum is the cornerstone of a child's educational journey, shaping their development in profound ways. It lays the groundwork for future learning and sets the stage for a successful academic and personal life. The curriculum should be well-rounded, adaptable and child-centred, fostering a love for learning and preparing young children for future success in school and in life.

Play is the primary mode of learning for young children. An effective EYFS curriculum should incorporate play-based activities that promote exploration, problem solving, and critical thinking. Play is essential for developing language, social skills and creativity. Children learn best when they are actively engaged in various activities that cater to their diverse needs.

Curriculum development is crucial because it ensures that education remains relevant, effective and adaptable to the evolving needs of children and society. It plays a vital role in shaping the quality of education and the outcomes for our children, making it an essential component of educational systems worldwide.

- High-Quality Teaching: staff in the EYFS should provide high-quality teaching that is adapted to meet the individual needs of each child. Teachers and practitioners should have a deep understanding of child development and how to support children's learning effectively.
- Exceptional Learning Outcomes: children's progress and development should be exceptional, with evidence of sustained progress across all areas of learning. Children should be making good progress and achieving their full potential.
- A Nurturing and Inclusive Environment: the setting should provide a safe, inclusive and nurturing environment where children feel secure, happy and engaged. Staff should create positive relationships with children and foster their wellbeing.
- Effective Leadership and Management: excellent EYFS provision demonstrates strong leadership and management, with leaders who have a clear vision for the EYFS and continually strive to improve outcomes for children.
- Partnerships with Parents and Carers: the setting should actively engage and involve parents and carers in their child's learning and development, fostering a strong partnership between the setting and families.
- Robust Self-Evaluation and Improvement: leaders should demonstrate a strong commitment to self-evaluation and continuous improvement. This includes the ability to identify areas for development and take effective action to address them.
- Safeguarding and Child Protection: there should be rigorous safeguarding and child protection procedures in place to ensure the safety and wellbeing of all children in the setting.
- Effective Assessment and Observation: the setting should have robust systems for assessing and tracking children's progress and development. This should be done in a way that is child centred and supports each child's unique learning journey.
- Adherence to Statutory Requirements: providers should meet all statutory requirements, including those set out in the EYFS framework.

The next contribution, presented by Fey Cole, FE Curriculum Manager for the Department of Health, Life and Personal Sciences, extends the theme of the significance of leadership, highlighting the impact of community support for Early Years.

Fey Cole: shaping provision through voluntary governance

It was my early years career that led to me contemplating taking on the role of a nursery and school Governor. Presuming initially that this would be a three-year post, I gladly found myself re-elected at the end of this term. Then the COVID-19 pandemic struck, followed by the collapse of the Northern Ireland Assembly, so the Department of Education requested during this time that all Governors remain in their post for continuity. Ten years on from being elected to be part of the school team, I find it a great honour to have been able to share my expertise and support a school who are laying a strong foundation for children in their early years.

Alongside this, I also provide training and mentorship to playgroup and nursery committees in my professional role as an Early Years Specialist. When implementing this, a focus is placed on the ethos and values of the shared team, evaluating how to include the children's voice in the development of provision and the shaping of policies. When out in the early years community delivering committee training, we move around the play space, learning from the experts leading play provision. A co-created mission statement becomes a living document for a team that recognises one another's strengths and expertise.

Often the voluntary role of governance comes in the evenings once little ones are tucked up in bed and this is the time when updates are shared. However, the real joy comes when time is spent with the children. During book week, we have been invited in to facilitate story times. We have enjoyed play mornings together and Christmas gatherings. It not only gives us time to get to know the children but also the opportunity to be absorbed into the routine and experience the positive community feeling that teachers have created through purposeful planning.

Over the past ten years we have seen the outdoor area of the nursery develop. As this progressed, we left the tables and went outside. Resources are explored, ideas suggested as we wander the paths played on during the sessions. In times outside of meetings, the nursery teacher has invited me in, knowing I have both a professional and personal interest in how the outdoor space is used. I have been able to observe how her vision has taken shape and developed. New tyres and milk crates added for differing heights to be investigated; little details added as play cues. The reflections from being within this space have been used in my own presentations as a lecturer in the further education classroom when with trainee Early Years educators, and also when presenting at conferences. I present photos and learning from these exchanges with pride, knowing that I am part of a nursery providing children with evidence-based, quality learning experiences.

Your position is one that places you at the heart of the community and provides you with the gift of building provision that is responsive to the needs of children, family, staff, volunteers and visitors. I am making a hopeful assumption that there will be no life-impacting setback that will mean further extension to my term of governing early years and primary provision, but I also feel some sadness as it draws to a necessary close. It is time to hand over the position, but I share this case study with the experience to state that I cannot recommend enough that using your skills as an EYE to volunteer in a governance post is worth every moment.

In this final contribution, Tamsin Grimmer, Principal Lecturer at Norland College, Early Years consultant and author, concludes this chapter by reminding us of the importance of a loving pedagogy, highlighting the importance of nurturing this beyond early years.

Tamsin Grimmer: adopting a loving pedagogy in early childhood: nurturing a whole setting approach

Effective pedagogy in early childhood education goes beyond the traditional notions of teaching and teaching methods; it encompasses a holistic approach that centres on love, care and a deep understanding of the unique needs of young learners. Educators are acting in 'loco parentis' as they nurture their children and are adopting a loving approach even if they do not use this term. I describe this as a loving pedagogy (Grimmer, 2021, 2023, 2024).

Defining loving pedagogy

A loving pedagogy combines the loving and caring nature of our role with our whole approach in action, for example, putting the needs of children first, holding them in mind and enjoying playing together (Grimmer, 2021). It is a pedagogical philosophy rooted in the belief that love and care are fundamental to fostering a positive learning climate. This approach recognises that children thrive when they feel safe, valued and loved by their caregivers and educators. A loving pedagogy acts as a foundation, underpinning everything we do, and can complement other pedagogical approaches.

At the heart of loving pedagogy lies the establishment of strong attachments between educators, caregivers and young learners (Bowlby, 1953; Gerhardt, 2015). These relationships contribute to a sense of belonging and I believe this will have a knock-on effect on their learning because they will associate education with positive emotions and are more likely to become enthusiastic, self-motivated learners. In addition, my own research highlighted how 'developing a loving pedagogy empowers children to feel safe, secure, valued, listened to and loved which in turn enables them to become self-assured and confident' (Grimmer, 2023: 535).

A loving approach also sees children's behaviour as communicating emotions, needs and wants. It nurtures self-regulation and essential social and emotional skills, such as empathy, compassion and conflict resolution, which are critical for success in later life. Children are not viewed as powerless but instead as competent beings who should be listened to, respected and have a voice within our schools and settings (Clark and Moss, 2017; Edwards, Gandini and Forman, 2012; Mainstone-Cotton, 2019).

Challenges of loving pedagogy

It would be naïve to suggest that a loving pedagogy is not without its challenges. Educators may face criticism around their use of the word love or may be fearful that their loving actions are misconstrued, particularly in relation to touch. They will need to reconcile legitimate safeguarding considerations with the use of appropriate positive touch within daily practice and ensure that their policies address these issues. In addition, many educators and parents will have different views about these complex ideas and these should be explored and discussed honestly and openly. I explore these and other challenges in my books *Developing a Loving Pedagogy in the Early Years* and *Loving Pedagogy Explained* (Grimmer, 2021, 2024) and believe that despite the challenges, a loving pedagogy is still an appropriate approach to adopt within early childhood.

What does a loving pedagogy look like in practice?

In practice, a loving approach underpins our day-to-day interactions with the children, and many educators would already see themselves as working in this way. For example, we can demonstrate our love for the children in our care by:

- Spending quality time with them;
- Keeping children's best interests at heart and holding them in mind;
- Showing a genuine interest in our children's lives;
- Using positive touch in interactions with children, e.g. offering a child a hug or a high 5 or allowing a child to sit on our lap during a story;
- Building positive relationships and secure attachments with children;
- Using positive, affirming and encouraging language, e.g. labelled praise and words that build self-esteem;
- Creating cosy corners for children to cuddle up with us and listen to a story;
- Building nurture times into our routine when children can re-fuel emotionally;
- Engaging in genuine consultation with children about issues that affect them, valuing their ideas and, whenever possible, acting upon them;
- Speaking their love languages (Chapman and Campbell, 2012);
- Role modelling acting in loving and caring ways ourselves;
- Sharing picture books specifically about love and special relationships;
- Ensuring that a loving pedagogy is defined and described within our policies.

A loving pedagogy prioritises love, care and emotional wellbeing which is important for life-long learning. By kind and caring actions Early Years educators express love on a daily basis. Children are then enabled to thrive in their learning and also become compassionate, resilient and successful individuals. This pedagogy demonstrates love's power in children's lives and helps them to grow into loving citizens. Therefore, it is imperative that schools and settings adopt a loving pedagogy and educators understand how this whole setting approach can shape the future through the hearts and mind of our youngest learners.

In conclusion

This chapter explores the significance of implementing EYFS principles across an entire school or setting, highlighting the transformative impact of a cohesive early years approach. It discusses how schools have adapted EYFS models beyond Reception, embedding child-centred methodologies into KS1 and beyond to enhance engagement, collaboration and holistic development. Contributions stress the need for an ongoing cycle of implementation and evaluation, ensuring adaptations remain relevant and aligned with developmental needs. The chapter also explores how an EYFS-informed approach supports well-being, fosters a nurturing learning environment and strengthens professional reflection and collaboration, ultimately creating an inclusive and progressive school culture.

Summary of key points

- A whole school/setting approach is possible if vision, intentions and aims are clearly communicated to all practitioners.
- A simple duplication of EYFS approaches/strategies needs to be observed in a professional conversation about the developmental needs of older children.
- Any supportive documentation which guides, scaffolds and challenges all adults involved in a school/setting would benefit from a commitment to health and wellbeing.
- Any changes made at a whole school/setting level should be part of an ongoing implementation and evaluation plan to ensure that they are integrated into provision.
- Refining current policies to ensure that they are developmentally appropriate would support the implementation of an EYFS approach as a whole school/setting.

References

Bowlby, J. (1953). *Childcare and the Growth of Love*. London, UK: Penguin books.

Chapman, G., and Campbell, R. (2012). *The 5 Love Languages of Children*. Chicago, IL: Northfield Publishing.

Clark, A., and Moss, P. (2017). *Listening to Young Children: A Guide to Understanding and Using the Mosaic Approach*. London: Jessica Kingsley.

DfE (2025). Early years foundation stage statutory framework for group and school-based providers. Setting the standards for learning, development and care for children from birth to five. Available at: https://assets.publishing.service.gov.uk/media/687105a381dd8f70f5de3ea9/EYFS_framework_for_group_and_school_based_providers_.pdf (Accessed 21 July 2025).

Edwards, C., Gandini, L., and Forman, G. (2012). *The Hundred Languages of Children: The Reggio Emilia Experience in Transformation* (3rd ed.). Santa Barbara, CA: Praeger.

Gerhardt, S. (2015). *Why Love Matters: How Affection Shapes a Baby's Brain* (2nd ed.). Hove: Routledge.

Grimmer, T. (2021). *Developing a Loving Pedagogy in the Early Years: How Love Fits with Professional Practice*. UK: Routledge.

Grimmer, T. (2023). Is there a place for love in an early childhood setting? *Early Years*, 44(3-4), pp. 525-538. https://doi.org/10.1080/09575146.2023.2182739

Grimmer, T. (2024). *Loving Pedagogy Explained*. UK: Routledge.

Hawkins, P, and McMahon, A. (2020). *Supervision in the Helping Professions* (5th ed.). McGraw-Hill Open University Press.

Mainstone-Cotton, S. (2019). *Listening to Young Children in Early Years Settings*. London: Jessica Kingsley.

Ofsted (2024). Strong foundations in the first years of school. Available at: Strong foundations in the first years of school - GOV.UK

Tickell, C. (2011). The Early Years: Foundations for life, health and learning. An Independent Report on the Early Years Foundation Stage to Her Majesty's Government. Available at: https://assets.publishing.service.gov.uk/media/5a7ac0ec40f0b66a2fc02915/DFE-00177-2011.pdf (last checked 4 September 2024).

16 Protected characteristics in the Early Years

Poppy Gibson

Introduction

In the UK, the Equality Act, 2010 protects people from discrimination based on specific characteristics. These 'protected characteristics' include age, disability, gender reassignment, marriage/civil partnership, pregnancy/maternity, race, religion/belief, sex and sexual orientation. The Act makes it unlawful to discriminate against someone because of any of these characteristics. This chapter highlights the statutory requirements included in the Equality Act, 2010 and explores, through ten contributors' additions that we have sought out, how the protected characteristics are both planned and taught to children from birth to five.

Pondering question: how can we discuss the protected characteristics with our youngest children sensitively?

Why should we teach about protected characteristics in the Early Years?

Teaching about protected characteristics in early years is crucial for fostering inclusivity and equality from a young age (Marjoribanks, Cookson, and Haygarth, 2022); protected characteristics include age, disability, gender reassignment, marriage/civil partnership, pregnancy/maternity, race, religion/belief, sex and sexual orientation. Early childhood is when children begin to develop their understanding of the world and their place in it. Introducing the concept of protected characteristics in EYFS helps even the youngest children to recognise and appreciate diversity in their community and world around them (Kurian, 2024).

The Equality Act, 2010 identifies nine protected characteristics: age, disability, gender reassignment, marriage and civil partnership, pregnancy and maternity, race, religion or belief, sex and sexual orientation. While some of these characteristics may seem complex for young children to learn about, the core message of the importance of treating everyone fairly and with respect can be effectively conveyed through age-appropriate methods (Hamilton, 2021).

For example, early years education provides an opportunity to introduce the basic concepts of fairness, respect and individual differences (Cerna et al., 2021). Children can learn that people may have different appearances, families, abilities, beliefs and backgrounds. When children learn about protected characteristics, they are more likely to feel included and valued for who they are. This fosters a sense of belonging, which is essential for their emotional wellbeing and development.

DOI: 10.4324/9781003505266-16

The role of the practitioner in exploring the protected characteristics in the early years

It is essential to use age-appropriate language and teaching strategies when discussing protected characteristics with young children. Some effective approaches include circle time discussions, role modelling and storytelling with books that feature characters with different protected characteristics and discuss their experiences (Alonge, 2024). Teaching about protected characteristics in the early years is not about political correctness or indoctrination. It is about equipping children with the knowledge, skills and values they need to thrive in a diverse and interconnected world. By fostering inclusivity, challenging prejudice and promoting respect, we can empower young children to become active, responsible and compassionate citizens as they grow up.

In this first contribution, Jessica Wythe, Lecturer in Early Childhood Studies at Birmingham City University, explains more about the value of exploring protected characteristics with very young children, and the positive impact this can have on an inclusive space for all.

Jessica Wythe: a graduated approach to SEND support in early years education

Protected characteristics play a crucial role in the development and wellbeing of children, especially in their early years. When we focus on disability within this context, it becomes paramount for Early Years practitioners to understand the significance of providing support tailored to the needs of each child, while also ensuring inclusivity and avoiding any form of isolation or differential treatment. First and foremost, it's essential to recognise that children with disabilities are just as deserving of a nurturing and supportive environment as their peers without disabilities. In fact, for these children, the early years are particularly critical for laying the foundation for their future growth and development. Early years practitioners can help mitigate potential challenges and promote the child's overall development by offering appropriate support and intervention in line with relative legislative documents, such as the Equality Act (2010) and the SEND Code of Practice (2015).

One of the key goals for Early Years practitioners should be to create an inclusive environment where every child feels valued and accepted regardless of their abilities. This means avoiding actions or attitudes that could potentially isolate or marginalise children with disabilities. Instead, practitioners should foster an atmosphere of understanding, empathy and respect for diversity. It is imperative for Early Years practitioners to consider the physical layout of their classrooms and learning spaces, both indoors and outdoors, to promote diversity and facilitate independence and autonomy. A key piece of advice I have carried with me throughout my career working in childcare and education is to get down low, sit on the floor and observe the classroom from the level of a child. Even though it might look bizarre to somebody walking past, this strategy has meant that I can adjust and adapt my learning spaces to ensure they are suitable for all children and young people, irrespective of any protected characteristics.

One practical approach is to focus on the child's strengths and abilities rather than solely on their limitations. By adopting a strengths-based perspective, practitioners can help children with disabilities recognise their own unique talents and capabilities, fostering a sense of confidence and self-worth. This approach also promotes the acquisition and development of critical independence and autonomy skills and encourages other children to see their peers with disabilities as individuals with valuable contributions to the group. Moreover, Early Years practitioners should strive to provide tailored support that meets each child's specific needs with a disability or learning impediment. This may involve implementing education health and care (EHC) plans, utilising assistive technologies or adapting activities to ensure accessibility for all children. By being proactive and responsive to the needs of each child, practitioners can create an inclusive learning environment where every child can thrive.

In this next contribution, Andrew Moffat, PD lead: Excelsior MAT and CEO: No Outsiders, shares the resources developed by the charity which support the teaching of protected characteristics in the Early Years.

Andrew Moffat: 'No Outsiders' and facilitating valuable discussions: teaching the protected characteristics in early years

We can teach about the protected characteristics in early years settings in an age-appropriate way. We don't need to list them or go through what they mean as we do in upper key stage 2, rather we can find ways to reference the characteristics in our resources and everyday language.

In 2006, I wrote my first resource for this age group: 'Challenging homophobia in Early Years'; thankfully this was never published. I say I'm thankful it wasn't published properly because I wouldn't want it used today. Does homophobia exist in early years? I'm not sure it does. Prejudice is learned later on. The reason I created the No Outsiders scheme was to move away from single issue lesson plans; we don't need one lesson in early years to challenge racism, another lesson to challenge sexism and another to challenge homophobia. I don't use any of those words in early years lessons.

A No Outsiders lesson will teach young children to think about difference and embrace diversity. I want children to be taught to explore who they are and be proud. I use picture books where different characters are seen to enjoy each other's differences and assemblies that champion real life stories where diversity wins.

The books I am currently using in the 'No Outsiders' resource in Reception are *You Choose* and *Red Rockets and Rainbow Jelly* by Sue Heap and Nick Sharratt, *Hello Hello* by Brendan Wenzel, *Blue Chameleon* by Emily Gravett, *The Family Book* by Todd Parr and *Super Duper You* by Sophy Henn. There are full lesson plans with activities for each of these books in the No Outsiders guide as well as guides for parents.

You Choose encourages children to consider choices; they are presented with colourful pictures of different objects and asked, 'which would you choose?' for your house, for your mode of transport, to eat, to wear and so on. *You Choose* provides the first step in teaching children it's okay to have different opinions; we can accept that we disagree over a favourite car or dinosaur. This concept is explored further in *Red Rockets and Rainbow Jelly*. We see characters Nick and Sue liking different things all through the text (ducks, socks, cats...) but remaining friends by the end. *Hello Hello* shows different animals with a range of shape, size and colour all saying 'Hello' to each other. No one is left out. *The Family Book* shows children that families come in many different shapes and sizes and in the lesson we all draw our own family. In *Blue Chameleon*, the chameleon is lonely and tries to make friends by changing shape and colour. Chameleon thinks you have to look like someone to be their friend; is that true? Finally *Super Duper You* is a wonderful celebration of all things that make us unique. We are not one thing; there are lots of ways you are you; we need to recognise 'all the brills you got'.

But the picture books themselves are not enough; it's a consistent language, an ethos that makes No Outsiders effective in early years. Every child in Reception understands how it feels to be left out and doesn't want to be left out, so a No Outsiders ethos is very powerful. 'No one is left out here because there are no outsiders!' It's relatable and it fits into a way of working that all schools will recognise. If I ask an eleven-year-old child in my school what No Outsiders is about, I would expect them to talk about the Equality Act and protected characteristics, British values and what they mean and list ways in our school we might be different. If I ask a four-year-old child in my school what No Outsiders is about, I would expect them to say something like, 'We play together,' and that is enough. We are absolutely talking about protected characteristics as a whole, but not individually. We can talk about them generally in a gentle, age-appropriate way that children understand and identify with.

We can prepare children for life in modern Britain in early years. We just have to be clever about it.

In this next contribution, Millie Overton, an EYFS class Teacher, continues the discussion on No Outsiders, explaining how it looks in her setting.

Millie Overton: everyone is welcome here—fostering mutual respect in the early years

The importance of facilitating discussions around the protected characteristics and fundamental British values, even to our youngest learners, are made clear to educators through legislation such as the Equality Act (2010). Ofsted (2024) states that schools should be promoting British values, raising respectful citizens, providing equal opportunities for all and creating an inclusive environment for all irrespective of their individual characteristics.

As a school this is something we pride ourselves in, however, promoting the protected characteristics in the early years can seem like a daunting subject to cover. However, this is something that we do every day within the classroom. In our early years setting, we are constantly having discussions surrounding individuality and uniqueness with the children, especially when they are completing independent learning through play. One particular topic that we cover early in the academic year surrounds families and the different family structures that we all live in. This is something that excites the children and hooks them in as it is a real-life scenario that they have all experienced. Suddenly the discussion moves from what that child's individual family looks like and progresses onto the similarities and differences between the families of every child in the class.

As a school, we made the decision to incorporate the No Outsiders scheme (Moffat, 2020) into our classrooms and this has allowed us to facilitate discussions surrounding the protected characteristics from our youngest learners all the way to our oldest by covering the same topics but in varied levels of depth appropriate for the age groups. This has allowed us to discretely introduce these topics into everyday learning by opening a dialog through which an understanding of the society that we live in can be developed and embedded.

In our early year's classrooms, we explore picture books and drama to start discussions surrounding the protected characteristics without explicitly labelling them, which creates a firm foundation on which future learning surrounding more complex and in-depth concepts can be built. One lesson taught to our youngest learners focused on the things that make us all different and unique. A picture book was introduced to the children and first read through without any comments or observations being made to allow the children to enjoy this new text. This book was then read again, this time taking the time to discuss and act out specific focus points within the book. By this point the children were hooked! The excitement created by a single text had unknowingly hooked them into a discussion surrounding the complex topic of protected characteristics. Using props, the discussion was deepened with the children looking for the similarities and differences between the animals that they were holding. Discretely through this discussion an understanding of uniqueness and individuality was raised and the understanding and meaning of mutual respect for others was deepened.

In this next contribution, Lisa Kelly, Foundation Lecturer at Chester University, advocates for a multifaceted approach to teaching and learning of protected characteristics in the early years. Highlighting the importance of providing commission for children is a theme which invites personal reflection.

Lisa Kelly: breaking apart to build again: diffracting the rhizome of protected characteristics in early years practice

Embracing protected characteristics in a complex and changing world can present unanticipated difficulties. As a practitioner, there is a legal obligation to promote equality and tackle discrimination. That being said, these are challenging terms and it can be difficult to separate our own personal understandings and biases from pedagogical and pastoral approaches. As educators, we are governed by the policies of our country as well as the wishes and beliefs of the parents and the potential influential nature of being strong voices during formative years. Crossing the boundaries set by stakeholders or being too assuming of our right to influence, can have destructive and career-ending outcomes. In building an equitable and diverse system, we have to navigate such important but potentially treacherous seas, avoiding narratives of deficits, community politics and, ultimately, we try to focus on the wards in our care. The challenge has to be meeting the needs of our young people and preparing them for the world that they will eventually have to enter.

McLeod (2011) notes that in order to meet the 'Every Child's a Talker' agenda that previously prevailed over early years communication strategies, a key factor was that teachers need to regain authority and ownership over their classrooms. She advocates for the more holistic European traditions where education is not separated into component parts and packaged as an exercise that offers only one route to quality. Significant difficulties in taking such ownership prevent practitioners from doing so and having agency in situations where uncertainty can arise (Robson and Fumoto, 2009: 49). This can be attributed to our need to label and homogenise our classrooms in the search for risk-free equality.

Philosophies that offer holistic pathways forward can be challenging to entrenched personal bias in the first instance, but they offer hope through the provision of a different vantage point. Seemingly abstract, these pathways encourage practitioners to step back and assume control by recognising that they aren't so different. Diffractive approaches borne of feminist identities (Barad, 2007, 2014) suggest that the ideologies of the sector might be reconsidered through a new framework—that nothing is binary and change is inherent. The philosophy encourages breaking ideas apart and reconstructing them anew. Barad creates a metaphor grounded in nature and growth, a rustic reminder of the balance and reinvigoration that already occurs in alignment with our natural surroundings.

> We might imagine re-turning as a multiplicity of processes, such as the kinds earthworms revel in while helping to make compost or otherwise being busy at work and at play: turning the soil over and over – ingesting and excreting it, tunnelling through it, burrowing, all means of aerating the soil, allowing oxygen in, opening it up and breathing new life into it.
>
> (Barad, 2014: 168)

Such recognition of the interconnectedness that affects us also exists within the rhizomatic philosophies of Deleuze and Guattari (1988), whose works are emerging more frequently within the early years field (Boldt, 2023). They offer a perception of learning that delineates mastery and recognises that it is a complexity built of multiplicities, ultimately known as 'assemblages' (Moss, 2018). Allowing children to bring their assemblages into the classroom environment can enrich and redirect learning if teachers and practitioners are given the time and space to embrace their individuality and identities. These encounters can encourage the lines of flight (trajectories of change) that develop from interactions with entities that are 'heterogeneous, [...] fluid and ephemeral in composition.' (p.115)

Why is this important for early years identity and for the inclusive practice of protected characteristics? Rather than a tokenistic approach to diversity, we can consider decolonising our approaches, adapting our pedagogies to reflect the interconnected worlds that exist within our learning environments and to commit to the recognition of the implications of experience and identity. We need to release the constrictions placed upon our processes and allow for the unexpected. Our research-led practice should embrace the varied nature of childhood and explore child-led curriculums that embrace innovation and manage risk and inclusivity. Once our concepts of quality are led by experience and the realities of our wards, rather than pre-conceived dominant notions of binary rights and wrongs, there is an eminent sense that a curriculum based on nurture, respect and care could emerge.

This next contribution, shared by Graeme McAvoy, Doctor of Education (EdD) student at the University of Strathclyde, explores an important aspect of the protective characteristics requirements; the under-representation of men in the early years.

Graeme McAvoy: where are all the men? An investigation into why men are under-represented in the Early Learning & Childcare (ELC) sector

A key theme reported in the literature surrounding the under-representation of men in Early Learning and Childcare related to supporting the sector to become more gender diverse.

This directly correlates to the impact of working with young children who do not have a positive male role model in their lives, and particularly those who do not have a father figure. This is further emphasised by the need to increase the visibility of men working in ELC and the positive impact this has on children. This viewpoint is also shared by Hedlin and Aberg (2012: 153), who argue that the increased presence of men in ELC would therefore impact children in a positive manner, by becoming a role model and acting as a 'father figure' for some children: 'A male teacher sees things from a male perspective. In preschools with no males, boys are disadvantaged. They are misunderstood and might be treated unfairly.'

It could be argued that this is further supported by men being role models for children whom they care for (Cushman, 2008; Haase, 2008). This viewpoint is consistent with Wood and Brownhill (2016), who undertook research with three primary school teachers into supporting children's social and emotional learning in their everyday practice. It was found that 'In order to advocate and encourage alternative, appropriate behaviours, they should act as 'replacement fathers' and become 'role models'' (p. 172). Furthermore, it also suggested that supporting children's social and emotional behaviours had a positive influence on children's emotional intelligence (Goleman, 1995). This is further emphasised by Demirkasimoglu and Taskin (2019: 430), who further support the idea that male practitioners are positive role models for young children: 'I had nothing but positive support from children - I even had students who were speaking and acting like me'.

Notwithstanding, Xu and Waniganayake (2018) found that male practitioners are expected to engage in play with children in a stereotypical manner, for example providing opportunities for children to take part in physical play experiences such as rough-and-tumble play, which further emphasises the role that men are expected to engage young children with, arguing: 'Male teachers are more passionate, more able to control activities, more playful when organising daily life and more capable of motivating children' (p.525). Beyond the Early Learning and Childcare sector, the presence of male practitioners has also been reported to positively impact relationships with parents, and in particular fathers (Bullough, 2015; Nentwich et al., 2013).

On the other hand, it is also suggested that male practitioners also act as a role model for other male practitioners, whom are in the minority in staff teams, as Hedlin and Aberg (2012: 154) suggest: 'More male preschool teachers also means that staff groups would be more gender-mixed.' This is further supported by Demirkasimoglu and Taskin (2019), who argue that male practitioners typically demonstrate positive relationships with colleagues and children in their care, highlighting that male practitioners often report having a positive and supportive relationship with the headteacher or manager of their settings.

In this next contribution, Troy Jenkinson, freelance lecturer, children's author and Equality, Diversity, Inclusion & Belonging specialist, provides additional ideas of how to plan and implement an effective protected characteristics curriculum in the Early Years.

Troy Jenkinson: successful teaching of the protected characteristics in EYFS.

Children come into early years from a wide range of backgrounds; all different but similar. The key to a successful introduction to the notion of protected characteristics is honesty, age appropriateness and seamlessness. This in essence celebrates each child's uniqueness (one of the overarching EYFS Statutory Framework principles), allowing them to feel included and supported with equal opportunity (Dfe, 2025: 7).

Honesty

What was once considered the traditional family make up (mum, dad and two children) is not representative of all families who enter our schools. We teach children from a range of backgrounds who may directly or indirectly relate to one or more of the protected characteristics; they may be disabled, follow a particular religion or in the future identify as part of the LGBTQ community. Alternatively, they may have close family members identifying with one of the protected characteristics. Either way, it is essential we do not marginalise children and families as they begin their educational career.

Children may already have experiences of differing characteristics (or witnessing potential prejudices). It is imperative that when questions are asked, we answer them honestly. We should tackle discriminative behaviour but children in the early years will be curious and will ask questions; this does not mean that innocent questions, perhaps about why someone has two mummies or why someone has a prosthetic leg, are ill-meant. Children need to hear the truth.

Age-appropriateness

To enable children to make sense of their world, we need to foster a sense of belonging within their schools. To do this, they need to have representation; to see themselves, and others like them, within their learning environment. Toys and books should be representative of all the youngsters in our care and we should use appropriate and correct terminology. When children ask about a person's clothing or religious artefacts for example, we should ensure we use the correct wording. The difficulty lies with more complex, controversial issues such as sexuality or gender identity. While you may not specifically use the term transgender with children in EYFS, children should feel comfortable in accessing dressing up clothes that may not represent their gender at birth. If a child feels comfortable playing with particular toys or wearing particular clothes, allow them to.

Seamlessness

EYFS being the introduction into educational life, should be a seamless transition from preschool experience into their continued learning journey. To make it seamless, children need to feel able to ask questions, to speak and hear the truth. They need to trust their educators. Likewise, parents are entrusting schools to care for their children to give them the very best start in life.

We work together with families to foster a safe environment to build trust. This trust enables us to have open conversations. This sometimes leads to challenging conversations when addressing stereotypes to empower children to continue developing curiosity that is respectful of all differences.

Conclusion

Stories and story time is powerful. Talk and learning through play and incidents of opportunity is important. We can use these times to give important messages of hope and inclusion. Once children are inspired by the stories and message, they will go on to re-enact their learning through play, enabling them to make sense of the modern world. There are many helpful lists of resources and book lists of stories that help to shape children's balanced learning of how we are same but different. As EYFS educators, we are in the prime position to offer honesty in an age-appropriate, seamless manner.

Dr Scott Michael Steele, Lecturer in Law at Anglia Ruskin University Peterborough, highlights the research around accessibility in the UK higher education system, offering an opportunity for evaluation and action planning.

Dr Scott Michael Steele: accessibility in the UK higher education system: a focus on the Equality Act 2010 and protected characteristics

Introduction

Accessibility within the UK education system is a critical issue that ensures all students, regardless of their background or personal characteristics, have equal opportunities to succeed. The Equality Act, 2010 plays a pivotal role in this by providing a legal framework to protect individuals from discrimination and promote equality.

The Equality Act, 2010

The Equality Act, 2010 consolidates previous anti-discrimination laws into a single piece of legislation, making it easier to understand and enforce. It identifies nine protected characteristics: age, disability, gender reassignment, marriage and civil partnership, pregnancy and maternity, race, religion or belief, sex and sexual orientation. These characteristics are crucial in ensuring that educational institutions do not discriminate against students based on these attributes.

Impact on Education

Educational institutions in the UK are required to comply with the Equality Act, 2010, which means they must take proactive steps to eliminate discrimination, advance equality of opportunity and foster good relations between people who share a protected characteristic and those who do not. This involves making reasonable adjustments to accommodate students with disabilities, ensuring that admissions processes are fair, and providing support services that cater to the diverse needs of the student population.

Reasonable adjustments and support

One of the key provisions of the Equality Act, 2010 is the requirement for institutions to make reasonable adjustments for students with disabilities. This can include physical adjustments to buildings, providing assistive technologies and offering alternative assessment methods. The goal is to remove barriers that might prevent students with disabilities from fully participating in education.

Reasonable adjustments

Under the Equality Act, nurseries and schools are required to make reasonable adjustments to support children with disabilities. These adjustments can take various forms:

- Adapted Learning Materials: Providing large print books, audio resources or braille materials.
- Flexible Teaching Methods: Using a variety of teaching strategies to accommodate different learning styles.
- Support Services: Offering additional support such as speech and language therapy, occupational therapy or one-on-one assistance.
- These adjustments are not just about compliance but about creating an environment where every child can thrive.

Accessibility in early years education

Creating an accessible environment involves both physical and educational adjustments. Physical accessibility ensures that the nursery or school is navigable for all children, including those with mobility challenges. This includes installing ramps, widening doorways and providing accessible toilets. Educational accessibility, on the other hand, involves using inclusive teaching materials and methods that cater to diverse learning needs. This might involve using visual aids, tactile resources and technology to support learning.

In this next contribution, Natalie Quinn-Walker, Public Health Lecturer and Deputy Course Lead MPH, presents a comprehensive account of the impact of support for pregnant students at universities.

Natalie Quinn-Walker: supporting pregnant university students: addressing the challenges and promoting equality

During pregnancy, a variety of physical, emotional and mental challenges can occur, and for university students, there is also the demand to navigate their education, thus further adding complexity. Unfortunately, there is this expectation that students will bounce back rapidly after giving birth, with minimum time off, particularly international students. Many cannot obtain access to any maternity benefits within the UK (University of Cumbria, 2023). Under the Equality Act (2010), a UK law that provides legal protection against discrimination and promotes equality, pregnancy and maternity are protected characteristics, yet adequate accommodations for their needs are not provided. Therefore, a more robust support service for pregnant students is needed to ensure they receive equal access to education. However, the management of services and adjustments varies across universities.

It is imperative for universities to adopt a united approach in providing specific accommodations for pregnant students. This collective effort, guided by transparent policies, will create an environment of support and encourage students to seek assistance. By working together, universities can reduce the dropout rate and promote a sense of inclusion and fairness. Furthermore, as Morgan (2024) highlights, many universities fail to recognize their students' caring responsibilities due to a lack of data collection. By gathering detailed data, universities can better understand the challenges their students face and ensure their policies and services are effective.

Morgan (2024) explains that individuals commonly experience financial hardships. Furthermore, the emotional experiences through pregnancy and post-birth are recognized. Childbirth and pregnancy should not be barriers to higher education. Instead, more supportive systems must be offered to ensure individuals are provided equal opportunities. Therefore, appropriate accommodations and an embedded culture of understanding ensure pregnant students can thrive without this fear of the need to bounce back prematurely.

Moving forward, further practical support is needed, which can include support services providing catch-up opportunities for students from academic sources. Furthermore, as noted students may experience financial difficulties, therefore additional hardship funding opportunities could be made available, in particular assisting with travel or other expenses. Although many universities offer supportive services, it is vital that students are aware of the services available. As Morgan (2024) explains, many are unaware of the facilities available. Building supportive relationships are needed whereby the student doesn't feel overwhelmed, stressed or pressured to leave their course. These supportive services need to be inclusive, recognising students who wish to disengage with their pregnancy will need to be offered potential different levels of support. Therefore, a recommendation of analysing and reviewing policies not only to ensure the Equality Act, 2010 is upheld, but also students feel voices and experiences are being heard and that they can engage with their course with the support of the university and not feel ostracised due to their pregnancy.

The penultimate contribution in this chapter, presented by Samantha Dholakia, coach, consultant, trainer: SPD Tuition & Coaching, explores how inclusivity can be placed at the forefront of a supported, respectful and authentic curriculum.

Samantha Dholakia: it all starts with the early years: a balanced approach for inclusive practice

Effective learning extends into the broader community. Derman-Sparks and Edwards (2020) state, 'Difference does not create bias. Children learn prejudice from prejudice–not diversity.'

Children thrive when their core needs are met. Feeling safe and supported leads to success. The Behaviour Balance System™ creates an inclusive, creative and safe environment where children feel valued and connected (Figure 16.1).

Early childhood shapes identity and social skills. Teaching about protected characteristics such as race, gender and disability must be age appropriate and part of everyday learning.

> TBBS, ART Framework: Ensuring inclusivity becomes a natural part of everyday learning, removing negative associations and judgements.
> Awareness
> Reflection
> Transformation
> TBBS Tips

Protected characteristics in the Early Years 207

Figure 16.1 The Behaviour Balance System

1. Safe, Supportive Environment
   Select resources that ensure every child sees themselves represented while being introduced to diverse characteristics reflecting the global community. Regularly assess the environment's accessibility and comfort, making sure all children feel safe and supported. Clear, collaborative expectations foster inclusion, making every child feel valued.
   Awareness Activity: Co-create a setting agreement using statements such as 'We are kind' and 'We celebrate all our differences.' Use visuals to make these rules accessible and refer back to them throughout the day.
2. Stage Appropriateness
   Supporting developmental stages rather than age makes learning accessible. Using age-appropriate stories, songs and activities promote kindness and understanding of differences when introducing protected characteristics. Focus on core concepts like fairness and sharing to help children internalise values of respect and inclusivity.
   Reflection Activity: Use storybooks like *We Are All Different* by Asa Gilland or *My Brain is Magic* by Prasha Sooful to encourage children to share what makes them special, using sentence scaffolds like 'Some people have… and some people have… I have…'
3. Emotional Regulation
   As children in the EYFS develop their ability to manage emotions, supporting emotional regulation is essential, especially when discussing sensitive topics.
   Awareness Activity: Use a visual emotions chart for children to indicate how they feel. During discussions, ask, 'How are you feeling?' to connect feelings to actions, like being kind to someone feeling left out.

4. Sensory Diets

    Varying sensory input helps with emotional regulation, communication and learning. TBBS settings promote every child having access to sensory tools. Sensory play enables exploration of textures, sounds and visuals, supporting development.

    Transformation Activity: Alongside sensory-rich play within your EYFS provision, create a Balance Zone™ where children can practise emotional regulation. This area supports up-regulation and down-regulation with tools like textured fabrics, movement spots and sensory baskets. Ensure accessibility by including adaptive seating and visual supports. Model the use of the zone to teach children how to navigate their emotions and sensory needs, supporting self-regulation.

5. Explorative Play

    Play builds confidence, teaches empathy and practises social skills. It allows children to explore different perspectives and characteristics.

    Awareness and Reflection Activity: Provide opportunities for children to practise inclusive behaviours through role-play or props like toy wheelchairs, dolls and a range of clothing. Support respectful discussions and encourage emotional expression.

6. An Inclusive Approach

    We are agents of change, ensuring success is accessible to all. Children learn through observation, so it is vital to demonstrate kindness and respect. Each interaction is an opportunity to model inclusivity.

    Transformation Activity: Populate your setting with diverse books and visuals. Use posters and select books featuring a diverse range of characters to increase familiarity and connection.

7. Celebrating Diversity

    Reflect a wide range of experiences and backgrounds in the setting. Use family photos and diverse materials to build familiarity and a sense of belonging, ensuring all children see their experiences reflected, as well as that of our global community.

    Awareness Activity: Assist children in creating family trees using photos or drawings, discussing the diversity of families and celebrating uniqueness (always ensure you are aware of any children in care).

8. Collaborative Community

    Families are crucial in shaping children's understanding of the world. Organising family workshops or inviting them to discuss their cultural or religious traditions reinforces the message of inclusivity both at school and at home.

    Awareness Activity: Invite members of the school community to share and show clothing, food, music, or favourite items with the class. These experiences help children appreciate the diversity within their community and learn about different cultural traditions in an interactive way.

All resources for The Behaviour Balance System™ and support materials for inclusive, collaborative, trauma-informed practice can be found in The Behaviour Bank™, the only online portal supporting teachers and parents with a holistic and systematic behaviour approach.

The final contribution in this chapter shared by Sophie Dent, Humanitarian Support Manager: local government authority, serves to remind us of the significance of the role of the adult in modelling an appropriate culture.

Sophie Dent: 'It's only a black eye when it's on white skin'—the importance of self-reflection and language choice in teaching protected characteristics

I was working in Children's Services; I had finished a safeguarding report to share with a social worker and I had written about an assault report involving a 'black eye'. My colleague pulled me to one side and asked me to change my report to from 'black eye' to 'bruising around the eye'. I queried her request, and she said, 'well it is only a black eye when it's on white skin'. We got into a complex discussion about how common terminology, even from professionals and statutory services, can demonstrate unconscious bias.

That conversation was almost 5 years ago, and I remember it vividly, partly because I felt a sense of shame in my bias, but also because it influenced the way I view protected characteristics and how we embed this with young children. Whilst there are numerous lesson plans, tools, toys and games we can use to teach protected characteristics, I realised that the first step in teaching protected characteristics to young children is one where professionals are aware of their unconscious biases, demonstrate awareness, promote acceptance and take accountability for their language and attitudes.

Black eye is a phrase I think many practitioners have probably said or used without considering race, but there are many other things we can say without realising how this undermines the protected characteristics we are trying to teach. Some examples:

'You're not old enough to do that by yourself'—is that child's age a reflection of their skills?
'You did so well to concentrate for so long—you normally struggle with your ADHD'—could we not just say 'well done'?
'Right boys and girls, let's go outside—are there only boys and girls?

Using protected characteristics as a guide, reflect on what language you may have used with or around children, and how you could adjust this to create the right culture in your setting. The language and the way we respond to children can help start a conversation with young children. I have given an example of how we can miss an opportunity or take an opportunity to discuss protected characteristics with children:

They don't want to be the daddy in my game
It's important to take turns, why don't you let them be the mummy instead?
Ok, they can be the mummy
That's very kind of you

The above response closes the conversation, and the children return to playing their game with one another. This could have been an opportunity to have a further discussion with the child and bring in alternative teaching resources:

They don't want to be the daddy in my game.
Maybe you could both be the mummy? Some families have two mummies.
No, they don't, I have a mummy and a daddy.
All families are different. Some families have two mummies, some have two daddies, and some have more than two parents.

More than two?

Yes, that's right. We have a book on the shelf about different families, shall we look at it together?

Teaching children is more than using a resource, a lesson plan or a game, it is creating the right culture for children to learn without realising they are learning. My own reflection and learning taught me that the way I engage in conversation and the language I use can be more powerful than a lesson plan, and I think this is pertinent when trying to teach protected characteristics to children.

In conclusion

This chapter explores the significance of teaching protected characteristics in early years education, aligning with the Equality Act, 2010, striving towards inclusivity, fairness and respect. Contributions from practitioners and researchers highlight approaches to embedding discussions on diversity, representation and identity within everyday learning experiences. Strategies include using age-appropriate storytelling, fostering open conversations and ensuring classroom environments reflect a wide range of backgrounds and identities. Through expert insights, practical examples and reflective guidance, this chapter reinforces the idea that early childhood education should cultivate belonging, challenge prejudice and prepare children for life in an increasingly diverse society.

Summary of key points

- **Inclusive environments are crucial**: early years settings must prioritise creating inclusive environments where all children, including those with disabilities, feel valued, respected and have equal opportunities to learn and grow.
- **Strengths-based approach**: emphasise each child's unique strengths and abilities rather than solely focusing on their limitations. This builds self-confidence and encourages other children to see their peers with disabilities as valued members of the group.
- **Key role in child development**: early years practitioners play a vital role in creating supportive and inclusive environments for all children, especially those with disabilities.
- **Embedding equality act principles through everyday practice**: rather than treating protected characteristics as separate inputs, practitioners can integrate them into daily interactions, storytelling and classroom discussions. This helps children naturally develop an understanding of diversity and inclusion, fostering environments where respect and belonging are seamlessly embedded into everyday learning experiences.
- **Encouraging conversations to promote critical thinking**: supporting children in exploring ideas of fairness, identity and respect through guided discussions allows them to develop confidence in expressing their thoughts. Using open-ended questions and reflective prompts helps children engage with complex topics in an age-appropriate way, ensuring they feel heard and valued.

References

Alonge, M. (2024). The role of multicultural children's books in fostering empathy and understanding across diverse cultures. *Journal of Professional Services Marketing*, [online] Available at: HAL Science Repository (Accessed 14 September 2025).

Barad, K. (2007). *Meeting the Universe Halfway: Quantum Physics and the Entanglement of Matter and Meaning*. Durham & London: Duke University Press.

Barad, K. (2014). Diffracting diffraction: Cutting together-apart. *Parallax*, 20(3), pp. 168-187.

Boldt, G. (2023). Working with Deleuze and Guattari in early childhood research and education. In L.E. Cohen, and S. Waite-Stupiansky (Ed.), *Theories of Early Childhood Education: Developmental, Behaviorist, and Critical* (2nd ed.). New York: Routledge, Taylor & Francis Group, pp. 210-219.

Bullough, R.V. (2015). Teaming and teaching in ECE: Neoliberal reforms, teacher metaphors, and identity in head start. *Journal of Research in Childhood Education*, 29(3), pp. 410-427. https://doi.org/10.1080/02568543.2015.1050563

Cerna, L., Mezzanotte, C., Rutigliano, A., Brussino, O., Santiago, P., Borgonovi, F., and Guthrie, C., (2021). Promoting inclusive education for diverse societies: A conceptual framework. *OECD Education Working Papers*, 260, pp. 0_1-57.

Cushman, P. (2008). So what exactly do you want? what principals mean when they say 'Male Role Model'. *Gender and Education*, 20(2), pp. 123-136.

Deleuze, G., and Guattari, F. (1988). *A Thousand Plateaus: Capitalism and Schizophrenia*. London: Athlone Press.

Demirkasimoglu, N., and Taskin, P. (2019). The career journey of the first male preschool teacher in Turkey: An optimistic perspective to a female dominated occupation. *Journal of Qualitative Research in Education*, 7(1), pp. 420-437. https://doi.org/10.14689/issn.2148-2624.1.7c1s.19m

Derman-Sparks, L., and Edwards, J.O. (2020). *Anti-Bias Education for Young Children and Ourselves*. (2nd ed.). Washington, DC: NAEYC.

Dfe (2025). Early Years foundation stage statutory framework for group and school-based providers. Setting the standards for learning, development and care for children from birth to five. Available at: https://assets.publishing.service.gov.uk/media/687105a381dd8f70f5de3ea9/EYFS_framework_for_group_and_school_based_providers_.pdf (Accessed 21 July 2025).

Equality Act (2010). HMSO.

Goleman, D. (1995). *Emotional Intelligence: Why It Can Matter More Than IQ*. New York: Bantam Books.

Haase, M. (2008). 'I don't do the mothering role that lots of female teachers do': Male teachers, gender, power and social organisation. *British Journal of Sociology of Education*, 29(6), pp. 597-608.

Hamilton, P. (2021). Diversity and marginalisation in childhood: A guide for inclusive thinking 0-11. Available at: Diversity and Marginalisation in Childhood: A Guide for Inclusive Thinking 0-11 - SAGE Publications Ltd - Torrossa.

Hedlin, M., and Aberg, M. (2012). The call for more male preschool teachers: Echoed and questioned by Swedish student teachers *Early Child Development and Care*, 183(1), pp. 149-162, https://doi.org/10.1177/1476718X18816347

Kurian, N., (2024). Building inclusive, multicultural Early Years classrooms: Strategies for a culturally responsive ethic of care. *Early Childhood Education Journal*, 52(5), pp. 863-878.

Marjoribanks, B., Cookson, L., and Haygarth, H., (2022). Promoting inclusive practice. In J. Guthrie et al. (Eds.), *The Early Childhood Graduate Practitioner Competencies: A Guide for Professional Practice*. Bingley, UK: Emerald Group Publishing Limited, p. 107.

McLeod, N. (2011). Exploring Early Years educators' ownership of language and communication knowledge and skills: a review of key policy and initial reflections on Every Child a Talker and its implementation. *Education 3-13*, 39(4), pp. 429-445.

Moffat, A. (2020). *No Outsiders: Everyone Different, Everyone Welcome*. Routledge.

Morgan, M. (2024). Student parents: What support should universities be providing? (UK) - Improving the Student Experience. [online] https://www.improvingthestudentexperience.com/. Available at: https://www.improvingthestudentexperience.com/support-for-student-parents/ (Accessed 22 September 2024).

Moss, P. (2018) *Alternative Narratives in Early Childhood: An Introduction for Students and Practitioners*. Oxford, UK: Taylor & Francis Group.

Nentwich, J.C., Poppen, W., Schälin, S., and Vogt, F. (2013). The same and the other: Male childcare workers managing identity dissonance. *International Review of Sociology*, 23(2), pp. 326-345. https://doi.org/10.1080/03906701.2013.804295

Ofsted (2024). *School Inspection Handbook*. [online] Available at: https://www.gov.uk/government/publications/school-inspection-handbook-eif/school-inspection-handbook-for-september-2023#evaluating-personal-development (Accessed 14 September 2025).

Robson, S., and Fumoto, H. (2009). Practitioners' experiences of personal ownership and autonomy in their support for young children's thinking. *Contemporary Issues in Early Childhood*, 10(1), pp. 43–54.

SEND Code of Practice (2015). *Special educational needs and disability code of practice: 0 to 25 years*. London: Department for Education and Department of Health.

University of Cumbria (2023). Student pregnancy & family leave policy. Available at: https://my.cumbria.ac.uk/media/MyCumbria/Documents/Student-Pregnancy-and-Family-Leave-Policy-(October-23-Update).pdf (Accessed 22 September 2024).

Wood, P., and Brownhill, S. (2016). 'Absent fathers', and children's social and emotional learning: An exploration of the perceptions of 'positive male role models' in the primary school sector. *Gender and Education*, 30(2), pp. 172–186. https://doi.org/10.1080/09540253.2016.1187264

Xu, Y., and Waniganayake, M. (2018). An exploratory study of gender and male teachers in early childhood education and care centres in China. *Compare: A Journal of Comparative and International Education*, 48(1), pp. 518–534, https://doi.org/10.1080/03050068.2022.2062950

17 Wellbeing

Poppy Gibson

Introduction

In this final chapter, we explore the concept of 'wellbeing' in the early years. You will have noticed that wellbeing runs through all of the chapters so far, but in this chapter we explicitly highlight purposeful wellbeing strategies that practitioners could consider for their own practice. The wellbeing of the early years children, the practitioners, and the children's parents and carers is paramount and all three groups must be nurtured; good communication and healthy boundaries are perhaps the key ways to help ensure all groups are heard and respected.

Eight experienced practitioners share valuable reflections and case studies around wellbeing in this chapter, encouraging personal reflection and next steps planning for improvement.

Pondering question: how can we ensure that the wellbeing of all staff and children is the golden thread of a school/setting?

What is wellbeing?

We all may interpret 'wellbeing' slightly differently, however we would likely all agree that wellbeing means 'being well', feeling physically and mentally well and able to conduct normal daily behaviours and functions. When we are struggling with our wellbeing, we may find it harder to regulate, to communicate and to connect with others. The importance of wellbeing in the Early Years is increasingly recognised as a critical factor in childrens overall development and future success. Wellbeing, encompassing physical, emotional, social and cognitive aspects, lays the foundation for children to thrive, learn and build resilience (Zarra-Nezhad, Suhonen, and Sajaniemi, 2024). This is especially important for children who may not have secure or healthy attachments in the home setting, or who have not been shown ways to co-regulate or self-regulate when they are angry, or sad, or frustrated (Marttila, Fukkink, and Silvén, 2024). Early years educators can support attachment and social skill development that can last a lifetime (Badea and Suditu, 2024).

The importance of supporting wellbeing for young children

Research consistently demonstrates the profound impact of wellbeing on young children's development. Studies have shown a strong correlation between children's wellbeing in the

DOI: 10.4324/9781003505266-17

early years and their later academic achievement. Children with higher levels of wellbeing tend to have better concentration, engagement and learning outcomes (OECD, 2015). Early years settings, therefore, play a vital role in promoting children's wellbeing as educators can create environments and implement practices that support children's emotional, social, physical and cognitive wellbeing.

Clearly, wellbeing in the early years is not just about happiness or comfort; it is a fundamental aspect of children's development that has far-reaching implications for their future. By prioritising and promoting wellbeing, I believe that we can provide children with the best possible start in life and help them to thrive in all areas of their development.

In the first contribution of this chapter, Rohit Sagoo, PhD Researcher, University of Bedfordshire, shares an insightful overview into 'social pedagogy' and the value in building relationships between early years children and staff.

Rohit Sagoo: Social pedagogy

A child's emotions and wellbeing significantly influence their learning and development. Social pedagogy, with its emphasis on personal development, social education and holistic wellbeing for children and practitioners, plays a crucial role in this. At the core of this practice are empowerment, participation and relational approaches that foster positivity and wellbeing in children and young people (Cameron and Moss, 2011). It provides a framework integrating development and practice within a broader societal context, encompassing personal, social and moral education (Gabriel, 2001). In early childhood education, social pedagogy is instrumental in blending learning and care to promote positive relationships, holistic development, cultural awareness and wellbeing.

From the lens of enhancing wellbeing in the early years, the application of social pedagogy recognises the importance of building relationships between practitioners and children (Eichsteller and Holthoff, 2012). The focus is on developing authentic, positive, happy and strong relationships in various early years educational environments in which the child participates (Kalagiakos, 2015). Nordström et al. (2021) place the notion of joy as being associated with positive wellbeing when children have affective sensoriality from play, storybooks and learning, consequently adding to positive wellbeing experiences for children in their early years. This emphasises social pedagogy, where 'care and education meet' (Cameron and Moss, 2011). From a social pedagogic lens, the child's wellbeing needs are met from a holistic perspective, providing reassurance about the comprehensive care provided to the child in their daily life within and beyond the walls of education. This comprehensive care is designed to meet the whole child's needs and instill confidence in practitioners (Petrie, 2020).

For practitioners, the 'Head, Heart, and Hands' (HHH) social pedagogic approach (McDermid et al., 2021) provides a comprehensive framework. The essence of the HHH approach is not just about making meaningful connections with children through education but also about the transformative impact it can have on vulnerable children, those marginalised, in poverty or foster care, by recognising their individual needs and wellbeing in early years settings.

HHH frameworks itself as a holistic dimensional approach and incorporates the three Ps: the professional, the personal and the practical self. In the following overview the principles are explored in more detail (Eichsteller and Holtoff, 2010; Petrie, 2011):

- The professional: theory and concepts, and being a reflective practitioner—the 'head'
- The personal: using one's personality positive attitude, building personal relationships, but keeping the 'private self' out—the 'heart'
- The practical: using specific methods and creative activities to build and maintain relationships with the child and responding to their needs—the 'hands'

In addition, the social pedagogic principle of 'haltung' is applied with the HHH framework; this translates to our attitudes, beliefs and values and how this guides our actions when working with children and expresses the connectedness we have with the needs of the child and their wellbeing (Eichsteller and Holthoff, 2011).

The image of a tree can be used to represent the HHH framework, with the tree symbolising 'wellbeing & personal growth', rooted in 'Haltung' (values, education, philosophy, sociology, psychology) and supported by critical societal thinkers. The tree's branches represent elements like communication, group dynamics, holistic learning, child-centeredness and empowerment, focusing on relationships, observing and reflecting, all nurturing children's rights and participation (Eichsteller and Holtoff, 2010).

In summary, social pedagogy emphasises holistic wellbeing in child development, integrating education, care and relationships. The Head, Heart, Hands framework guides practitioners in fostering empowerment, participation and positive connections rooted in values and societal context.

Here are three practical ways practitioners can enhance their wellbeing from a social pedagogic lens:

1. Reflect regularly on experiences to align practice with core values and reduce stress.
2. Build supportive relationships with colleagues and children to foster a positive work environment.
3. Engage in creative, joyful activities to reduce burnout and increase fulfillment.

In this next contribution, Kelsie Lee, Primary Education Graduate, reminds us of the value not just in building relationships through social pedagogy, but through considering how staff wellbeing may translate into pupils' outcomes.

Kelsie Lee: healthy and happy teachers

Healthy and happy teachers are the most important school resource because they are crucial stakeholders in determining the educational success of all pupils (McCallum and Price, 2016). Therefore, imbalances in teacher mental health and wellbeing can pose risks to running an effective school system (Travers, 2017). I conducted my own research to explore the importance of teacher wellbeing in influencing pupils' positive functioning and educational outcomes in primary school. The teachers expressed that when they are not experiencing their best state of wellbeing then this has a 'knock-on effect' in their classroom, which links to social contagion theory (Mercer and Gregersen, 2020). As a result, this permits poorer classroom experiences for the pupils in terms of lower-quality instruction, which negatively affects pupil achievement (Turner and Theikling, 2019).

The teachers in my study identified that having a 'support network' in school was a key contributor to their positive wellbeing experiences, particularly when this is considered as a 'high priority' to the school. Gearhart et al. (2022) and Fox's (2021) studies also support this finding. A member from the Senior Leadership Team (SLT) from the same school agreed by stating that 'communication and relationships are everything in a school', hence it is their responsibility to find strategies to ensure that strong, supportive staff relationships are fostered. Furthermore, the member of the SLT recognised that good staff relationships help them to identify forms of pressure or stress that are affecting their teachers before they reach a point of 'poor performance', in which pupil motivation and attainment is negatively impacted.

In addition to emphasising the importance of strong staff relationships to support staff wellbeing in school, the participants in my study listed some strategies that are in place at their school to support staff wellbeing. It is significant that these strategies do not correspond with the medical and scientific nature of the underutilised and low-impacting strategies, which are often explored in literature (Gearhart et al., 2022; Iancu et al., 2017). Instead, the strategies my participants listed are personalised to the individual teachers at school level.

Along with ensuring establishment of strong staff relationships, I recommend that SLTs consider implementing some of the strategies that my participants listed as effective in their school for supporting staff wellbeing, which will help promote children's best school experiences pertaining to their highest wellbeing and educational outcomes. Listed below are the strategies my participants informed me of:

- Having an open-door policy for all staff members.
- Staff recharge sessions—run every half-term for all staff members to get together in the staff room to informally catch up with each other over coffee and cake.
- Having at least one professional development day dedicated to supporting staff wellbeing—encouraging every staff member to take that day to do something to support their own wellbeing. It is highly encouraged that this does not mean doing schoolwork. However, if this is something that would support a teacher's wellbeing, then this should not be discredited.
- Access to a school counsellor—if the school budget allows, anonymous access to a school counsellor that is free to use for all staff members.
- Informal staff meetings that use fun activities to get all staff members socialising together—e.g. doing a quiz.
- Chocolate bar Fridays—if the school budget allows, all staff members being given a chocolate bar from the headteacher on a Friday.
- Inclusion manager being mental health trained for staff as well as pupils—helps to build the staff network and their access to well-trained support.

In this next contribution, Helen Bartle, Assistant Headteacher at Ackton Pastures Primary Academy, illuminates the notion of 'belonging' and shares personal reflections of how this can be embedded in the early years curriculum.

Helen Bartle: belonging and wellbeing

My feelings around belonging can be best summed up from the following quote I saw on a visit to Manchester Museum (source unknown):

> Belonging is fundamental to our sense of purpose, our wellbeing and knowing who we are. Belonging helps us to face our fears and inspires us to create and make better futures. We can know belonging through relationships, everyday objects, places, movements and actions. A sense of belonging aims to inspire empathy, bringing you into worlds which may feel familiar and sometimes taking you to places you can only imagine.

For me this details why creating a sense of belonging is so important in the early years and we try to create belonging in different ways.

Building relationships quickly with our children is the most important thing. We take the time to get to know our children, through preschool visits, transition visits, meetings with parents and meeting picnics. But crucially we recognise that we all have different stories and lived experiences and value each and every one of these. This information feeds into our curriculum and classroom provision so that we can adapt our planning to reflect our children so that everyone feels valued.

We recognise that the classroom space is one which they curate, driven by their learning and interests. Before children start school they are given the opportunity to design their own peg label which is then proudly displayed on their peg ready for their first day. Already before the school year has started the classroom space is their space not our (the practitioners) space.

The books and resources we use provide mirrors of their lives. We intentionally choose books, authors and illustrators that reflect our children. Visual timetables include representations of everyone's homes, brick houses, flats, chalets and trailers. Seeing themselves in the classroom is crucial to feeling like they belong.

Pupil agency is important to us. Children vote for the story they want to hear at the end of the day, the songs they want to sing. They create their own small worlds, which are displayed in the classroom, with their choices being respected. We write down the children's stories and keep them in books, acting them out for others to see. These stories are precious to us and valued just as much as any on our bookshelves. Their play, their choices, their voices matter to us and we respect them.

We learn about our local area and create worlds in the classroom with pictures of ourselves and our own homes. We learn about people who help us in our school and local community and help to keep it tidy, taking part in local litter picks. Our community matters to us.

Creating an environment and curriculum that is reflective of the children, driven by our relationships with the children has really fostered a sense of belonging in our classrooms and this can be seen through their behaviour and wellbeing and we hope that it develops their empathy and inspires them to create better futures… I guess only time will tell.

In this next contribution, Elenaor Milligan, Lecturer in Education, University of East Anglia, invites reflections on the practice of mindfulness, exploring its use in supporting the mental health and wellbeing of practitioners in the early years.

Eleanor Milligan: mindfulness in the Early Years

Early years educators play a crucial role in shaping the developmental journeys of young children. Their work, however, is often demanding, both physically and emotionally. The pressures of managing a classroom or setting, meeting the diverse needs of children, maintaining communication with parents, keeping up to date with policy or curriculum expectations and experiences of external scrutiny can lead to significant stress and burnout (Early Years Alliance, 2023; TES, 2024). This is where mindfulness becomes an invaluable tool for sustaining their wellbeing.

Mindfulness, the practice of maintaining a moment-by-moment awareness of ones thoughts, feelings, bodily sensations and surrounding environment, has been widely recognized for its potential to reduce stress, enhance emotional regulation and improve overall mental health (Flook et al., 2013). For Early Years educators, who are frequently faced with high levels of stress, mindfulness offers a way to cultivate self-compassion and resilience, enhance job satisfaction and ultimately, create and maintain better environments for, and relationships with, the children in their care (Almaguer-Botero et al., 2023; Erwin 2020; Jennings, 2015).

Mindfulness helps educators to become more attuned to their internal experiences and external demands, allowing them to respond to challenges with greater clarity, calmness and intention (Skinner and Beers, 2016). By regularly engaging in mindfulness practices, educators can develop a greater capacity for acceptance and patience, which are essential qualities in the classroom. Additionally, mindfulness promotes self-compassion, helping educators to manage the inevitable challenges of teaching with kindness towards themselves rather than self-criticism (Emerson et al., 2017). This not only enhances their own wellbeing but also provides a positive role model for the children in their care (Bernay, 2014; Mukadam, 2023).

The foundations of practicing mindfulness are built upon three core components: attention, attitude and intention (Shapiro et al., 2006). This is articulated clearly in the writing of Kabat-Zinn (2012), developer and founder of the Mindfulness-Based Stress Reduction programme,

> Mindfulness is awareness, cultivated by paying attention in a sustained and particular way: on purpose, in the present moment, and non-judgmentally.
>
> (p. 1)

Practitioners can apply this to their everyday lives both inside and outside of the school environment through simple mindful strategies.

1. Breath Awareness: taking a few moments throughout the day to focus on breathing can help educators to centre themselves, reduce stress and bring attention back to the present moment. This simple practice can be done anytime, even during a busy classroom session.
2. Body Scan: at the beginning or end of the day, educators can perform a body scan, where they mentally focus their attention or 'scan' each part of their body, noticing sensations without judgment. This practice helps in recognising areas of tension and promotes relaxation.

3. Mindful Walking: walking mindfully, paying attention to the sensation of each step, can be a grounding exercise. Educators can incorporate this during short breaks or transitions between activities.
4. Five Senses Exercise: engaging the five senses—sight, sound, smell, taste and touch—by noticing details in the immediate environment that link to these senses can help educators ground themselves in the present moment, reducing anxiety and promoting calm.

By integrating these simple activities into their daily routines, Early Years educators can create a more balanced and resilient approach. This not only benefits their own mental and emotional health but also enhances their ability to provide high-quality care and education to the children they nurture.

Rachael Summerscales, founder of Honest Childhood, presents a compelling case study to continue the narrative on the significance of supporting practitioner mental health and wellbeing.

Rachael summerscales: Case study: From policy to practice: how Sunny Days Nursery enhances staff wellbeing

Background: Sunny Days Nursery caters to children aged six months to five years and employs 20 staff members. Recognising the critical impact of staff wellbeing on the quality of care and education, the nursery's leadership implemented a comprehensive wellbeing programme aligned with the Early Years Foundation Stage (EYFS) framework.

Implementing Wellbeing Initiatives Leadership Commitment and Policy Development: The nursery's management team prioritised staff wellbeing by developing a clear policy. This included regular supervision meetings, professional development opportunities and health and wellness activities to reduce unnecessary workload and provide a supportive environment.

Regular Supervision Meetings: Sunny Days Nursery established monthly supervision meetings between staff and leaders. These meetings provided a platform for discussing concerns, reflecting on practice and setting personal and professional development goals. This practice aligns with the EYFS framework's requirements for ongoing professional development and support.

Professional Development and Training: The nursery offered various training programmes focusing on stress management, resilience and mental health awareness. These sessions equipped staff with tools to manage their workloads effectively and maintain their wellbeing. Creating a Supportive Environment: Sunny Days Nursery fostered a positive work culture through open communication channels and a recognition initiative. The leadership encouraged staff to voice their concerns and suggestions, ensuring they felt heard and valued. Regular staff meetings and feedback sessions were implemented to maintain transparency and promote a collaborative environment.

Health and Wellness Support: The nursery introduced various health and wellness initiatives, including weekly yoga classes, mindfulness sessions and access to counselling services. These activities aimed to help staff manage stress and maintain a healthy work-life balance. The nursery also organised team-building events and social gatherings to strengthen relationships and build a sense of community among the staff. Monitoring and Evaluation: To assess the effectiveness of these initiatives, Sunny Days Nursery conducted regular staff surveys and monitored key metrics such as absenteeism and staff turnover rates. Feedback collected was used to make informed adjustments to the wellbeing programme, ensuring it met the evolving needs of the staff. This continuous improvement approach ensured that wellbeing remained a dynamic and integral part of the nursery's culture. The implementation of wellbeing initiatives at Sunny Days Nursery led to significant positive outcomes, including higher job satisfaction and reduced stress among staff, and the supportive environment enhanced teamwork and collaboration.

One staff member, Jane, a room leader at Sunny Days, noted, 'The regular supervision sessions have been incredibly beneficial. They give me a chance to discuss any challenges and receive valuable feedback, which has significantly improved my practice and wellbeing.' The nursery's comprehensive approach, focusing on regular supervision, professional development, supportive leadership and health and wellness programmes, demonstrates the value of integrating wellbeing into early years settings. This strategy not only benefits employees but also improves the overall quality of care and education provided.

In her second contribution in this chapter, Eleanor Milligan provides a very useful overview of the importance of a collaborative approach to practitioners' mental health and the importance of open and honest conversations.

Eleanor Milligan: the golden thread of staff wellbeing

Staff wellbeing is recognised as a key aspect of effective leadership (Ofsted, 2024a, 2024b). Poor wellbeing can lead to higher levels of staff illness, absence, turnover and conflict (CIPD, 2022). Staff wellbeing also impacts children's wellbeing (Mainstone-Cotton, 2017; Mukadam, 2023, Foundation Years no date). Whilst it is acknowledged that policy and systemic change are critical for the long-term wellbeing of staff at all levels, the most recent teacher and school wellbeing reports indicate high levels of stress within settings and a need to improve communication channels, organisational culture and systems (Education Support, 2023, 2024; TES, 2024).

Specifically in the early years sector, underfunding, lack of recognition, increased staff to child ratios, pay levels, access to training and increasing numbers of children with special needs have left the workforce strained and in a recruitment and retention crisis (Anna Freud Anna, 2022, Early Education and Childcare Coalition, 2023, Early Years Alliance, 2021).

So, how can we ensure that the wellbeing of all staff is the golden thread of a school/setting?

Staff wellbeing needs to be seen holistically and includes personal, social, mental and physical wellbeing alongside professional identity and development. Advice and guidance specifically designed for early years staff and setting leadership (Anna Freud n.d.; Foundation Years, n.d.; Mainstone-Cotton, 2017; Mukadam, 2023) has been combined with recommendations from TesWorld (2024), where a panel drew on their expertise across the sector to offer strategies for leaders and teachers in achieving a professional working space which holds staff wellbeing in mind.

Leaders

- Recognise and support mental health and wellbeing
- Establish a staff wellbeing framework/policy
- Allocate time to survey staff, using established questionnaires to ensure benchmarks are available
- Ensure clarity of communication on vision and systems
- Provide good overall organisation—ensuring strong systems are in place
- Ensure roles and responsibilities are allocated with sustainability in mind
- Ensure the boundaries of job/roles are articulated clearly and maintained
- Offer professional trust in staff
- Develop a culture of compassion
- Provide flexible working practices
- Demonstrate recognition and appreciation of staff

Leaders and teachers

- Be aware of workload/the role and strategies to manage it
- Ensure you prioritise what can be achieved and what can have the greatest impact
- Reduce that which will not make a significant difference to children
- Develop understanding of high-quality inclusive practice
- Promote professional training and development, understanding pedagogy, accessing research and contributing to research
- Recognise what impacts morale
- Enable staff to take responsibility for understanding their wellbeing and how to manage it
- Recognise the importance of relationships and networks
- Value sleep, exercise and nutrition
- Utilise available guides and support resources

Key points

- Staff wellbeing is important and impacts on children's wellbeing
- Wellbeing is the responsibility of both staff individually and leaders working with their staff collaboratively
- Empowering staff wellbeing comes through a range of strategies
- There are tools, guidance, resources and advice on strategies widely available.

In this next contribution, Angela Hodgkins, Senior Lecturer, Department for Children and Families, University of Worcester, explores the fundamental aspect of empathy, summarising the power of this skill as part of a holistic approach to mental health and wellbeing.

Angela Hodgkins: the value of empathy

Most people would agree that empathy is a crucial skill for those working with young children. However, empathy is notoriously difficult to define, as it is understood in different ways in different disciplines (e.g. developmental psychology, neuroscience and social psychology). Hoffman (2000: 30), a leading writer on empathy, says 'the more I study empathy, the more complex it becomes!' The majority of people identify empathy as the ability to understand something from someone else's point of view; to *walk in their shoes* or *see the world through their eyes*. Carl Rogers (1980: 85) described empathy as the 'sensitive ability and willingness to understand the client's thoughts, feelings and struggles from the client's point of view'. Although primarily a counselling and therapy theory, Rogers believed that empathy is an interpersonal skill that is beneficial for anyone working with people. As Early Years practitioners, we understand the importance of understanding what the children are feeling, and of trying to look at situations from their point of view.

Empathy is a precursor to compassion; we must understand suffering from someone else's point of view in order to be motivated to take action and help. There are two possible outcomes of empathy: compassionate action or empathic distress. There is evidence that taking compassionate action (acting to relieve hurt in others) also affects our own mood; we feel better when we can help others (Hoffman, 2000). This is why we feel slightly better about world suffering when we give money to charity. But there may be times, in Early Years practice, when it is not possible to take compassionate action, due to barriers such as setting policies and procedures. For example, you may know that a child wants to be held and carried but work in a setting that discourages this. Feeling empathy for the child and not being able to take action can lead to empathic distress.

Empathic distress is a particular stress which results from the very close empathic relationships that practitioners have with the children in their care. Whilst empathy is essential, at times we can feel overloaded with emotion, which can result in our own distress. In empathic distress, the emotion is internalised, we feel the distress of others ourselves. This can lead to burnout and absenteeism if it is not managed. Research suggests that managers should prioritise the emotional experiences of their staff to promote job satisfaction. Whilst supervision in early years settings is mandatory, in practice it is variable in its usefulness. Elfer et al. (2018) call for emotional supervision in early years settings, where practitioners are encouraged to talk about the emotional impact of the work.

It is important to note that empathy can also result in empathic satisfaction. Experiencing empathy for those who are joyful can create an atmosphere of positivity and happiness. Positive effects include the fulfilment and pride that come with being an Early Years practitioner. Building close relationships with children and families can be highly rewarding. It is widely accepted that there is a strong relationship between emotion and job satisfaction. Williams et al. (2023) identified pride, joy, happiness, contentment, hope and optimism as the emotions that impact on high job satisfaction.

In this challenging profession, full of emotional highs and lows, supporting each other through tough times and celebrating happy times together is fundamental.

In this next contribution, Amber Browne, Crisis Care Practitioner at Northumbria University, focuses on effective support for mothers with anxiety. By offering guidance for personal reflection, this contribution provides a comprehensive summary for improvement.

Amber Browne: supporting mothers with anxiety through pregnancy and beyond

The psychological health of a mother during pregnancy and the post-partum period is such an important yet often overlooked part of a baby coming into the world. Those with well-meaning intentions may often focus on the excitement of a new baby but sometimes forget mum in the process.

Feeling worried during pregnancy and after having a baby is normal, however maternal anxiety may be present when this worry and fear is persistent and disrupts daily life. Up to 20% of women may experience significant levels of anxiety during the perinatal period (Harrison, et al. 2020). Often, mums may worry about stigma and are reluctant to admit how they are feeling or seek help; they may worry about being judged or perceived as a 'bad mother' (McCarthy, et al. 2021).

It is important for Early Years practitioners to have an understanding of maternal anxiety as they will regularly come across pregnant women or women in the post-partum period when dropping older children off to nursery or school. Practitioners may be able to see the signs of maternal anxiety and be a safe space for a mum to open up about how she is feeling as they are someone she already knows and is familiar with. Around 50% of cases of perinatal depression and anxiety will go undetected (Public Health England, 2021), therefore if a practitioner is able to spot the signs and support a mum, this could make a real difference to both mum and the family as a whole.

Signs of maternal anxiety may be but are not limited to:

- Fear or anxiety that impacts daily tasks and/or an uncontrollable sense of anxiousness
- Panic attacks
- Feeling irritable, restless or on edge
- Difficulty relaxing or sleeping
- Fear or anxiety that might make mum reluctant to go out with baby
- Anxiety or worries that keeping coming into mum's mind that are difficult to stop or control.

(Cope, 2023)

The ways in which an early years practitioner could support a mum:

- Simply asking questions such as 'how are you feeling?', 'how have you been managing?', 'is there anything we can do to support you?' –these simple questions can often mean the most and leave an opening for a mum to reach out if she wants to.
- Communicate regularly; a mum might not feel she can open up initially, however regular check-ins create an open, honest and safe environment.
- In the education setting, have leaflets and information available about maternal mental health–this raises awareness as well as reduces stigma
- Be extra supportive and understanding around situations such as if mum is running late or has forgotten something.

If a mum is struggling with their mental health, Early Years practitioners could:

- Encourage them to talk to their health visitor, midwife or GP
- Point them in the direction of their local NHS therapy and counselling service
- Suggest local charities such as MIND and Maternal Mental Health Alliance
- Suggest a local support group so they can meet other people in similar circumstances and share thoughts and feelings

In this final contribution to this chapter, Rachel Lehart, Childcare Assessor/Lecturer, provides a comprehensive and insightful narrative, emphasising the paramountcy of investing in the wellbeing for all.

Rachel Lehart: wellbeing starts with you!

As an Early Years practitioner, your primary focus is naturally on supporting the development and wellbeing of the children in your care. It's the foundation of everything you do. But how often do you pause and reflect on your own wellbeing?

In my own experience, I have neglected my personal wellbeing, pushing through the demands of previous roles without considering the toll it was taking on me. Over time, I realised this approach was not sustainable, and the expectations I placed on myself were unreasonable. Through consistent self-work and a commitment to nurturing my own wellbeing, I've discovered several valuable strategies that can make a difference.

Reflection has been one of the most important tools I have adopted. When was the last time you took a moment to reflect on yourself, your role and how well you're truly doing? Regular reflection can prevent feelings of stress and overwhelm from building up. Simple practices like writing down your thoughts or setting time aside for reflective practices each day can truly make a difference.

Prioritising your wellbeing is not only beneficial for you but essential for the work you do. Without taking care of yourself, it's difficult to effectively contribute to the education and care of children. Here are some simple, yet impactful steps that can support you in this journey, provided they are practised consistently:

Self-care—Self-care is important, whatever makes you feel good and like you feel looked after. This could be a pamper evening, it could be going for a run, it could be reading a book. It can be easy to say 'I don't have time', however, making self-care a priority will actually improve your time management in the future.

Priorities—Upon arrival to work, consider your priorities for the day. Write them down and focus only on a manageable chunk of your 'to do list'. Tasks and things you need to do can wait, focus only on the things that can't. This will support you to feel less overwhelmed and set you up for a more productive day.

Talk to others—Talk to others, share the workload. A problem shared is a problem halved; it is important to know others will be feeling how you are. Sharing problems or concerns can help your own mental health as well as your workload.

Setting healthy boundaries—Boundaries are not selfish, they are a form of self-care and will actually benefit you long term in relation to limiting stress levels. Give yourself the time and space to recharge and make this a priority for yourself.

Being fully present and attentive is something we initially expect to be able to do. However, this is not the case if we are not taking steps as educators to prioritise wellbeing. Fostering an environment with a sense of wellbeing at its focus will help to facilitate an overall calm and effective learning environment for all staff and children involved, leading to positive outcomes in the future.

In conclusion

This final chapter examines the critical role of wellbeing in early years education, showing its interconnected impact on children, practitioners and families. While wellbeing has been a recurring theme throughout previous chapters, this section explicitly highlights strategies for embedding meaningful wellbeing practices into daily educational environments. The chapter stresses that nurturing relationships, setting healthy boundaries and fostering supportive environments are essential for maintaining mental and emotional health. It also examines the influence of leadership in sustaining a culture where wellbeing is the 'golden thread' running through all aspects of school life. Through case studies, practitioner perspectives and research-based strategies, this chapter advocates for a holistic approach that prioritises wellbeing as a foundation for learning, development and resilience.

Summary of key points

- It is important as an Early Years practitioner to set healthy boundaries to nurture your wellbeing and avoid burnout.
- A child's emotions and wellbeing significantly influence their learning and development. Social pedagogy, with its emphasis on personal development, social education and holistic wellbeing for children and practitioners, plays a crucial role in this.
- Good communication between home and the early years setting creates a partnership where everyone's wellbeing is considered.
- Wellbeing in the early years extends beyond children. By fostering environments that support mental, emotional and physical health for all, schools and settings can create sustainable practices that nurture resilience, engagement and positive relationships across the entire learning community.
- Truly impactful wellbeing initiatives are not standalone activities but are woven into the fabric of daily interactions, pedagogy and school culture. Viewing wellbeing as a fundamental component of early years education ensures that it is consistently prioritised in policies, decision-making and everyday practice.

References

Almaguer-Botero, A.P., Miller, E.L., Chen, R.K. et al. (2023). Effects of a mindfulness intervention to improve teachers' wellbeing. *Trends in Psychology*. https://doi.org/10.1007/s43076-023-00318-3

Anna, F. (2022). Supporting staff wellbeing in Early Years settings. Uploaded 17 January Available at: https://www.youtube.com/watch?v=Ddnz19sC1VA&t=24s (Accessed 22 July 2024).

Anna, F. (n.d.) *Wellbeing Measurement for Early Years Settings*. Available at: https://www.annafreud.org/resources/under-fives-wellbeing/wellbeing-measurement-for-early-years-settings/#:~:text=Wellbeing%20measurement%20in%20early%20years%20settings,-Dr%20Abi%20Miranda&text=Our%20Wellbeing%20measurement%20for%20early,measure%20wellbeing%20robustly%20and%20consistently (Accessed 22 July 2024).

Badea, M., and Suditu, M. (Eds.). (2024). *Modern Early Childhood Teacher Education: Theories and Practice: Theories and Practice*. Bucharest: University of Bucharest Publishing House.

Bernay, R.S. (2014). Mindfulness and the beginning teacher. *Australian Journal of Teacher Education*, 39(7), pp. 78-90.

Cameron, C., and Moss, P. (2011). *Social Pedagogy and Working with Children and Young People: Where Care and Education Meet*. London: Jessica Kingsley.

Chartered Institute of Professional Development (CIPD) (2022). *Supporting the Mental Health at Work: Guide for People Mangers*. Available at: https://www.cipd.org/uk/knowledge/guides/mental-health-support-guide/ (Accessed 22 July 2024).

Cope (2023). Perinatal anxiety. Available at: https://www.cope.org.au/health-professionals/health-professionals-3/perinatal-mental-health-disorders/perinatal-anxiety/#:~:text=Constantly%20feeling%20irritable%2C%20restless%20or,going%20out%20with%20her%20baby

Early Education and Childcare Coalition (2023). Retention and return: Delivering the expansion of Early Years entitlement in England. Available at: https://static1.squarespace.com/static/646ca30371a2ef6a657e9309/t/65482050ded6710668b8b62a/1699225681784/Retention+and+Return.pdf (Accessed 22 July 2024).

Early Years Alliance (2021). *Breaking Point: The impact of recruitment and retention challenges on the Early Years sector in England*. https://www.eyalliance.org.uk/breaking-point-impact-recruitment-and-retention-challenges-early-years-sector-england (Accessed 22 July 2024).

Early Years Alliance (2023). *Minds Still Matter*. Available at: https://www.eyalliance.org.uk/sites/default/files/minds_still_matter_6_nov.pdf?utm_source=website&utm_medium=inpagelinks&utm_campaign=MSM

Education Support (2023). *Teacher Wellbeing Index*. Available at: https://www.educationsupport.org.uk/media/0h4jd5pt/twix_2023.pdf (Accessed 22 July 2024).

Education Support (2024). *Ofsted - The need for change in the English inspection system for schools*. Available at: https://www.educationsupport.org.uk/media/0xzpguq0/ofsted-s-big-listen-response-from-education-support.pdf (Accessed 22 July 2024).

Eichsteller, G., and Holthoff, S. (2011). Conceptual foundations of social pedagogy: A transnational perspective from Germany. In Cameron, C., and Moss, P. (Eds.). *Social Pedagogy and Working with Children and Young People: Where Care and Education Meet*. London: Jessica Kingsley Publishers, pp. 36-37.

Eichsteller, G., and Holthoff, S. (2012). The art of being a social pedagogue: developing cultural change in children's homes in Essex. *International Journal of Social Pedagogy*, 1(1). https://doi.org/10.14324/111.444.ijsp.2012.v1.1.004

Eichsteller, G., and Holtoff, S. (2010). *Foundations of Social Pedagogy: A Holistic Approach to Working with Children and Young People*. London: Social Pedagogy UK.

Elfer, P., Page, J., and Salmon, N. (2018). *Working with Babies and Children: From Principles to Practice*. (2nd ed.). London: Routledge.

Emerson, L.M., Leyland, A., Hudson, K. et al. (2017). Teaching mindfulness to teachers: A systematic review and narrative synthesis. *Mindfulness* **8**, pp. 1136-1149. https://doi.org/10.1007/s12671-017-0691-4

Erwin, E. (2020). *The Power of Presence: A Guide to Mindfulness Practices in Early Childhood*. Lewisville, NC: Gryphon House Inc.

Flook, L., Goldberg, S.B., Pinger, L., Bonus, K. and Davidson, R.J., (2013). Mindfulness for teachers: A pilot study to assess effects on stress, burnout, and teaching efficacy. *Mind, Brain, and Education*, 7(3), pp. 182-195.

Foundation years (n.d.). *Practitioner Wellbeing: useful information and resources*. Available at: https://www.foundationyears.org.uk/2024/05/practitioner-wellbeing-useful-information-and-resources/ (Accessed 22 July 2024).

Fox, H.B. (2021). *A Mixed Method Item Response Theory Investigation of Teacher wellbeing*. PhD Thesis. The George Washington University. Available at: https://scholarspace.library.gwu.edu/etd/5999n424n

Gabriel, T. (2001). Social Pedagogy and Residential care in Germany. Unpublished report for the Thomas Coram Research Unit, Institute of Education, University of London.

Gearhart, C.A., Blaydes, M., and McCarthy, C.J. (2022). Barriers to and facilitators for teacher's wellbeing. *Frontiers in Psychology*, 13, p. 867433. https://doi.org/10.3389/fpsyg.2022.867433

Harrison, V., Moore, D., and Lazard, L. (2020). Supporting perinatal anxiety in the digital age; a qualitative exploration of stressors and support strategies. *BMC Pregnancy Childbirth*, 20, 363. https://doi.org/10.1186/s12884-020-02990-0

Hoffman, M.L. (2000). *Empathy and Moral Development: Implications for Caring and Justice*. Cambridge: Cambridge University Press.

Iancu, A.E., Rusu, A., Maroiu, C., Pacurar, R., and Maricutoiu, L.P. (2017). The effectiveness of interventions aimed at reducing teacher burnout: a meta-analysis. *Educational Psychology Review*, 30, pp. 373-396. Available at: https://doi.org/10.1007/s10648-017-9420-8

Jennings, P. (2015). Early childhood teachers' wellbeing, mindfulness, and self-compassion in relation to classroom quality and attitudes towards challenging students. *Mindfulness*, 6, pp. 732-743. https://doi.org/10.1007/s12671-014-0312-4

Kabat-Zinn, J. (2012). *Mindfulness for beginners: Reclaiming the present moment – and your life/Jon Kabat-Zinn*. Sounds True.

Kalagiakos, P. (2015). Social pedagogy under very difficult conditions: The case of the multicultural school of Athens. *International Journal of Social Pedagogy*, 4(1). https://doi.org/10.14324/111.444.ijsp.2015.v4.1.008

Mainstone-Cotton, S. (2017). *Promoting Emotional Wellbeing in Early Years Staff. Mainstone-Cotton, Sonia*. London: Jessica Kingsley Publishers.

Marttila, J., Fukkink, R., and Silvén, M. (2024). Enhancing early childhood education student teachers' mentalization, interaction, and relationships: An online intervention. *European Early Childhood Education Research Journal*, 32(4), pp. 545–561.

McCallum, F. and Price, D. (2016). *Nurturing Wellbeing Development in Education: From little things, big things grow*. London: Routledge.

McCarthy, M. Houghton, C., and Matvienko-Sikar, K. (2021). Women's experiences and perceptions of anxiety and stress during the perinatal period: a systematic review and qualitative evidence synthesis. *BMC Pregnancy and Childbirth*, 21, p. 811. https://doi.org/10.1186/s12884-021-04271-w

McDermid, S., Trivedi, H., Holmes, L., and Boddy, J. (2021). Foster carers' receptiveness to new innovations and programmes: An example from the introduction of social pedagogy to UK foster care. *The British Journal of Social Work*, 52(3), pp. 1213-1230. https://doi.org/10.1093/bjsw/bcab152

Mercer, S. and Gregersen, T. (2020). *Teacher Wellbeing*. Oxford: Oxford University Press.

Mukadam, Y. (2023). *Mindfulness in Early Years; Strategies and Approaches to Nurturing Young Minds*. London: Routledge.

Nordström, A., Kumpulainen, K., and Rajala, A. (2021). Unfolding joy in young children's literacy practices in a Finnish Early Years classroom. *Journal of Early Childhood Literacy*, 24(1), pp. 3-19. https://doi.org/10.1177/14687984211038662

OECD. (2015). PISA 2015 Results Students' Well-Being Volume III. Available at: https://www.oecd.org/content/dam/oecd/en/publications/reports/2017/04/pisa-2015-results-volume-iii_g1g787cb/9789264273856-en.pdf

Ofsted (2024a). *Early Years Inspection Handbook* GOV.UK. Available at: https://www.gov.uk/government/publications/early-years-inspection-handbook-eif (Accessed 22 July 2024).

Ofsted (2024b). *School Inspection Handbook* GOV.UK Available at: https://www.gov.uk/government/publications/school-inspection-handbook-eif (Accessed 22 July 2024).

Petrie, P. (2011). *Communication Skills for Working with Children and Young People Introducing Social Pedagogy*. London: Jessica Kingsley Publishers.

Petrie, P. (2020). Taking social pedagogy forward: Its fit with official UK statements on promoting wellbeing. *International Journal of Social Pedagogy*, 9(1), p. 17. https://doi.org/10.14324/111.444.ijsp.2020.v9.x.017

Public Health England. (2021). Early years high impact area 2: Supporting maternal and family mental health. [online] gov.uk. Available at: https://www.gov.uk/government/publications/commissioning-of-public-health-services-for-children/early-years-high-impact-area-2-supporting-maternal-and-family-mental-health

Rogers, C.R., (1980). *A Way of Being*. Boston: Houghton Mifflin.

Shapiro, S.L., Carlson, L.E., Astin, J.A., and Freedman, B. (2006). Mechanisms of mindfulness. *Journal of Clinical Psychology*, 62(3), pp. 373-386. https://doi.org/10.1002/jclp.20237

Skinner, E., and Beers, J. (2016). Mindfulness and teachers' coping in the classroom: A developmental model of teacher stress, coping, and everyday resilience. In Schonert-Reichl, K. and Roeser, R. (Eds.), *Handbook of Mindfulness in Education*. Mindfulness in Behavioral Health. New York, NY: Springer. https://doi.org/10.1007/978-1-4939-3506-2_7

TES (2024). *School Wellbeing Report 2024*: UK. Available at: https://assets.tes.com/marketing/s3fs-public/documents/2024-03/Tes_School_Wellbeing_Report_UK_2024.pdf (Accessed 22 July 2024).

TesWorld (2024). *The Big Debate: Discussing the Tes School Wellbeing Report 2024 Results*. Uploaded 22 March. Available at: https://www.youtube.com/watch?v=ZIjezjIP8WQ (Accessed: 22 July 2024).

Travers, C. (2017). Current knowledge on the nature, prevalence, sources and potential impact of teacher stress. In McIntyre, T.M., McIntyre, S.E., and Francis, D.J. (Eds.), *Sducator Stress: An Occupational Health Perspective*. Cham: Springer International Publishing AG, pp. 23-54.

Turner, K. and Theikling, M. (2019). Teacher wellbeing: Its effects on teaching practice and student learning. *Issues in Educational Research, 29*(3), pp. 938-960.

Williams, M., Mainstone-Cotton, S., and Mukadam, Y. (2023). *Wellbeing in the Early Years: A Practical Guide for Practitioners*. London: Jessica Kingsley Publishers.

Zarra-Nezhad, M., Suhonen, K., and Sajaniemi, N. (2024). Keeping early social-emotional learning developmental: The development, implementation, and preliminary evaluation of a preventive intervention program for early childhood education and care. *International Journal of Developmental Science, 17*(4), pp. 113-125.

INDEX

Pages in **bold** refer to tables

action research 97, 169
ADHD 209
adult-child interaction 160, 164
agency 126, 131, 133, 161, 175, 181
anxiety 11, 27, 65; maths anxiety 109; mothers with anxiety 223
art 27, 43, 126, 129
assessment 147-158
assessment for learning 155-156
autism 48, 69, 100, 101
autonomy 26, 80, 86

baby room 65
behaviour 74, 117, 193
'Birth to Five Matters' 4-5
Bokashi composting 124-125
books 131, 166, 194
breathing techniques 65

care home (visit) 128-129
carpet time 109, 189
childminder, childminding 34, 156
coaching 206
collaboration 179, 183
communication and language development 79-91, 82
community 89, 103, 127
composting 124-125
continuing professional development (CPD) 110, 114, 139, 199
COVID-19 38, 58, 60, 66, 69
creativity 75, 101, 103, 109, 117

dance 135-136
development matters 4, 98, 153, 178
digital 44, 123
displays 10, 12, 72
drama 135-136, 141
Dweck, Carol 109, 121, 163

early career teacher 190
effective learning 173, 186, 206, 225
empathy 73, 130, 144, 152, 175-176
environments 167, 168, 174
expressive arts and design 135-146

faith 129-130
feedback 146, 149, 158
fundamental British values 199
funding 42-43, 206

gender 151, 168
gender stereotypes 67, 168
grouping 169, 187

handover 38, 43, 154
happiness 58, 67, 72
home learning 39

imagination 75, 83, 119, 129
inclusion 130, 169, 184, 202

joyful 60, 114, 215, 222

kindness 70, 105, 207, 208, 218

leadership 80, 216, 219-220, 225
learning centres 14
learning environment: indoors 4-18; outdoors 19-31
literacy 94-106

maternal anxiety 223
mathematics 108-122
maths anxiety 109
mental health 19, 24, 29, 44, 48, 51
mentoring 189-190, 192
mindfulness 65, 217-218
Montessori, Maria 6, 161, 175, 179
motivation 7, 24, 29, 46, 57

motor skills 57–58, 106
multi-agency 80
museums 103, 125–127
music 126, 135–136

nursery 138, 154, 162

observation 147–158, 177, 185, 200, 208
Ofsted 9, 49, 57, 114, 136

parent partnership 33–35
parental empowerment 39
parental engagement 39
physical development 46–61
physical literacy skills 46
playground 20, 22, 25, 37, 131
playgroup 173, 192
protected characteristics 196–210
personal, social, and emotional development (PSED) 64–77

questioning 67, 88–89, 90

reading 167, 187, 224
Reggio Emilia approach 5
relationships 202, 206, 214, 217–220
religious studies 129, 130
resilience 142, 144, 162, 163, 174

resources: natural resources 12, 13, 17, 101, 142; organising resources 13
routine 21, 29, 50

seating 208
self-esteem 146, 162, 179
SEND Code of Practice 197
sensory-aware 75–76, 208
STEAM 11
STEM 24–25, 67
storytelling 72–73, 89
sustainability 17, 23–24, 175–176

technology 11, 24, 35, 51
timetable **58**, 85, 167, 217
training 219–221
trauma 66–67, 176, 208
trauma informed practice 66

understanding the world 123–133
UNICEF 67

verbal feedback 34, 50, 95, 97, 104, 111
visits 39, 217
visual arts 136, 145

wellbeing 135, 146
world 123–133

For Product Safety Concerns and Information please contact our EU representative GPSR@taylorandfrancis.com
Taylor & Francis Verlag GmbH, Kaufingerstraße 24, 80331 München, Germany

www.ingramcontent.com/pod-product-compliance
Lightning Source LLC
Chambersburg PA
CBHW080613230426
43664CB00019B/2874